Scala for the Impatient

Second Edition

Scala for the Impatient

Second Edition

Cay S. Horstmann

✦✦Addison-Wesley

Boston • Columbus • Indianapolis • New York • San Francisco • Amsterdam • Cape Town
Dubai • London • Madrid • Milan • Munich • Paris • Montreal • Toronto • Delhi • Mexico City
São Paulo • Sydney • Hong Kong • Seoul • Singapore • Taipei • Tokyo

For information about buying this title in bulk quantities, or for special sales opportunities (which may include electronic versions; custom cover designs; and content particular to your business, training goals, marketing focus, or branding interests), please contact our corporate sales department at corpsales@pearsoned.com or (800) 382–3419.

For government sales inquiries, please contact governmentsales@pearsoned.com.

For questions about sales outside the United States, please contact intlcs@pearson.com.

Visit us on the Web: informit.com/aw

Library of Congress Control Number: 2016954825

Copyright © 2017 Pearson Education, Inc.

ISBN-13: 978-0-13-454056-6
ISBN-10: 0-13-454056-5

33614080390775

Text printed in the United States of America.

1   16

To my wife, who made writing this book possible,
and to my children, who made it necessary.

Contents

Foreword to the First Edition

When I met Cay Horstmann some years ago he told me that Scala needed a better introductory book. My own book had come out a little bit earlier, so of course I had to ask him what he thought was wrong with it. He responded that it was great but too long; his students would not have the patience to read through the eight hundred pages of *Programming in Scala*. I conceded that he had a point. And he set out to correct the situation by writing *Scala for the Impatient*.

I am very happy that his book has finally arrived because it really delivers on what the title says. It gives an eminently practical introduction to Scala, explains what's particular about it, how it differs from Java, how to overcome some common hurdles to learning it, and how to write good Scala code.

Scala is a highly expressive and flexible language. It lets library writers use highly sophisticated abstractions, so that library users can express themselves simply and intuitively. Therefore, depending on what kind of code you look at, it might seem very simple or very complex.

A year ago, I tried to provide some clarification by defining a set of levels for Scala and its standard library. There were three levels each for application programmers and for library designers. The junior levels could be learned quickly and would be sufficient to program productively. Intermediate levels would make programs more concise and more functional and would make libraries more flexible to use. The highest levels were for experts solving specialized tasks. At the time I wrote:

I hope this will help newcomers to the language decide in what order to pick subjects to learn, and that it will give some advice to teachers and book authors in what order to present the material.

Cay's book is the first to have systematically applied this idea. Every chapter is tagged with a level that tells you how easy or hard it is and whether it's oriented towards library writers or application programmers.

As you would expect, the first chapters give a fast-paced introduction to the basic Scala capabilities. But the book does not stop there. It also covers many of the more "senior" concepts and finally progresses to very advanced material which is not commonly covered in a language introduction, such as how to write parser combinators or make use of delimited continuations. The level tags serve as a guideline for what to pick up when. And Cay manages admirably to make even the most advanced concepts simple to understand.

I liked the concept of *Scala for the Impatient* so much that I asked Cay and his editor, Greg Doench, whether we could get the first part of the book as a free download on the Typesafe web site. They have gracefully agreed to my request, and I would like to thank them for that. That way, everybody can quickly access what I believe is currently the best compact introduction to Scala.

Martin Odersky

January 2012

Preface

The evolution of traditional languages such as Java, C#, and C++ has slowed down considerably, and programmers who are eager to use more modern language features are looking elsewhere. Scala is an attractive choice; in fact, I think it is by far the most attractive choice for programmers who want to improve their productivity. Scala has a concise syntax that is refreshing after the Java boilerplate. It runs on the Java virtual machine, providing access to a huge set of libraries and tools. And Scala doesn't just target the Java virtual machine. The ScalaJS project emits JavaScript code, enabling you to write both the server-side and client-side parts of a web application in a language that isn't JavaScript. Scala embraces the functional programming style without abandoning object orientation, giving you an incremental learning path to a new paradigm. The Scala interpreter lets you run quick experiments, which makes learning Scala very enjoyable. Last but not least, Scala is statically typed, enabling the compiler to find errors, so that you don't waste time finding them—or not—later in the running program.

I wrote this book for *impatient* readers who want to start programming in Scala right away. I assume you know Java, C#, or C++, and I don't bore you with explaining variables, loops, or classes. I don't exhaustively list all the features of the language, I don't lecture you about the superiority of one paradigm over another, and I don't make you suffer through long and contrived examples. Instead, you will get the information that you need in compact chunks that you can read and review as needed.

Scala is a big language, but you can use it effectively without knowing all of its details intimately. Martin Odersky, the creator of Scala, has identified levels of expertise for application programmers and library designers—as shown in the following table.

Application Programmer	Library Designer	Overall Scala Level
Beginning **A1**		Beginning
Intermediate **A2**	Junior **L1**	Intermediate
Expert **A3**	Senior **L2**	Advanced
	Expert **L3**	Expert

For each chapter (and occasionally for individual sections), I indicate the experience level required. The chapters progress through levels **A1**, **L1**, **A2**, **L2**, **A3**, **L3**. Even if you don't want to design your own libraries, knowing about the tools that Scala provides for library designers can make you a more effective library user.

This is the second edition of this book, and I updated it thoroughly for Scala 2.12. I added coverage of recent Scala features such as string interpolation, dynamic invocation, implicit classes, and futures, and updated all chapters to reflect current Scala usage.

I hope you enjoy learning Scala with this book. If you find errors or have suggestions for improvement, please visit http://horstmann.com/scala and leave a comment. On that page, you will also find a link to an archive file containing all code examples from the book.

I am very grateful to Dmitry Kirsanov and Alina Kirsanova who turned my manuscript from XHTML into a beautiful book, allowing me to concentrate on the content instead of fussing with the format. Every author should have it so good!

Reviewers include Adrian Cumiskey, Mike Davis, Rob Dickens, Steve Haines, Susan Potter, Daniel Sobral, Craig Tataryn, David Walend, and William Wheeler. Thanks so much for your comments and suggestions!

Finally, as always, my gratitude goes to my editor, Greg Doench, for encouraging me to write this book, and for his insights during the development process.

Cay Horstmann
San Francisco, 2016

About the Author

Cay S. Horstmann is author of *Core Java™, Volumes I & II, Tenth Edition* (Prentice Hall, 2016), as well as a dozen other books for professional programmers and computer science students. He is a professor of computer science at San Jose State University and a Java Champion.

The Basics

Topics in This Chapter `A1`

Chapter 1

In this chapter, you will learn how to use Scala as an industrial-strength pocket calculator, working interactively with numbers and arithmetic operations. We introduce a number of important Scala concepts and idioms along the way. You will also learn how to browse the Scaladoc documentation at a beginner's level.

Highlights of this introduction are:

* Using the Scala interpreter
* Defining variables with var and val
* Numeric types
* Using operators and functions
* Navigating Scaladoc

1.1 The Scala Interpreter

To start the Scala interpreter:

1. Install Scala.
2. Make sure that the scala/bin directory is on the PATH.
3. Open a command shell in your operating system.
4. Type scala followed by the Enter key.

Now type commands followed by Enter. Each time, the interpreter displays the answer, as shown in Figure 1–1. For example, if you type 8 * 5 + 2 (as shown in boldface below), you get 42.

```
scala> 8 * 5 + 2
res0: Int = 42
```

The answer is given the name res0. You can use that name in subsequent computations:

```
scala> 0.5 * res0
res1: Double = 21.0
scala> "Hello, " + res0
res2: java.lang.String = Hello, 42
```

As you can see, the interpreter also displays the type of the result—in our examples, Int, Double, and java.lang.String.

```
Terminal                                                            _ □ ×
~$ scala
Welcome to Scala 2.12.0-M4 (Java HotSpot(TM) 64-Bit Server VM, Java 1.8.0_92).
Type in expressions for evaluation. Or try :help.

scala> 8 * 5 + 2
res0: Int = 42

scala> 0.5 * res0
res1: Double = 21.0

scala> "Hello, " + res0
res2: String = Hello, 42

scala> █
```

Figure 1–1   The Scala Interpreter

 TIP: Don't like the command shell? Several integrated development environments that support Scala have a "worksheet" feature for entering expressions and displaying their result whenever the sheet is saved. Figure 1–2 shows a worksheet in the Eclipse-based Scala IDE.

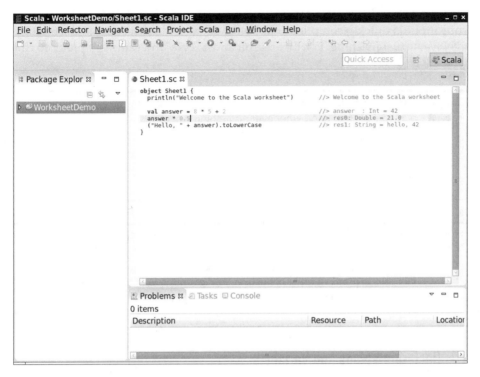

Figure 1–2   A Scala Worksheet

When calling methods, try using *tab completion* for method names. Type res2.to and then hit the Tab key. If the interpreter offers choices such as

    toCharArray   toLowerCase   toString   toUpperCase

this means tab completion works in your environment. Type a U and hit the Tab key again. You now get a single completion:

    res2.toUpperCase

Hit the Enter key, and the answer is displayed. (If you can't use tab completion in your environment, you'll have to type the complete method name yourself.)

Also try hitting the ↑ and ↓ arrow keys. In most implementations, you will see the previously issued commands, and you can edit them. Use the ←, →, and Del keys to change the last command to

    res2.toLowerCase

As you can see, the Scala interpreter reads an expression, evaluates it, prints it, and reads the next expression. This is called the *read-eval-print loop*, or REPL.

Technically speaking, the scala program is *not* an interpreter. Behind the scenes, your input is quickly compiled into bytecode, and the bytecode is executed by the Java virtual machine. For that reason, most Scala programmers prefer to call it "the REPL".

TIP: The REPL is your friend. Instant feedback encourages experimenting, and you will feel good whenever something works.

It is a good idea to keep an editor window open at the same time, so you can copy and paste successful code snippets for later use. Also, as you try more complex examples, you may want to compose them in the editor and then paste them into the REPL.

TIP: In the REPL, type :help to see a list of useful commands. All commands start with a colon. For example, the :warnings command gives more detailed information about the most recent compiler warning. You only have to enter the unique prefix of each command. For example, :w is the same as :warnings—at least for now, since there isn't currently another command starting with w.

1.2 Declaring Values and Variables

Instead of using res0, res1, and so on, you can define your own names:

```
scala> val answer = 8 * 5 + 2
answer: Int = 42
```

You can use these names in subsequent expressions:

```
scala> 0.5 * answer
res3: Double = 21.0
```

A value declared with val is actually a constant—you can't change its contents:

```
scala> answer = 0
<console>:6: error: reassignment to val
```

To declare a variable whose contents can vary, use a var:

```
var counter = 0
counter = 1 // OK, can change a var
```

In Scala, you are encouraged to use a val unless you really need to change the contents. Perhaps surprisingly for Java or C++ programmers, most programs don't need many var variables.

Note that you need not specify the type of a value or variable. It is inferred from the type of the expression with which you initialize it. (It is an error to declare a value or variable without initializing it.)

However, you can specify the type if necessary. For example,

```
val greeting: String = null
val greeting: Any = "Hello"
```

 NOTE: In Scala, the type of a variable or function is written *after* the name of the variable or function. This makes it easier to read declarations with complex types.

As I move back and forth between Scala and Java, I find that my fingers write Java declarations such as String greeting on autopilot, so I have to rewrite them as greeting: String. This is a bit annoying, but when I work with complex Scala programs, I really appreciate that I don't have to decrypt C-style type declarations.

 NOTE: You may have noticed that there were no semicolons after variable declarations or assignments. In Scala, semicolons are only required if you have multiple statements on the same line.

You can declare multiple values or variables together:

```
val xmax, ymax = 100 // Sets xmax and ymax to 100
var greeting, message: String = null
    // greeting and message are both strings, initialized with null
```

1.3 Commonly Used Types

You have already seen some of the data types of Scala, such as Int and Double. Like Java, Scala has seven numeric types: Byte, Char, Short, Int, Long, Float, and Double, and a Boolean type. However, unlike Java, these types are *classes*. There is no distinction between primitive types and class types in Scala. You can invoke methods on numbers, for example:

```
1.toString() // Yields the string "1"
```

or, more excitingly,

```
1.to(10) // Yields Range(1, 2, 3, 4, 5, 6, 7, 8, 9, 10)
```

(We will discuss the Range class in Chapter 13. For now, just view it as a collection of numbers.)

In Scala, there is no need for wrapper types. It is the job of the Scala compiler to convert between primitive types and wrappers. For example, if you make an array of Int, you get an int[] array in the virtual machine.

As you saw in Section 1.1, "The Scala Interpreter," on page 1, Scala relies on the underlying java.lang.String class for strings. However, it augments that class with well over a hundred operations in the StringOps class. For example, the intersect method yields the characters that are common to two strings:

```
"Hello".intersect("World") // Yields "lo"
```

In this expression, the java.lang.String object "Hello" is implicitly converted to a StringOps object, and then the intersect method of the StringOps class is applied. So, remember to look into the StringOps class when you use the Scala documentation (see Section 1.7, "Scaladoc," on page 10).

Similarly, there are classes RichInt, RichDouble, RichChar, and so on. Each of them has a small set of convenience methods for acting on their poor cousins—Int, Double, or Char. The to method that you saw above is actually a method of the RichInt class. In the expression

```
1.to(10)
```

the Int value 1 is first converted to a RichInt, and the to method is applied to that value.

Finally, there are classes BigInt and BigDecimal for computations with an arbitrary (but finite) number of digits. These are backed by the java.math.BigInteger and java.math.BigDecimal classes, but, as you will see in the next section, they are much more convenient because you can use them with the usual mathematical operators.

 NOTE: In Scala, you use methods, not casts, to convert between numeric types. For example, 99.44.toInt is 99, and 99.toChar is 'c'. Of course, as in Java, the toString method converts any object to a string.

To convert a string containing a number into the number, use toInt or toDouble. For example, "99.44".toDouble is 99.44.

1.4 Arithmetic and Operator Overloading

Arithmetic operators in Scala work just as you would expect in Java or C++:

```
val answer = 8 * 5 + 2
```

The + - * / % operators do their usual job, as do the bit operators & | ^ >> <<. There is just one surprising aspect: These operators are actually methods. For example,

```
a + b
```

is a shorthand for

```
a.+(b)
```

Here, + is the name of the method. Scala has no silly prejudice against non-alphanumeric characters in method names. You can define methods with just about any symbols for names. For example, the `BigInt` class defines a method called /% that returns a pair containing the quotient and remainder of a division.

In general, you can write

a *method* b

as a shorthand for

a.*method*(b)

where *method* is a method with two parameters (one implicit, one explicit). For example, instead of

```
1.to(10)
```

you can write

```
1 to 10
```

Use whatever you think is easier to read. Beginning Scala programmers tend to stick to the Java syntax, and that's fine. Of course, even the most hardened Java programmers seem to prefer a + b over a.+(b).

There is one notable difference between Scala and Java or C++. Scala does not have ++ or -- operators. Instead, simply use +=1 or -=1:

```
counter+=1 // Increments counter—Scala has no ++
```

Some people wonder if there is any deep reason for Scala's refusal to provide a ++ operator. (Note that you can't simply implement a method called ++. Since the Int class is immutable, such a method cannot change an integer value.) The Scala designers decided it wasn't worth having yet another special rule just to save one keystroke.

You can use the usual mathematical operators with `BigInt` and `BigDecimal` objects:

```
val x: BigInt = 1234567890
x * x * x // Yields 1881676371789154860897069000
```

That's much better than Java, where you would have had to call x.multiply(x).multiply(x).

NOTE: In Java, you cannot overload operators, and the Java designers claimed this is a good thing because it stops you from inventing crazy operators like !@$&＊ that would make your program impossible to read. Of course, that's silly; you can make your programs just as unreadable by using crazy method names like qxywz. Scala allows you to define operators, leaving it up to you to use this feature with restraint and good taste.

1.5 More about Calling Methods

You have already seen how to call methods on objects, such as

```
"Hello".intersect("World")
```

If the method has no parameters, you don't have to use parentheses. For example, the API of the StringOps class shows a method sorted, without (), which yields a new string with the letters in sorted order. Call it as

```
"Bonjour".sorted // Yields the string "Bjnooru"
```

The rule of thumb is that a parameterless method that doesn't modify the object has no parentheses. We discuss this further in Chapter 5.

In Java, mathematical methods such as sqrt are defined as static methods of the Math class. In Scala, you define such methods in *singleton objects*, which we will discuss in detail in Chapter 6. A package can have a *package object*. In that case, you can import the package and use the methods of the package object without any prefix:

```
import scala.math._ // In Scala, the _ character is a "wildcard," like * in Java
sqrt(2) // Yields 1.4142135623730951
pow(2, 4) // Yields 16.0
min(3, Pi) // Yields 3.0
```

If you don't import the scala.math package, add the package name:

```
scala.math.sqrt(2)
```

NOTE: If a package that starts with scala., you can omit the scala prefix. For example, import math._ is equivalent to import scala.math._, and math.sqrt(2) is the same as scala.math.sqrt(2). However, in this book, we always use the scala prefix for clarity.

You can find more information about the import statement in Chapter 7. For now, just use import *packageName*._ whenever you need to import a particular package.

Often, a class has a *companion object* whose methods act just like static methods do in Java. For example, the BigInt companion object to the scala.math.BigInt class has a method `probablePrime` that generates a random prime number with a given number of bits:

```
BigInt.probablePrime(100, scala.util.Random)
```

Here, `Random` is a singleton random number generator object, defined in the scala.util package. Try this in the REPL; you'll get a number such as 1039447980491200275486540240713.

1.6 The apply Method

In Scala, it is common to use a syntax that looks like a function call. For example, if s is a string, then s(i) is the ith character of the string. (In C++, you would write s[i]; in Java, s.charAt(i).) Try it out in the REPL:

```
val s = "Hello"
s(4) // Yields 'o'
```

You can think of this as an overloaded form of the () operator. It is implemented as a method with the name `apply`. For example, in the documentation of the `StringOps` class, you will find a method

```
def apply(n: Int): Char
```

That is, s(4) is a shortcut for

```
s.apply(4)
```

Why not use the [] operator? You can think of a sequence s of element type T as a function from { 0, 1, . . . , $n - 1$ } to T that maps i to s(i), the ith element of the sequence.

This argument is even more convincing for maps. As you will see in Chapter 4, you look up a map value for a given key as map(key). Conceptually, a map is a function from keys to values, and it makes sense to use the function notation.

 CAUTION: Occasionally, the () notation conflicts with another Scala feature: implicit parameters. For example, the expression

```
"Bonjour".sorted(3)
```

yields an error because the `sorted` method can optionally be called with an ordering, but 3 is not a valid ordering. You can use parentheses:

```
("Bonjour".sorted)(3)
```

or call `apply` explicitly:

```
"Bonjour".sorted.apply(3)
```

When you look at the documentation for the BigInt companion object, you will see apply methods that let you convert strings or numbers to BigInt objects. For example, the call

```
BigInt("1234567890")
```

is a shortcut for

```
BigInt.apply("1234567890")
```

It yields a new BigInt object, *without having to use* new. For example:

```
BigInt("1234567890") * BigInt("112358111321")
```

Using the apply method of a companion object is a common Scala idiom for constructing objects. For example, Array(1, 4, 9, 16) returns an array, thanks to the apply method of the Array companion object.

 NOTE: All through this chapter, we have assumed that Scala code is executed on the Java virtual machine. That is in fact true for the standard Scala distribution. However, the Scala.js project (www.scala-js.org) provides tools to translate Scala to JavaScript. If you take advantage of that project, you can write both the client-side and the server-side code of web applications in Scala.

1.7 Scaladoc

Java programmers use Javadoc to navigate the Java API. Scala has its own variant, called Scaladoc (see Figure 1–3).

Using Scaladoc can be a bit more overwhelming than Javadoc. Scala classes tend to have many more convenience methods than Java classes. Some methods use advanced features that are more meaningful to library implementors than to library users.

Here are some tips for navigating Scaladoc as a newcomer to the language.

You can browse Scaladoc online at www.scala-lang.org/api, but it is a good idea to download a copy from http://scala-lang.org/download/all.html and install it locally.

Unlike Javadoc, which presents an alphabetical listing of classes, Scaladoc is organized by packages. If you know a class or method name, don't bother navigating to the package. Simply use the search bar on the top of the entry page (see Figure 1–4).

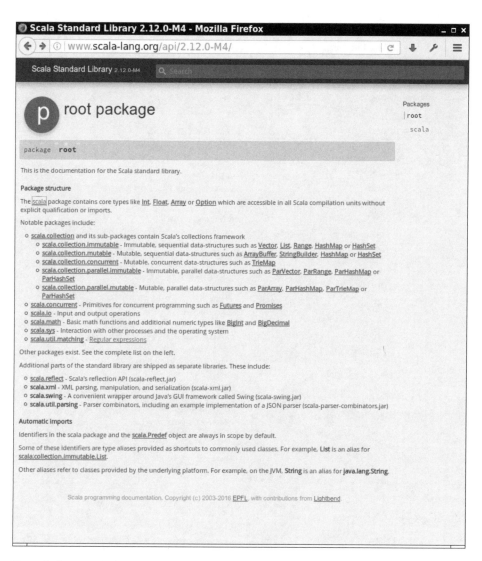

Figure 1–3   The entry page for Scaladoc

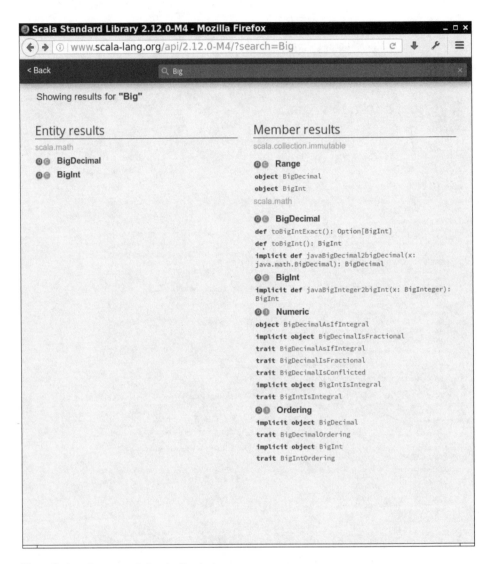

Figure 1–4   The search bar in Scaladoc

Click on the X symbol to clear the search pattern, or click on a matching class or method (Figure 1–5).

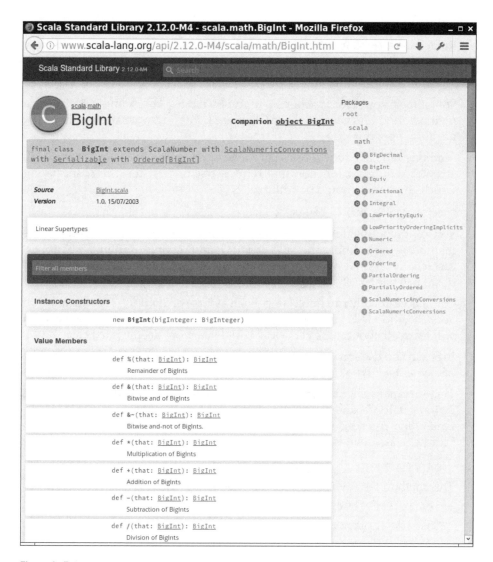

Figure 1–5   Class documentation in Scaladoc

Note the C and O symbols next to the class name. They let you navigate to the class (C) or the companion object (O). For traits (which are similar to Java interfaces), you see t and O symbols instead.

Keep these tips in mind:

- Remember to look into `RichInt`, `RichDouble`, and so on, if you want to know how to work with numeric types. Similarly, to work with strings, look into `StringOps`.

- The mathematical functions are in the *package* `scala.math`, not in any class.

- Sometimes, you'll see functions with funny names. For example, `BigInt` has a method `unary_-`. As you will see in Chapter 11, this is how you define the prefix negation operator `-x`.

- Methods can have functions as parameters. For example, the `count` method in `StringOps` requires a function that returns `true` or `false` for a `Char`, specifying which characters should be counted:

  ```
  def count(p: (Char) => Boolean) : Int
  ```

  You supply a function, often in a very compact notation, when you call the method. As an example, the call `s.count(_.isUpper)` counts the number of upper-case characters. We will discuss this style of programming in much more detail in Chapter 12.

- You'll occasionally run into classes such as `Range` or `Seq[Char]`. They mean what your intuition tells you—a range of numbers, a sequence of characters. You will learn all about these classes as you delve more deeply into Scala.

- In Scala, you use square brackets for type parameters. A `Seq[Char]` is a sequence of elements of type `Char`, and `Seq[A]` is a sequence of elements of some type `A`.

- There are many slightly different types for sequences such as `GenSeq`, `GenIterable`, `GenTraversableOnce`, and so on. The differences between them are rarely important. When you see such a construct, just think "sequence." For example, the `StringOps` class defines a method

  ```
  def containsSlice[B](that: GenSeq[B]): Boolean
  ```

  This method tests whether the string contains with a given sequence. If you like, you can pass a `Range`:

  ```
  "Bierstube".containsSlice('r'.to('u'))
    // Yields true since the string contains Range('r', 's', 't', 'u')
  ```

- Don't get discouraged that there are so many methods. It's the Scala way to provide lots of methods for every conceivable use case. When you need to solve a particular problem, just look for a method that is useful. More often than not, there is one that addresses your task, which means you don't have to write so much code yourself.

- Some methods have an "implicit" parameter. For example, the `sorted` method of `StringOps` is declared as

  ```
  def sorted[B >: Char](implicit ord: math.Ordering[B]): String
  ```

That means that an ordering is supplied "implicitly," using a mechanism that we will discuss in detail in Chapter 21. You can ignore these implicit parameters for now.

- Finally, don't worry if you run into the occasional indecipherable incantation, such as the [B >: Char] in the declaration of sorted. The expression B >: Char means "any supertype of Char," but for now, ignore that generality.

- Whenever you are confused what a method does, just try it out in the REPL:

```scala
"Scala".sorted // Yields "Saacl"
```

Now you can clearly see that the method returns a new string that consists of the characters in sorted order.

Exercises

1. In the Scala REPL, type 3. followed by the Tab key. What methods can be applied?

2. In the Scala REPL, compute the square root of 3, and then square that value. By how much does the result differ from 3? (Hint: The res variables are your friend.)

3. Are the res variables val or var?

4. Scala lets you multiply a string with a number—try out "crazy" * 3 in the REPL. What does this operation do? Where can you find it in Scaladoc?

5. What does 10 max 2 mean? In which class is the max method defined?

6. Using BigInt, compute 2^{1024}.

7. What do you need to import so that you can get a random prime as probablePrime(100, Random), without any qualifiers before probablePrime and Random?

8. One way to create random file or directory names is to produce a random BigInt and convert it to base 36, yielding a string such as "qsnvbevtomcj38o06kul". Poke around Scaladoc to find a way of doing this in Scala.

9. How do you get the first character of a string in Scala? The last character?

10. What do the take, drop, takeRight, and dropRight string functions do? What advantage or disadvantage do they have over using substring?

Control Structures and Functions

Topics in This Chapter A1

Chapter 2

In this chapter, you will learn how to implement conditions, loops, and functions in Scala. You will encounter a fundamental difference between Scala and other programming languages. In Java or C++, we differentiate between *expressions* (such as 3 + 4) and *statements* (for example, an if statement). An expression has a value; a statement carries out an action. In Scala, almost all constructs have values. This feature can make programs more concise and easier to read.

Here are the highlights of this chapter:

* An if expression has a value.

* A block has a value—the value of its last expression.

* The Scala for loop is like an "enhanced" Java for loop.

* Semicolons are (mostly) optional.

* The void type is Unit.

* Avoid using return in a function.

* Beware of missing = in a function definition.

* Exceptions work just like in Java or C++, but you use a "pattern matching" syntax for catch.

* Scala has no checked exceptions.

2.1 Conditional Expressions

Scala has an if/else construct with the same syntax as in Java or C++. However, in Scala, an if/else has a value, namely the value of the expression that follows the if or else. For example,

```
if (x > 0) 1 else -1
```

has a value of 1 or -1, depending on the value of x. You can put that value in a variable:

```
val s = if (x > 0) 1 else -1
```

This has the same effect as

```
if (x > 0) s = 1 else s = -1
```

However, the first form is better because it can be used to initialize a val. In the second form, s needs to be a var.

(As already mentioned, semicolons are mostly optional in Scala—see Section 2.2, "Statement Termination," on page 19.)

Java and C++ have a ?: operator for this purpose. The expression

```
x > 0 ? 1 : -1 // Java or C++
```

is equivalent to the Scala expression if (x > 0) 1 else -1. However, you can't put statements inside a ?: expression. The Scala if/else combines the if/else and ?: constructs that are separate in Java and C++.

In Scala, every expression has a type. For example, the expression if (x > 0) 1 else -1 has the type Int because both branches have the type Int. The type of a mixed-type expression, such as

```
if (x > 0) "positive" else -1
```

is the common supertype of both branches. In this example, one branch is a java.lang.String, and the other an Int. Their common supertype is called Any. (See Section 8.11, "The Scala Inheritance Hierarchy," on page 100 for details.)

If the else part is omitted, for example in

```
if (x > 0) 1
```

then it is possible that the if statement yields no value. However, in Scala, every expression is supposed to have *some* value. This is finessed by introducing a class Unit that has one value, written as (). The if statement without an else is equivalent to

```
if (x > 0) 1 else ()
```

Think of () as a placeholder for "no useful value," and of Unit as an analog of void in Java or C++.

(Technically speaking, void has no value whereas Unit has one value that signifies "no value." If you are so inclined, you can ponder the difference between an empty wallet and a wallet with a bill labeled "no dollars.")

NOTE: Scala has no switch statement, but it has a much more powerful pattern matching mechanism that we will discuss in Chapter 14. For now, just use a sequence of if statements.

CAUTION: The REPL is more nearsighted than the compiler—it only sees one line of code at a time. For example, when you type

```
if (x > 0) 1
else if (x == 0) 0 else -1
```

the REPL executes if (x > 0) 1 and shows the answer. Then it gets confused about the else keyword.

If you want to break the line before the else, use braces:

```
if (x > 0) { 1
} else if (x == 0) 0 else -1
```

This is only a concern in the REPL. In a compiled program, the parser will find the else on the next line.

TIP: If you want to paste a block of code into the REPL without worrying about its nearsightedness, use *paste mode*. Type

```
:paste
```

Then paste in the code block and type Ctrl+D. The REPL will then analyze the block in its entirety.

2.2 Statement Termination

In Java and C++, every statement ends with a semicolon. In Scala—like in JavaScript and other scripting languages—a semicolon is never required if it falls just before the end of the line. A semicolon is also optional before an }, an else, and similar locations where it is clear from context that the end of a statement has been reached.

However, if you want to have more than one statement on a single line, you need to separate them with semicolons. For example,

```
if (n > 0) { r = r * n; n -= 1 }
```

A semicolon is needed to separate r = r * n and n -= 1. Because of the }, no semicolon is needed after the second statement.

If you want to continue a long statement over two lines, make sure that the first line ends in a symbol that *cannot be* the end of a statement. An operator is often a good choice:

```
s = s0 + (v - v0) * t + // The + tells the parser that this is not the end
  0.5 * (a - a0) * t * t
```

In practice, long expressions usually involve function or method calls, and then you don't need to worry much—after an opening (, the compiler won't infer the end of a statement until it has seen the matching).

In the same spirit, Scala programmers favor the Kernighan & Ritchie brace style:

```
if (n > 0) {
  r = r * n
  n -= 1
}
```

The line ending with a { sends a clear signal that there is more to come.

Many programmers coming from Java or C++ are initially uncomfortable about omitting semicolons. If you prefer to put them in, feel free to—they do no harm.

2.3 Block Expressions and Assignments

In Java or C++, a block statement is a sequence of statements enclosed in { }. You use a block statement whenever you need to put multiple actions in the body of a branch or loop statement.

In Scala, a { } block contains a sequence of *expressions*, and the result is also an expression. The value of the block is the value of the last expression.

This feature can be useful if the initialization of a val takes more than one step. For example,

```
val distance = { val dx = x - x0; val dy = y - y0; sqrt(dx * dx + dy * dy) }
```

The value of the { } block is the last expression, shown here in bold. The variables dx and dy, which were only needed as intermediate values in the computation, are neatly hidden from the rest of the program.

In Scala, assignments have no value—or, strictly speaking, they have a value of type Unit. Recall that the Unit type is the equivalent of the void type in Java and C++, with a single value written as ().

A block that ends with an assignment, such as

```
{ r = r * n; n -= 1 }
```

has a Unit value. This is not a problem, just something to be aware of when defining functions—see Section 2.7, "Functions," on page 25.

Since assignments have Unit value, don't chain them together.

```
x = y = 1 // No
```

The value of y = 1 is (), and it's highly unlikely that you wanted to assign a Unit to x. (In contrast, in Java and C++, the value of an assignment is the value that is being assigned. In those languages, chained assignments are useful.)

2.4 Input and Output

To print a value, use the print or println function. The latter adds a newline character after the printout. For example,

```
print("Answer: ")
println(42)
```

yields the same output as

```
println("Answer: " + 42)
```

There is also a printf function with a C-style format string:

```
printf("Hello, %s! You are %d years old.%n", name, age)
```

Or better, use *string interpolation*

```
print(f"Hello, $name! In six months, you'll be ${age + 0.5}%7.2f years old.%n")
```

A formatted string is prefixed with the letter f. It contains expressions that are prefixed with $ and optionally followed by C-style format strings. The expression $name is replaced with the value of the variable name. The expression ${age + 0.5}%7.2f is replaced with the value of age + 0.5, formatted as a floating-point number of width 7 and precision 2. You need ${...} around expressions that are not variable names.

Using the f interpolator is better than using the printf method because it is type-safe. If you accidentally use %f with an expression that isn't a number, the compiler reports an error.

NOTE: Formatted strings are one of three predefined string interpolators in the Scala library. With a prefix of s, strings can contain expressions but not format directives. With a prefix of raw, escape sequences in a string are not evaluated. For example, raw"\n is a newline" starts with a backslash and the letter n, not a newline character.

To include a $ sign in an interpolated string, double it. For example, s"$$$price" yields a dollar sign followed by the value of price.

You can also define your own interpolators—see Exercise 11 on page 32. However, interpolators that produce compile-time errors (such as the f interpolator) need to be implemented as "macros," an experimental Scala feature that is beyond the scope of this book.

You can read a line of input from the console with the readLine method of the scala.io.StdIn class. To read a numeric, Boolean, or character value, use readInt, readDouble, readByte, readShort, readLong, readFloat, readBoolean, or readChar. The readLine method, but not the other ones, takes a prompt string:

```
import scala.io
val name = StdIn.readLine("Your name: ")
print("Your age: ")
val age = StdIn.readInt()
println(s"Hello, ${name}! Next year, you will be ${age + 1}.")
```

2.5 Loops

Scala has the same while and do loops as Java and C++. For example,

```
while (n > 0) {
  r = r * n
  n -= 1
}
```

Scala has no direct analog of the for (*initialize*; *test*; *update*) loop. If you need such a loop, you have two choices. You can use a while loop. Or, you can use a for statement like this:

```
for (i <- 1 to n)
  r = r * i
```

You saw the to method of the RichInt class in Chapter 1. The call 1 to n returns a Range of the numbers from 1 to n (inclusive).

The construct

```
for (i <- expr)
```

makes the variable i traverse all values of the expression to the right of the <-. Exactly how that traversal works depends on the type of the expression. For a Scala collection, such as a Range, the loop makes i assume each value in turn.

 NOTE: There is no val or var before the variable in the for loop. The type of the variable is the element type of the collection. The scope of the loop variable extends until the end of the loop.

When traversing a string, you can loop over the index values:

```
val s = "Hello"
var sum = 0
for (i <- 0 to s.length - 1)
  sum += s(i)
```

In this example, there is actually no need to use indexes. You can directly loop over the characters:

```
var sum = 0
for (ch <- "Hello") sum += ch
```

In Scala, loops are not used as often as in other languages. As you will see in Chapter 12, you can often process the values in a sequence by applying a function to all of them, which can be done with a single method call.

 NOTE: Scala has no break or continue statements to break out of a loop. What to do if you need a break? Here are a few options:

- Use a Boolean control variable.

- Use nested functions—you can return from the middle of a function.

- Use the break method in the Breaks object:

  ```
  import scala.util.control.Breaks._
  breakable {
    for (...) {
      if (...) break; // Exits the breakable block
      ...
    }
  }
  ```

  Here, the control transfer is done by throwing and catching an exception, so you should avoid this mechanism when time is of essence.

NOTE: In Java, you cannot have two local variables with the same name and overlapping scope. In Scala, there is no such prohibition, and the normal shadowing rule applies. For example, the following is perfectly legal:

```
val n = ...
for (n <- 1 to 10) {
  // Here n refers to the loop variable
}
```

2.6 Advanced for Loops

In the preceding section, you saw the basic form of the for loop. However, this construct is much richer in Scala than in Java or C++. This section covers the advanced features.

You can have multiple *generators* of the form *variable <- expression*. Separate them by semicolons. For example,

```
for (i <- 1 to 3; j <- 1 to 3) print(f"${10 * i + j}%3d")
  // Prints 11 12 13 21 22 23 31 32 33
```

Each generator can have a *guard*, a Boolean condition preceded by if:

```
for (i <- 1 to 3; j <- 1 to 3 if i != j) print(f"${10 * i + j}%3d")
  // Prints 12 13 21 23 31 32
```

Note that there is no semicolon before the if.

You can have any number of *definitions*, introducing variables that can be used inside the loop:

```
for (i <- 1 to 3; from = 4 - i; j <- from to 3) print(f"${10 * i + j}%3d")
  // Prints 13 22 23 31 32 33
```

When the body of the for loop starts with yield, the loop constructs a collection of values, one for each iteration:

```
for (i <- 1 to 10) yield i % 3
  // Yields Vector(1, 2, 0, 1, 2, 0, 1, 2, 0, 1)
```

This type of loop is called a for *comprehension*.

The generated collection is compatible with the first generator.

```
for (c <- "Hello"; i <- 0 to 1) yield (c + i).toChar
  // Yields "HIeflmlmop"
for (i <- 0 to 1; c <- "Hello") yield (c + i).toChar
  // Yields Vector('H', 'e', 'l', 'l', 'o', 'I', 'f', 'm', 'm', 'p')
```

NOTE: If you prefer, you can enclose the generators, guards, and definitions of a for loop in braces, and you can use newlines instead of semicolons to separate them:

```
for { i <- 1 to 3
  from = 4 - i
  j <- from to 3 }
```

2.7 Functions

Scala has functions in addition to methods. A method operates on an object, but a function doesn't. C++ has functions as well, but in Java, you have to imitate them with static methods.

To define a function, specify the function's name, parameters, and body like this:

```
def abs(x: Double) = if (x >= 0) x else -x
```

You must specify the types of all parameters. However, as long as the function is not recursive, you need not specify the return type. The Scala compiler determines the return type from the type of the expression to the right of the = symbol.

If the body of the function requires more than one expression, use a block. The last expression of the block becomes the value that the function returns. For example, the following function returns the value of r after the for loop.

```
def fac(n : Int) = {
  var r = 1
  for (i <- 1 to n) r = r * i
  r
}
```

There is no need for the return keyword in this example. It is possible to use return as in Java or C++, to exit a function immediately, but that is not commonly done in Scala.

TIP: While there is nothing wrong with using return in a named function (except the waste of seven keystrokes), it is a good idea to get used to life without return. Pretty soon, you will be using lots of *anonymous functions*, and there, return doesn't return a value to the caller but breaks out to the enclosing named function. Think of return as a kind of break statement for functions, and only use it when you want that breakout functionality.

With a recursive function, you must specify the return type. For example,

```
def fac(n: Int): Int = if (n <= 0) 1 else n * fac(n - 1)
```

Without the return type, the Scala compiler couldn't verify that the type of n * fac(n - 1) is an Int.

 NOTE: Some programming languages (such as ML and Haskell) *can* infer the type of a recursive function, using the Hindley-Milner algorithm. However, this doesn't work well in an object-oriented language. Extending the Hindley-Milner algorithm so it can handle subtypes is still a research problem.

2.8 Default and Named Arguments L1

You can provide default arguments for functions that are used when you don't specify explicit values. For example,

```
def decorate(str: String, left: String = "[", right: String = "]") =
  left + str + right
```

This function has two parameters, left and right, with default arguments "[" and "]".

If you call decorate("Hello"), you get "[Hello]". If you don't like the defaults, supply your own: decorate("Hello", "<<<", ">>>").

If you supply fewer arguments than there are parameters, the defaults are applied from the end. For example, decorate("Hello", ">>>[") uses the default value of the right parameter, yielding ">>>[Hello]".

You can also specify the parameter names when you supply the arguments. For example,

```
decorate(left = "<<<", str = "Hello", right = ">>>")
```

The result is "<<<Hello>>>". Note that the named arguments need not be in the same order as the parameters.

Named arguments can make a function call more readable. They are also useful if a function has many default parameters.

You can mix unnamed and named arguments, provided the unnamed ones come first:

```
decorate("Hello", right = "]<<<") // Calls decorate("Hello", "[", "]<<<")
```

2.9 Variable Arguments L1

Sometimes, it is convenient to implement a function that can take a variable number of arguments. The following example shows the syntax:

```
def sum(args: Int*) = {
  var result = 0
  for (arg <- args) result += arg
  result
}
```

You can call this function with as many arguments as you like.

```
val s = sum(1, 4, 9, 16, 25)
```

The function receives a single parameter of type Seq, which we will discuss in Chapter 13. For now, all you need to know is that you can use a for loop to visit each element.

If you already have a sequence of values, you cannot pass it directly to such a function. For example, the following is not correct:

```
val s = sum(1 to 5) // Error
```

If the sum function is called with one argument, that must be a single integer, not a range of integers. The remedy is to tell the compiler that you want the parameter to be considered an argument sequence. Append : _*, like this:

```
val s = sum(1 to 5: _*) // Consider 1 to 5 as an argument sequence
```

This call syntax is needed in a recursive definition:

```
def recursiveSum(args: Int*) : Int = {
  if (args.length == 0) 0
  else args.head + recursiveSum(args.tail : _*)
}
```

Here, the head of a sequence is its initial element, and tail is a sequence of all other elements. That's again a Seq, and we have to use : _* to convert it to an argument sequence.

CAUTION: When you call a Java method with variable arguments of type Object, such as PrintStream.printf or MessageFormat.format, you need to convert any primitive types by hand. For example,

```
val str = MessageFormat.format("The answer to {0} is {1}",
  "everything", 42.asInstanceOf[AnyRef])
```

This is the case for any Object parameter, but I mention it here because it is most common with varargs methods.

2.10 Procedures

Scala has a special notation for a function that returns no value. If the function body is enclosed in braces *without a preceding = symbol*, then the return type is Unit. Such a function is called a *procedure*. A procedure returns no value, and you only call it for its side effect. For example, the following procedure prints a string inside a box, like

```
-------
|Hello|
-------
```

Since the procedure doesn't return any value, we omit the = symbol.

```
def box(s : String) { // Look carefully: no =
  val border = "-" * (s.length + 2)
  print(f"$border%n|$s|%n$border%n")
}
```

Some people (not me) dislike this concise syntax for procedures and suggest that you always use an explicit return type of Unit:

```
def box(s : String): Unit = {
  ...
}
```

 CAUTION: The concise procedure syntax can be a surprise for Java and C++ programmers. It is a common error to accidentally omit the = in a function definition. You then get an error message at the point where the function is called: You are told that Unit is not acceptable at that location.

2.11 Lazy Values [L1]

When a val is declared as lazy, its initialization is deferred until it is accessed for the first time. For example,

```
lazy val words = scala.io.Source.fromFile("/usr/share/dict/words").mkString
```

(We will discuss file operations in Chapter 9. For now, just take it for granted that this call reads all characters from a file into a string.)

If the program never accesses words, the file is never opened. To verify this, try it out in the REPL, but misspell the file name. There will be no error when the initialization statement is executed. However, if you access words, you will get an error message that the file is not found.

Lazy values are useful to delay costly initialization statements. They can also deal with other initialization issues, such as circular dependencies. Moreover, they are essential for developing lazy data structures—see Section 13.12, "Streams," on page 189.

You can think of lazy values as halfway between val and def. Compare

```
val words = scala.io.Source.fromFile("/usr/share/dict/words").mkString
  // Evaluated as soon as words is defined
lazy val words = scala.io.Source.fromFile("/usr/share/dict/words").mkString
  // Evaluated the first time words is used
def words = scala.io.Source.fromFile("/usr/share/dict/words").mkString
  // Evaluated every time words is used
```

 NOTE: Laziness is not cost-free. Every time a lazy value is accessed, a method is called that checks, in a threadsafe manner, whether the value has already been initialized.

2.12 Exceptions

Scala exceptions work the same way as in Java or C++. When you throw an exception, for example

```
throw new IllegalArgumentException("x should not be negative")
```

the current computation is aborted, and the runtime system looks for an exception handler that can accept an IllegalArgumentException. Control resumes with the innermost such handler. If no such handler exists, the program terminates.

As in Java, the objects that you throw need to belong to a subclass of java.lang.Throwable. However, unlike Java, Scala has no "checked" exceptions—you never have to declare that a function or method might throw an exception.

 NOTE: In Java, "checked" exceptions are checked at compile time. If your method might throw an IOException, you must declare it. This forces programmers to think where those exceptions should be handled, which is a laudable goal. Unfortunately, it can also give rise to monstrous method signatures such as void doSomething() throws IOException, InterruptedException, ClassNotFoundException. Many Java programmers detest this feature and end up defeating it by either catching exceptions too early or using excessively general exception classes. The Scala designers decided against checked exceptions, recognizing that thorough compile-time checking isn't *always* a good thing.

A throw expression has the special type Nothing. That is useful in if/else expressions. If one branch has type Nothing, the type of the if/else expression is the type of the other branch. For example, consider

```
if (x >= 0) { sqrt(x)
} else throw new IllegalArgumentException("x should not be negative")
```

The first branch has type Double, the second has type Nothing. Therefore, the if/else expression also has type Double.

The syntax for catching exceptions is modeled after the pattern matching syntax (see Chapter 14).

```
val url = new URL("http://horstmann.com/fred-tiny.gif")
try {
  process(url)
} catch {
  case _: MalformedURLException => println(s"Bad URL: $url")
  case ex: IOException => ex.printStackTrace()
}
```

As in Java or C++, the more general exception types should come after the more specific ones.

Note that you can use _ for the variable name if you don't need it.

The try/finally statement lets you dispose of a resource whether or not an exception has occurred. For example:

```
val in = new URL("http://horstmann.com/fred.gif").openStream()
try {
  process(in)
} finally {
  in.close()
}
```

The finally clause is executed whether or not the process function throws an exception. The reader is always closed.

This code is a bit subtle, and it raises several issues.

- What if the URL constructor or the openStream method throws an exception? Then the try block is never entered, and neither is the finally clause. That's just as well—in was never initialized, so it makes no sense to invoke close on it.

- Why isn't val in = new URL(...).openStream() inside the try block? Then the scope of in would not extend to the finally clause.

- What if in.close() throws an exception? Then that exception is thrown out of the statement, superseding any earlier one. (This is just like in Java, and it isn't very nice. Ideally, the old exception would stay attached to the new one.)

Note that try/catch and try/finally have complementary goals. The try/catch statement handles exceptions, and the try/finally statement takes some action (usually cleanup) when an exception is not handled. You can combine them into a single try/catch/finally statement:

```
try { ... } catch { ... } finally { ... }
```

This is the same as

```
try { try { ... } catch { ... } } finally { ... }
```

However, that combination is rarely useful.

NOTE: Scala does not have an analog to the Java try-with-resources statement. Consider using the scala-ARM library (http://jsuereth.com/scala-arm). Then you can write

```
import resource._
import java.nio.file._
for (in <- resource(Files.newBufferedReader(inPath));
     out <- resource(Files.newBufferedWriter(outPath))) {
  ...
}
```

NOTE: The Try class is designed to work with computations that may fail with exceptions. We will look at it more closely in Chapter 17. Here is a simple example:

```
import scala.io._
val result =
  for (a <- Try { StdIn.readLine("a: ").toInt };
       b <- Try { StdIn.readLine("b: ").toInt })
    yield a / b
```

If an exception occurs in either of the calls to toInt, or because of division by zero, then result is a Failure object, containing the exception that caused the computation to fail. Otherwise, result is a Success object holding the result of the computation.

Exercises

1. The *signum* of a number is 1 if the number is positive, –1 if it is negative, and 0 if it is zero. Write a function that computes this value.

2. What is the value of an empty block expression {}? What is its type?

3. Come up with one situation where the assignment x = y = 1 is valid in Scala. (Hint: Pick a suitable type for x.)

4. Write a Scala equivalent for the Java loop

   ```
   for (int i = 10; i >= 0; i--) System.out.println(i);
   ```

5. Write a procedure countdown(n: Int) that prints the numbers from n to 0.

6. Write a for loop for computing the product of the Unicode codes of all letters in a string. For example, the product of the characters in "Hello" is 9415087488L.

7. Solve the preceding exercise without writing a loop. (Hint: Look at the StringOps Scaladoc.)

8. Write a function product(s : String) that computes the product, as described in the preceding exercises.

9. Make the function of the preceding exercise a recursive function.

10. Write a function that computes x^n, where n is an integer. Use the following recursive definition:

    - $x^n = y \cdot y$ if n is even and positive, where $y = x^{n/2}$.
    - $x^n = x \cdot x^{n-1}$ if n is odd and positive.
    - $x^0 = 1$.
    - $x^n = 1 / x^{-n}$ if n is negative.

    Don't use a return statement.

11. Define a string interpolator date so that you can define a java.time.LocalDate as date"$year-$month-$day". You need to define an "implicit" class with a date method, like this:

    ```
    implicit class DateInterpolator(val sc: StringContext) extends AnyVal {
      def date(args: Any*): LocalDate = . . .
    }
    ```

    args(i) is the value of the ith expression. Convert each to a string and then to an integer, and pass them to the LocalDate.of method. If you already know some Scala, add error handling. Throw an exception if there aren't three arguments, or if they aren't integers, or if they aren't separated by dashes. (You get the strings in between the expressions as sc.parts.)

Working with Arrays

Topics in This Chapter A1

Chapter 3

In this chapter, you will learn how to work with arrays in Scala. Java and C++ programmers usually choose an array or its close relation (such as array lists or vectors) when they need to collect a bunch of elements. In Scala, there are other choices (see Chapter 13), but for now, I'll assume you are impatient and just want to get going with arrays.

Key points of this chapter:

- Use an `Array` if the length is fixed, and an `ArrayBuffer` if the length can vary.
- Don't use `new` when supplying initial values.
- Use () to access elements.
- Use `for (elem <- arr)` to traverse the elements.
- Use `for (elem <- arr if ... ) ... yield ...` to transform into a new array.
- Scala and Java arrays are interoperable; with `ArrayBuffer`, use `scala.collection.JavaConversions`.

3.1 Fixed-Length Arrays

If you need an array whose length doesn't change, use the `Array` type in Scala. For example,

```
val nums = new Array[Int](10)
  // An array of ten integers, all initialized with zero
val a = new Array[String](10)
  // A string array with ten elements, all initialized with null
val s = Array("Hello", "World")
  // An Array[String] of length 2—the type is inferred
  // Note: No new when you supply initial values
s(0) = "Goodbye"
  // Array("Goodbye", "World")
  // Use () instead of [] to access elements
```

Inside the JVM, a Scala Array is implemented as a Java array. The arrays in the preceding example have the type java.lang.String[] inside the JVM. An array of Int, Double, or another equivalent of the Java primitive types is a primitive type array. For example, Array(2,3,5,7,11) is an int[] in the JVM.

3.2 Variable-Length Arrays: Array Buffers

Java has ArrayList and C++ has vector for arrays that grow and shrink on demand. The equivalent in Scala is the ArrayBuffer.

```
import scala.collection.mutable.ArrayBuffer
val b = ArrayBuffer[Int]()
  // Or new ArrayBuffer[Int]
  // An empty array buffer, ready to hold integers
b += 1
  // ArrayBuffer(1)
  // Add an element at the end with +=
b += (1, 2, 3, 5)
  // ArrayBuffer(1, 1, 2, 3, 5)
  // Add multiple elements at the end by enclosing them in parentheses
b ++= Array(8, 13, 21)
  // ArrayBuffer(1, 1, 2, 3, 5, 8, 13, 21)
  // You can append any collection with the ++= operator
b.trimEnd(5)
  // ArrayBuffer(1, 1, 2)
  // Removes the last five elements
```

Adding or removing elements at the end of an array buffer is an efficient ("amortized constant time") operation.

You can also insert and remove elements at an arbitrary location, but those operations are not as efficient—all elements after that location must be shifted. For example:

```
b.insert(2, 6)
  // ArrayBuffer(1, 1, 6, 2)
  // Insert before index 2
b.insert(2, 7, 8, 9)
  // ArrayBuffer(1, 1, 7, 8, 9, 6, 2)
  // You can insert as many elements as you like
b.remove(2)
  // ArrayBuffer(1, 1, 8, 9, 6, 2)
b.remove(2, 3)
  // ArrayBuffer(1, 1, 2)
  // The second parameter tells how many elements to remove
```

Sometimes, you want to build up an `Array`, but you don't yet know how many elements you will need. In that case, first make an array buffer, then call

```
b.toArray
  // Array(1, 1, 2)
```

Conversely, call `a.toBuffer` to convert the array a to an array buffer.

3.3 Traversing Arrays and Array Buffers

In Java and C++, there are several syntactical differences between arrays and array lists/vectors. Scala is much more uniform. Most of the time, you can use the same code for both.

Here is how you traverse an array or array buffer with a for loop:

```
for (i <- 0 until a.length)
  println(s"$i: ${a(i)}")
```

The `until` method is similar to the `to` method, except that it excludes the last value. Therefore, the variable i goes from 0 to `a.length - 1`.

In general, the construct

```
for (i <- range)
```

makes the variable i traverse all values of the range. In our case, the loop variable i assumes the values 0, 1, and so on until (but not including) `a.length`.

To visit every second element, let i traverse

```
0 until a.length by 2
  // Range(0, 2, 4, ...)
```

To visit the elements starting from the end of the array, traverse

```
0 until a.length by -1
  // Range(..., 2, 1, 0)
```

 TIP: Instead of 0 until a.length or 0 until a.length by -1, you can use
a.indices or a.indices.reverse.

If you don't need the array index in the loop body, visit the array elements
directly:

```
for (elem <- a)
  println(elem)
```

This is similar to the "enhanced" for loop in Java or the "range-based" for loop
in C++. The variable elem is set to a(0), then a(1), and so on.

3.4 Transforming Arrays

In the preceding sections, you saw how to work with arrays just like you
would in Java or C++. But in Scala, you can go further. It is easy to take an array
(or array buffer) and transform it in some way. Such transformations don't modify
the original array but yield a new one.

Use a for comprehension like this:

```
val a = Array(2, 3, 5, 7, 11)
val result = for (elem <- a) yield 2 * elem
  // result is Array(4, 6, 10, 14, 22)
```

The for/yield loop creates a new collection of the same type as the original collection. If you started with an array, you get another array. If you started with an
array buffer, that's what you get from for/yield.

The result contains the expressions after the yield, one for each iteration of the loop.

Oftentimes, when you traverse a collection, you only want to process the elements
that match a particular condition. This is achieved with a *guard*: an if inside the
for. Here we double every even element, dropping the odd ones:

```
for (elem <- a if elem % 2 == 0) yield 2 * elem
```

Keep in mind that the result is a new collection—the original collection is not
affected.

NOTE: Alternatively, you could write

```
a.filter(_ % 2 == 0).map(2 * _)
```

or even

```
a filter { _ % 2 == 0 } map { 2 * _ }
```

Some programmers with experience in functional programming prefer `filter` and `map` to guards and `yield`. That's just a matter of style—the `for/yield` loop does exactly the same work. Use whichever you find easier.

Suppose we want to remove all negative elements from an array buffer of integers. A traditional sequential solution might traverse the array buffer and remove unwanted elements as they are encountered.

```
var n = a.length
var i = 0
while (i < n) {
  if (a(i) >= 0) i += 1
  else { a.remove(i); n -= 1 }
}
```

That's a bit fussy—you have to remember *not* to increment i when you remove the element, and to decrement n instead. It is also not efficient to remove elements from the middle of the array buffer. This loop unnecessarily moves elements that will later be removed.

In Scala, the obvious solution is to use a `for/yield` loop and keep all non-negative elements:

```
val result = for (elem <- a if elem >= 0) yield elem
```

The result is a new array buffer. Suppose that we want to modify the original array buffer instead, removing the unwanted elements. Then we can collect their positions:

```
val positionsToRemove = for (i <- a.indices if a(i) < 0) yield i
```

Now remove the elements at those positions, starting from the back:

```
for (i <- positionsToRemove.reverse) a.remove(i)
```

Or better, remember the positions to keep, copy them over, and then shorten the buffer:

```
val positionsToKeep = for (i <- a.indices if a(i) >= 0) yield i
for (j <- positionsToKeep.indices) a(j) = a(positionsToKeep(j))
a.trimEnd(a.length - positionsToKeep.length)
```

The key observation is that it is better to have *all index values together* instead of seeing them one by one.

3.5 Common Algorithms

It is often said that a large percentage of business computations are nothing but computing sums and sorting. Fortunately, Scala has built-in functions for these tasks.

```
Array(1, 7, 2, 9).sum
  // 19
  // Works for ArrayBuffer too
```

In order to use the sum method, the element type must be a numeric type: either an integral or floating-point type or BigInteger/BigDecimal.

Similarly, the min and max methods yield the smallest and largest element in an array or array buffer.

```
ArrayBuffer("Mary", "had", "a", "little", "lamb").max
  // "little"
```

The sorted method sorts an array or array buffer and *returns* the sorted array or array buffer, without modifying the original:

```
val b = ArrayBuffer(1, 7, 2, 9)
val bSorted = b.sorted
  // b is unchanged; bSorted is ArrayBuffer(1, 2, 7, 9)
```

You can also supply a comparison function, but then you should use the sortWith method:

```
val bDescending = b.sortWith(_ > _) // ArrayBuffer(9, 7, 2, 1)
```

See Chapter 12 for the function syntax.

You can sort an array, but not an array buffer, in place:

```
val a = Array(1, 7, 2, 9)
scala.util.Sorting.quickSort(a)
  // a is now Array(1, 2, 7, 9)
```

For the min, max, and quickSort methods, the element type must have a comparison operation. This is the case for numbers, strings, and other types with the Ordered trait.

Finally, if you want to display the contents of an array or array buffer, the mkString method lets you specify the separator between elements. A second variant has parameters for the prefix and suffix. For example,

```
a.mkString(" and ")
  // "1 and 2 and 7 and 9"
a.mkString("<", ",", ">")
  // "<1,2,7,9>"
```

Contrast with `toString`:

```
a.toString
  // "[I@b73e5"
  // This is the useless toString method from Java
b.toString
  // "ArrayBuffer(1, 7, 2, 9)"
  // The toString method reports the type, which is useful for debugging
```

3.6 Deciphering Scaladoc

There are lots of useful methods on arrays and array buffers, and it is a good idea to browse the Scala documentation to get an idea of what's there.

Scala has a richer type system than Java, so you may encounter some strange-looking syntax as you browse the Scala documentation. Fortunately, you don't have to understand all nuances of the type system to do useful work. Use Table 3–1 as a "decoder ring."

Table 3–1 Scaladoc Decoder Ring

Scaladoc	Explanation
`def count(p: (A) => Boolean): Int`	This method takes a *predicate*, a function from A to Boolean. It counts for how many elements the function is true. For example, `a.count(_ > 0)` counts how many elements of a are positive.
`def append(elems: A*): Unit`	This method takes *zero or more* arguments of type A. For example, `b.append(1, 7, 2, 9)` appends four elements to b.
`def appendAll(xs: TraversableOnce[A]): Unit`	The xs parameter can be any collection with the TraversableOnce trait, a trait in the Scala collections hierarchy. Other common traits that you may encounter in Scaladoc are Traversable and Iterable. All Scala collections implement these traits, and the difference between them is academic for library users. Simply think "any collection" when you see one of these.

(Continues)

Table 3–1 Scaladoc Decoder Ring *(Continued)*

Scaladoc	Explanation
`def containsSlice[B](that: GenSeq[B]): Boolean`	A `GenSeq` or `Seq` is a collection whose elements are arranged in sequential order. Think "array, list, or string."
`def += (elem: A): ArrayBuffer.this.type`	This method returns `this`, which allows you to chain calls, for example: `b += 4 -= 5`. When you work with an `ArrayBuffer[A]`, you can just think of the method as `def += (elem: A) : ArrayBuffer[A]`. If someone forms a subclass of `ArrayBuffer`, then the return type of `+=` is that subclass.
`def copyToArray[B >: A] (xs: Array[B]): Unit`	Note that the function copies an `ArrayBuffer[A]` into an `Array[B]`. Here, `B` is allowed to be a *supertype* of `A`. For example, you can copy from an `ArrayBuffer[Int]` to an `Array[Any]`. At first reading, just ignore the `[B >: A]` and replace `B` with `A`.
`def sorted[B >: A] (implicit cmp: Ordering[B]): ArrayBuffer[A]`	The element type `A` must have a supertype `B` for which an "implicit" object of type `Ordering[B]` exists. Such an ordering exists for numbers, strings, and other types with the `Ordered` trait, as well as for classes that implement the Java `Comparable` interface.

`def ++:[B >: A, That](that: collection.Traversable[B])(implicit bf: CanBuildFrom[ArrayBuffer[A], B, That]): That`	This declaration happens when the method creates a new collection. Most of the time, Scaladoc hides such complex descriptions and shows a simpler one tagged with "[use case]". In this case, it doesn't. You can simplify the declaration in your mind to a "happy day scenario," like this:
	
	`def ++:(that: ArrayBuffer[A]) : ArrayBuffer[A]`
	
	What if that is an `ArrayBuffer[B]` or some other collection? Try it out in the REPL:
	
	`ArrayBuffer('a', 'b') ++: "cd" // Yields a string "abcd"`

3.7 Multidimensional Arrays

Like in Java, multidimensional arrays are implemented as arrays of arrays. For example, a two-dimensional array of `Double` values has the type `Array[Array[Double]]`. To construct such an array, use the `ofDim` method:

```
val matrix = Array.ofDim[Double](3, 4) // Three rows, four columns
```

To access an element, use two pairs of parentheses:

```
matrix(row)(column) = 42
```

You can make ragged arrays, with varying row lengths:

```
val triangle = new Array[Array[Int]](10)
for (i <- triangle.indices)
  triangle(i) = new Array[Int](i + 1)
```

3.8 Interoperating with Java

Since Scala arrays are implemented as Java arrays, you can pass them back and forth between Java and Scala.

This works in almost all cases, except if the array element type isn't an exact match. In Java, an array of a given type is automatically converted to an array of a supertype. For example, a Java String[] array can be passed to a method that expects a Java Object[] array. Scala does not permit this automatic conversion because it is unsafe. (See Chapter 18 for a detailed explanation.)

Suppose you want to invoke a Java method with an Object[] parameter, such as java.util.Arrays.binarySearch(Object[] a, Object key):

```
val a = Array("Mary", "a", "had", "lamb", "little")
java.util.Arrays.binarySearch(a, "beef") // Does not work
```

This does not work because Scala will not convert an Array[String] into an Array[Object]. You can force the conversion like this:

```
java.util.Arrays.binarySearch(a.asInstanceOf[Array[Object]], "beef")
```

 NOTE: This is just an example to show how to overcome element type differences. If you want to carry out binary search in Scala, do it like this:

```
import scala.collection.Searching._
val result = a.search("beef")
```

The result is Found(n) if the element was found at position n or InsertionPoint(n) if the element was not found but should be inserted before position n.

If you call a Java method that receives or returns a java.util.List, you could, of course, use a Java ArrayList in your Scala code—but that is unattractive. Instead, import the implicit conversion methods in scala.collection.JavaConversions. Then you can use Scala buffers in your code, and they automatically get wrapped into Java lists when calling a Java method.

For example, the java.lang.ProcessBuilder class has a constructor with a List<String> parameter. Here is how you can call it from Scala:

```
import scala.collection.JavaConversions.bufferAsJavaList
import scala.collection.mutable.ArrayBuffer
val command = ArrayBuffer("ls", "-al", "/home/cay")
val pb = new ProcessBuilder(command) // Scala to Java
```

The Scala buffer is wrapped into an object of a Java class that implements the java.util.List interface.

Conversely, when a Java method returns a java.util.List, you can have it automatically converted into a Buffer:

```
import scala.collection.JavaConversions.asScalaBuffer
import scala.collection.mutable.Buffer
val cmd : Buffer[String] = pb.command() // Java to Scala
    // You can't use ArrayBuffer—the wrapped object is only guaranteed to be a Buffer
```

If the Java method returns a wrapped Scala buffer, then the implicit conversion unwraps the original object. In our example, cmd == command.

Exercises

1. Write a code snippet that sets a to an array of n random integers between 0 (inclusive) and n (exclusive).

2. Write a loop that swaps adjacent elements of an array of integers. For example, Array(1, 2, 3, 4, 5) becomes Array(2, 1, 4, 3, 5).

3. Repeat the preceding assignment, but produce a new array with the swapped values. Use for/yield.

4. Given an array of integers, produce a new array that contains all positive values of the original array, in their original order, followed by all values that are zero or negative, in their original order.

5. How do you compute the average of an Array[Double]?

6. How do you rearrange the elements of an Array[Int] so that they appear in reverse sorted order? How do you do the same with an ArrayBuffer[Int]?

7. Write a code snippet that produces all values from an array with duplicates removed. (Hint: Look at Scaladoc.)

8. Suppose you are given an array buffer of integers and want to remove all but the first negative number. Here is a sequential solution that sets a flag when the first negative number is called, then removes all elements beyond.

```
var first = true
var n = a.length
var i = 0
while (i < n) {
  if (a(i) >= 0) i += 1
  else {
    if (first) { first = false; i += 1 }
    else { a.remove(i); n -= 1 }
  }
}
```

This is a complex and inefficient solution. Rewrite it in Scala by collecting positions of the negative elements, dropping the first element, reversing the sequence, and calling a.remove(i) for each index.

9. Improve the solution of the preceding exercise by collecting the positions that should be moved and their target positions. Make those moves and truncate the buffer. Don't copy any elements before the first unwanted element.

10. Make a collection of all time zones returned by java.util.TimeZone.getAvailableIDs that are in America. Strip off the "America/" prefix and sort the result.

11. Import java.awt.datatransfer._ and make an object of type SystemFlavorMap with the call

```
val flavors = SystemFlavorMap.getDefaultFlavorMap().asInstanceOf[SystemFlavorMap]
```

Then call the getNativesForFlavor method with parameter DataFlavor.imageFlavor and get the return value as a Scala buffer. (Why this obscure class? It's hard to find uses of java.util.List in the standard Java library.)

Maps and Tuples

Chapter 4

A classic programmer's saying is, "If you can only have one data structure, make it a hash table." Hash tables—or, more generally, maps—are among the most versatile data structures. As you will see in this chapter, Scala makes it particularly easy to use them.

Maps are collections of key/value pairs. Scala has a general notion of tuples— aggregates of n objects, not necessarily of the same type. A pair is simply a tuple with $n = 2$. Tuples are useful whenever you need to aggregate two or more values together, and we briefly discuss the syntax at the end of this chapter.

Highlights of the chapter are:

- Scala has a pleasant syntax for creating, querying, and traversing maps.
- You need to choose between mutable and immutable maps.
- By default, you get a hash map, but you can also get a tree map.
- You can easily convert between Scala and Java maps.
- Tuples are useful for aggregating values.

4.1 Constructing a Map

You can construct a map as

```
val scores = Map("Alice" -> 10, "Bob" -> 3, "Cindy" -> 8)
```

This constructs an immutable Map[String, Int] whose contents can't be changed. If you want a mutable map, use

```
val scores = scala.collection.mutable.Map("Alice" -> 10, "Bob" -> 3, "Cindy" -> 8)
```

If you want to start out with a blank map, you have to supply type parameters:

```
val scores = scala.collection.mutable.Map[String, Int]()
```

In Scala, a map is a collection of *pairs*. A pair is simply a grouping of two values, not necessarily of the same type, such as ("Alice", 10).

The -> operator makes a pair. The value of

```
"Alice" -> 10
```

is

```
("Alice", 10)
```

You could have equally well defined the map as

```
val scores = Map(("Alice", 10), ("Bob", 3), ("Cindy", 8))
```

The -> operator is just a little easier on the eyes than the parentheses. It also supports the intuition that a map data structure is a kind of function that maps keys to values. The difference is that a function computes values, and a map just looks them up.

4.2 Accessing Map Values

In Scala, the analogy between functions and maps is particularly close because you use the () notation to look up key values.

```
val bobsScore = scores("Bob") // Like scores.get("Bob") in Java
```

If the map doesn't contain a value for the requested key, an exception is thrown.

To check whether there is a key with the given value, call the contains method:

```
val bobsScore = if (scores.contains("Bob")) scores("Bob") else 0
```

Since this call combination is so common, there is a shortcut:

```
val bobsScore = scores.getOrElse("Bob", 0)
  // If the map contains the key "Bob", return the value; otherwise, return 0.
```

Finally, the call *map*.get(*key*) returns an Option object that is either Some(*value for key*) or None. We discuss the Option class in Chapter 14.

NOTE: Given an immutable map, you can turn it into a map with a fixed default value for keys that are not present, or a function to compute such values.

```
val scores1 = scores.withDefaultValue(0)
val zeldasScore1 = scores1.get("Zelda")
  // Yields 0 since "Zelda" is not present
val scores2 = scores.withDefault(_.length)
val zeldasScore2 = scores2.get("Zelda")
  // Yields 5, applying the length function to the key that is not present
```

4.3 Updating Map Values

In a mutable map, you can update a map value, or add a new one, with a () to the left of an = sign:

```
scores("Bob") = 10
  // Updates the existing value for the key "Bob" (assuming scores is mutable)
scores("Fred") = 7
  // Adds a new key/value pair to scores (assuming it is mutable)
```

Alternatively, you can use the += operation to add multiple associations:

```
scores += ("Bob" -> 10, "Fred" -> 7)
```

To remove a key and its associated value, use the -= operator:

```
scores -= "Alice"
```

You can't update an immutable map, but you can do something that's just as useful—obtain a new map that has the desired update:

```
val newScores = scores + ("Bob" -> 10, "Fred" -> 7) // New map with update
```

The newScores map contains the same associations as scores, except that "Bob" has been updated and "Fred" added.

Instead of saving the result as a new value, you can update a var:

```
var scores = ...
scores = scores + ("Bob" -> 10, "Fred" -> 7)
```

You can even use the += operator:

```
scores += ("Bob" -> 10, "Fred" -> 7)
```

Similarly, to remove a key from an immutable map, use the - operator to obtain a new map without the key:

```
scores = scores - "Alice"
```

or

```
scores -= "Alice"
```

You might think that it is inefficient to keep constructing new maps, but that is not the case. The old and new maps share most of their structure. (This is possible because they are immutable.)

4.4 Iterating over Maps

The following amazingly simple loop iterates over all key/value pairs of a map:

```
for ((k, v) <- map) process k and v
```

The magic here is that you can use pattern matching in a Scala for loop. (Chapter 14 has all the details.) That way, you get the key and value of each pair in the map without tedious method calls.

If for some reason you want to visit only the keys or values, use the keySet and values methods, as you would in Java. The values method returns an Iterable that you can use in a for loop.

```
scores.keySet // A set such as Set("Bob", "Cindy", "Fred", "Alice")
for (v <- scores.values) println(v) // Prints 10 8 7 10 or some permutation thereof
```

To reverse a map—that is, switch keys and values—use

```
for ((k, v) <- map) yield (v, k)
```

4.5 Sorted Maps

There are two common implementation strategies for maps: hash tables and balanced trees. Hash tables use the hash codes of the keys to scramble entries, so iterating over the elements yields them in unpredictable order. By default, Scala gives you a map based on a hash table because it is usually more efficient. If you need to visit the keys in sorted order, use a SortedMap instead.

```
val scores = scala.collection.mutable.SortedMap("Alice" -> 10,
  "Fred" -> 7, "Bob" -> 3, "Cindy" -> 8)
```

 TIP: If you want to visit the keys in insertion order, use a LinkedHashMap. For example,

```
val months = scala.collection.mutable.LinkedHashMap("January" -> 1,
  "February" -> 2, "March" -> 3, "April" -> 4, "May" -> 5, ...)
```

4.6 Interoperating with Java

If you get a Java map from calling a Java method, you may want to convert it to a Scala map so that you can use the pleasant Scala map API. This is also useful if you want to work with a mutable tree map, which Scala doesn't provide.

Simply add an import statement:

```
import scala.collection.JavaConversions.mapAsScalaMap
```

Then trigger the conversion by specifying the Scala map type:

```
val scores: scala.collection.mutable.Map[String, Int] =
  new java.util.TreeMap[String, Int]
```

In addition, you can get a conversion from java.util.Properties to a Map[String, String]:

```
import scala.collection.JavaConversions.propertiesAsScalaMap
val props: scala.collection.Map[String, String] = System.getProperties()
```

Conversely, to pass a Scala map to a method that expects a Java map, provide the opposite implicit conversion. For example:

```
import scala.collection.JavaConversions.mapAsJavaMap
import java.awt.font.TextAttribute._ // Import keys for map below
val attrs = Map(FAMILY -> "Serif", SIZE -> 12) // A Scala map
val font = new java.awt.Font(attrs) // Expects a Java map
```

4.7 Tuples

Maps are collections of key/value pairs. Pairs are the simplest case of *tuples*—aggregates of values of different types.

A tuple value is formed by enclosing individual values in parentheses. For example,

```
(1, 3.14, "Fred")
```

is a tuple of type

```
Tuple3[Int, Double, java.lang.String]
```

which is also written as

```
(Int, Double, java.lang.String)
```

If you have a tuple, say,

```
val t = (1, 3.14, "Fred")
```

then you can access its components with the methods _1, _2, _3, for example:

```
val second = t._2 // Sets second to 3.14
```

Unlike array or string positions, the component positions of a tuple start with 1, not 0.

NOTE: You can write t._2 as t _2 (with a space instead of a period), but not t_2.

Usually, it is better to use pattern matching to get at the components of a tuple, for example

```
val (first, second, third) = t // Sets first to 1, second to 3.14, third to "Fred"
```

You can use a _ if you don't need all components:

```
val (first, second, _) = t
```

Tuples are useful for functions that return more than one value. For example, the partition method of the StringOps class returns a pair of strings, containing the characters that fulfill a condition and those that don't:

```
"New York".partition(_.isUpper) // Yields the pair ("NY", "ew ork")
```

4.8 Zipping

One reason for using tuples is to bundle together values so that they can be processed together. This is commonly done with the zip method. For example, the code

```
val symbols = Array("<", "-", ">")
val counts = Array(2, 10, 2)
val pairs = symbols.zip(counts)
```

yields an array of pairs

```
Array(("<", 2), ("-", 10), (">", 2))
```

The pairs can then be processed together:

```
for ((s, n) <- pairs) print(s * n) // Prints <<---------->>
```

 TIP: The toMap method turns a collection of pairs into a map.

If you have a collection of keys and a parallel collection of values, zip them up and turn them into a map like this:

```
keys.zip(values).toMap
```

Exercises

1. Set up a map of prices for a number of gizmos that you covet. Then produce a second map with the same keys and the prices at a 10 percent discount.

2. Write a program that reads words from a file. Use a mutable map to count how often each word appears. To read the words, simply use a java.util.Scanner:

```
val in = new java.util.Scanner(new java.io.File("myfile.txt"))
while (in.hasNext()) process in.next()
```

Or look at Chapter 9 for a Scalaesque way.

At the end, print out all words and their counts.

3. Repeat the preceding exercise with an immutable map.

4. Repeat the preceding exercise with a sorted map, so that the words are printed in sorted order.

5. Repeat the preceding exercise with a java.util.TreeMap that you adapt to the Scala API.

6. Define a linked hash map that maps "Monday" to java.util.Calendar.MONDAY, and similarly for the other weekdays. Demonstrate that the elements are visited in insertion order.

7. Print a table of all Java properties reported by the getProperties method of the java.lang.System class, like this:

```
java.runtime.name         | Java(TM) SE Runtime Environment
sun.boot.library.path     | /home/apps/jdk1.6.0_21/jre/lib/i386
java.vm.version           | 17.0-b16
java.vm.vendor            | Sun Microsystems Inc.
java.vendor.url           | http://java.sun.com/
path.separator            | :
java.vm.name              | Java HotSpot(TM) Server VM
```

You need to find the length of the longest key before you can print the table.

8. Write a function minmax(values: Array[Int]) that returns a pair containing the smallest and the largest values in the array.

9. Write a function lteqgt(values: Array[Int], v: Int) that returns a triple containing the counts of values less than v, equal to v, and greater than v.

10. What happens when you zip together two strings, such as "Hello".zip("World")? Come up with a plausible use case.

Classes

Chapter 5

In this chapter, you will learn how to implement classes in Scala. If you know classes in Java or C++, you won't find this difficult, and you will enjoy the much more concise notation of Scala.

The key points of this chapter are:

- Fields in classes automatically come with getters and setters.

- You can replace a field with a custom getter/setter without changing the client of a class—that is the "uniform access principle."

- Use the @BeanProperty annotation to generate the JavaBeans get*Xxx*/set*Xxx* methods.

- Every class has a primary constructor that is "interwoven" with the class definition. Its parameters turn into the fields of the class. The primary constructor executes all statements in the body of the class.

- Auxiliary constructors are optional. They are called this.

5.1 Simple Classes and Parameterless Methods

In its simplest form, a Scala class looks very much like its equivalent in Java or C++:

```
class Counter {
  private var value = 0 // You must initialize the field
  def increment() { value += 1 } // Methods are public by default
  def current() = value
}
```

In Scala, a class is not declared as `public`. A Scala source file can contain multiple classes, and all of them have public visibility.

To use this class, you construct objects and invoke methods in the usual way:

```
val myCounter = new Counter // Or new Counter()
myCounter.increment()
println(myCounter.current)
```

You can call a parameterless method (such as `current`) with or without parentheses:

```
myCounter.current // OK
myCounter.current() // Also OK
```

Which form should you use? It is considered good style to use () for a *mutator* method (a method that changes the object state), and to drop the () for an *accessor* method (a method that does not change the object state).

That's what we did in our example:

```
myCounter.increment() // Use () with mutator
println(myCounter.current) // Don't use () with accessor
```

You can enforce this style by declaring `current` without ():

```
class Counter {
  ...
  def current = value // No () in definition
}
```

Now class users must use `myCounter.current`, without parentheses.

5.2 Properties with Getters and Setters

When writing a Java class, we don't like to use public fields:

```
public class Person { // This is Java
  public int age; // Frowned upon in Java
}
```

With a public field, anyone could write to `fred.age`, making Fred younger or older. That's why we prefer to use getter and setter methods:

```
public class Person { // This is Java
  private int age;
  public int getAge() { return age; }
  public void setAge(int age) { this.age = age; }
}
```

A getter/setter pair such as this one is often called a *property*. We say that the class Person has an age property.

Why is this any better? By itself, it isn't. Anyone can call fred.setAge(21), keeping him forever twenty-one.

But if that becomes a problem, we can guard against it:

```
public void setAge(int newValue) { if (newValue > age) age = newValue; }
  // Can't get younger
```

Getters and setters are better than public fields because they let you start with simple get/set semantics and evolve them as needed.

 NOTE: Just because getters and setters are better than public fields doesn't mean they are always good. Often, it is plainly bad if every client can get or set bits and pieces of an object's state. In this section, I show you how to implement properties in Scala. It is up to you to choose wisely when a gettable/settable property is an appropriate design.

Scala provides getter and setter methods for every field. Here, we define a public field:

```
class Person {
  var age = 0
}
```

Scala generates a class for the JVM with a *private* age field and getter and setter methods. These methods are public because we did not declare age as private. (For a private field, the getter and setter methods are private.)

In Scala, the getter and setter methods are called age and age_=. For example,

```
println(fred.age) // Calls the method fred.age()
fred.age = 21 // Calls fred.age_=(21)
```

In Scala, the getters and setters are not named get*Xxx* and set*Xxx*, but they fulfill the same purpose. Section 5.5, "Bean Properties," on page 61 shows how to generate Java-style get*Xxx* and set*Xxx* methods, so that your Scala classes can interoperate with Java tools.

NOTE: To see these methods with your own eyes, compile the Person class and then look at the bytecode with javap:

```
$ scalac Person.scala
$ javap -private Person
Compiled from "Person.scala"
public class Person extends java.lang.Object implements scala.ScalaObject{
  private int age;
  public int age(); public void age_$eq(int);
  public Person();
}
```

As you can see, the compiler created methods age and age_$eq. (The = symbol is translated to $eq because the JVM does not allow an = in a method name.)

TIP: You can run the javap command inside the REPL as

```
:javap -private Person
```

At any time, you can redefine the getter and setter methods yourself. For example,

```
class Person {
  private var privateAge = 0 // Make private and rename

  def age = privateAge
  def age_=(newValue: Int) {
    if (newValue > privateAge) privateAge = newValue; // Can't get younger
  }
}
```

The user of your class still accesses fred.age, but now Fred can't get younger:

```
val fred = new Person
fred.age = 30
fred.age = 21
println(fred.age) // 30
```

NOTE: Bertrand Meyer, the inventor of the influential Eiffel language, formulated the *Uniform Access Principle* that states: "All services offered by a module should be available through a uniform notation, which does not betray whether they are implemented through storage or through computation." In Scala, the caller of fred.age doesn't know whether age is implemented through a field or a method. (Of course, in the JVM, the service is *always* implemented through a method, either synthesized or programmer-supplied.)

 TIP: It may sound scary that Scala generates getter and setter methods for every field. But you have some control over this process.

- If the field is private, the getter and setter are private.

- If the field is a val, only a getter is generated.

- If you don't want any getter or setter, declare the field as private[this] (see Section 5.4, "Object-Private Fields," on page 60).

5.3 Properties with Only Getters

Sometimes you want a *read-only property* with a getter but no setter. If the value of the property never changes after the object has been constructed, use a val field:

```
class Message {
  val timeStamp = java.time.Instant.now
  ...
}
```

The Scala compiler produces a Java class with a private final field and a public getter method, but no setter.

Sometimes, however, you want a property that a client can't set at will, but that is mutated in some other way. The Counter class from Section 5.1, "Simple Classes and Parameterless Methods," on page 55 is a good example. Conceptually, the counter has a current property that is updated when the increment method is called, but there is no setter for the property.

You can't implement such a property with a val—a val never changes. Instead, provide a private field and a property getter, like this:

```
class Counter {
  private var value = 0
  def increment() { value += 1 }
  def current = value // No () in declaration
}
```

Note that there are no () in the definition of the getter method. Therefore, you *must* call the method without parentheses:

```
val n = myCounter.current // Calling myCounter.current() is a syntax error
```

To summarize, you have four choices for implementing properties:

1. var foo: Scala synthesizes a getter and a setter.

2. val foo: Scala synthesizes a getter.

3. You define methods foo and foo_=.

4. You define a method foo.

 NOTE: In Scala, you cannot have a write-only property (that is, a property with a setter and no getter).

 TIP: When you see a field in a Scala class, remember that it is not the same as a field in Java or C++. It is a private field *together with* a getter (for a val field) or a getter and a setter (for a var field).

5.4 Object–Private Fields

In Scala (as well as in Java or C++), a method can access the private fields of *all* objects of its class. For example,

```
class Counter {
  private var value = 0
  def increment() { value += 1 }

  def isLess(other : Counter) = value < other.value
    // Can access private field of other object
}
```

Accessing other.value is legal because other is also a Counter object.

Scala allows an even more severe access restriction with the private[this] qualifier:

```
private[this] var value = 0 // Accessing someObject.value is not allowed
```

Now, the methods of the Counter class can only access the value field of the current object, not of other objects of type Counter. This access is sometimes called *object-private*, and it is common in some OO languages such as SmallTalk.

With a class-private field, Scala generates private getter and setter methods. However, for an object-private field, no getters and setters are generated at all.

NOTE: Scala allows you to grant access rights to specific classes. The private[*ClassName*] qualifier states that only methods of the given class can access the given field. Here, the *ClassName* must be the name of the class being defined or an enclosing class. (See Section 5.8, "Nested Classes," on page 66 for a discussion of inner classes.)

In this case, the implementation will generate auxiliary getter and setter methods that allow the enclosing class to access the field. These methods will be public because the JVM does not have a fine-grained access control system, and they will have implementation-dependent names.

5.5 Bean Properties ▇

As you saw in the preceding sections, Scala provides getter and setter methods for the fields that you define. However, the names of these methods are not what Java tools expect. The JavaBeans specification (www.oracle.com/technetwork/articles/javaee/spec-136004.html) defines a Java property as a pair of getFoo/setFoo methods (or just a getFoo method for a read-only property). Many Java tools rely on this naming convention.

When you annotate a Scala field with @BeanProperty, then such methods are automatically generated. For example,

```
import scala.beans.BeanProperty

class Person {
  @BeanProperty var name: String = _
}
```

generates *four* methods:

1. `name: String`

2. `name_=(newValue: String): Unit`

3. `getName(): String`

4. `setName(newValue: String): Unit`

Table 5–1 shows which methods are generated in all cases.

Table 5–1 Generated Methods for Fields

Scala Field	Generated Methods	When to Use
val/var name	public name name_= (var only)	To implement a property that is publicly accessible and backed by a field.
@BeanProperty val/var name	public name getName() name_= (var only) setName(...) (var only)	To interoperate with JavaBeans.
private val/var name	private name name_= (var only)	To confine the field to the methods of this class, just like in Java. Use private unless you really want a public property.
private[this] val/var name	none	To confine the field to methods invoked on the same object. Not commonly used.
private[*ClassName*] val/var name	implementation-dependent	To grant access to an enclosing class. Not commonly used.

 NOTE: If you define a field as a primary constructor parameter (see Section 5.7, "The Primary Constructor," on page 63), and you want JavaBeans getters and setters, annotate the constructor parameter like this:

```
class Person(@BeanProperty var name: String)
```

5.6 Auxiliary Constructors

As in Java or C++, a Scala class can have as many constructors as you like. However, a Scala class has one constructor that is more important than all the others, called the *primary constructor*. In addition, a class may have any number of *auxiliary constructors*.

We discuss auxiliary constructors first because they are easier to understand. They are similar to constructors in Java or C++, with just two differences.

1. The auxiliary constructors are called this. (In Java or C++, constructors have the same name as the class—which is not so convenient if you rename the class.)

2. Each auxiliary constructor *must* start with a call to a previously defined auxiliary constructor or the primary constructor.

Here is a class with two auxiliary constructors:

```scala
class Person {
  private var name = ""
  private var age = 0

  def this(name: String) { // An auxiliary constructor
    this() // Calls primary constructor
    this.name = name
  }

  def this(name: String, age: Int) { // Another auxiliary constructor
    this(name) // Calls previous auxiliary constructor
    this.age = age
  }
}
```

We will look at the primary constructor in the next section. For now, it is sufficient to know that a class for which you don't define a primary constructor has a primary constructor with no arguments.

You can construct objects of this class in three ways:

```scala
val p1 = new Person // Primary constructor
val p2 = new Person("Fred") // First auxiliary constructor
val p3 = new Person("Fred", 42) // Second auxiliary constructor
```

5.7 The Primary Constructor

In Scala, every class has a primary constructor. The primary constructor is not defined with a this method. Instead, it is interwoven with the class definition.

1. The parameters of the primary constructor are placed *immediately after the class name*.

   ```scala
   class Person(val name: String, val age: Int) {
     // Parameters of primary constructor in (...)
     ...
   }
   ```

   Parameters of the primary constructor turn into fields that are initialized with the construction parameters. In our example, name and age become fields of the Person class. A constructor call such as new Person("Fred", 42) sets the name and age fields.

   Half a line of Scala is the equivalent of seven lines of Java:

```
public class Person { // This is Java
  private String name; private int age; public Person(String name, int age) {
    this.name = name; this.age = age;
  }
  public String name() { return this.name; } public int age() { return this.age; }
  ...
}
```

2. The primary constructor executes *all statements in the class definition*. For example, in the following class

```
class Person(val name: String, val age: Int) {
  println("Just constructed another person")
  def description = s"$name is $age years old"
}
```

the `println` statement is a part of the primary constructor. It is executed whenever an object is constructed.

This is useful when you need to configure a field during construction. For example:

```
class MyProg {
  private val props = new Properties
  props.load(new FileReader("myprog.properties"))
    // The statement above is a part of the primary constructor
  ...
}
```

NOTE: If there are no parameters after the class name, then the class has a primary constructor with no parameters. That constructor simply executes all statements in the body of the class.

TIP: You can often eliminate auxiliary constructors by using default arguments in the primary constructor. For example:

```
class Person(val name: String = "", val age: Int = 0)
```

Primary constructor parameters can have any of the forms in Table 5–1. For example,

```
class Person(val name: String, private var age: Int)
```

declares and initializes fields

```
val name: String
private var age: Int
```

Construction parameters can also be regular method parameters, without val or var. How these parameters are processed depends on their usage inside the class.

- If a parameter without val or var is used inside at least one method, it becomes a field. For example,

```scala
class Person(name: String, age: Int) {
  def description = s"$name is $age years old"
}
```

  declares and initializes immutable fields name and age that are object-private.

  Such a field is the equivalent of a private[this] val field (see Section 5.4, "Object-Private Fields," on page 60).

- Otherwise, the parameter is not saved as a field. It's just a regular parameter that can be accessed in the code of the primary constructor. (Strictly speaking, this is an implementation-specific optimization.)

Table 5–2 summarizes the fields and methods that are generated for different kinds of primary constructor parameters.

Table 5–2 Fields and Methods Generated for Primary Constructor Parameters

Primary Constructor Parameter	Generated Field/Methods
name: String	object-private field, or no field if no method uses name
private val/var name: String	private field, private getter/setter
val/var name: String	private field, public getter/setter
@BeanProperty val/var name: String	private field, public Scala and JavaBeans getters/setters

If you find the primary constructor notation confusing, you don't need to use it. Just provide one or more auxiliary constructors in the usual way, but remember to call this() if you don't chain to another auxiliary constructor.

However, many programmers like the concise syntax. Martin Odersky suggests to think about it this way: In Scala, classes take parameters, just like methods do.

 NOTE: When you think of the primary constructor's parameters as class parameters, parameters without val or var become easier to understand. The scope of such a parameter is the entire class. Therefore, you can use the parameter in methods. If you do, it is the compiler's job to save it in a field.

TIP: The Scala designers think that *every keystroke is precious*, so they let you combine a class with its primary constructor. When reading a Scala class, you need to disentangle the two. For example, when you see

```scala
class Person(val name: String) {
  var age = 0
  def description = s"$name is $age years old"
}
```

take this definition apart into a class definition:

```scala
class Person(val name: String) {
  var age = 0
  def description = s"$name is $age years old"
}
```

and a constructor definition:

```scala
class Person(val name: String) {
  var age = 0
  def description = s"$name is $age years old"
}
```

NOTE: To make the primary constructor private, place the keyword private like this:

```scala
class Person private(val id: Int) { ... }
```

A class user must then use an auxiliary constructor to construct a Person object.

5.8 Nested Classes L1

In Scala, you can nest just about anything inside anything. You can define functions inside other functions, and classes inside other classes. Here is a simple example of the latter:

```scala
import scala.collection.mutable.ArrayBuffer
class Network {
  class Member(val name: String) {
    val contacts = new ArrayBuffer[Member]
  }

  private val members = new ArrayBuffer[Member]

  def join(name: String) = {
    val m = new Member(name)
    members += m
```

```
        m
    }
}
```

Consider two networks:

```
val chatter = new Network
val myFace = new Network
```

In Scala, each *instance* has its own class Member, just like each instance has its own field members. That is, chatter.Member and myFace.Member are *different classes.*

> **NOTE:** This is different from Java, where an inner class belongs to the outer class.
>
> The Scala approach is more regular. For example, to make a new inner object, you simply use new with the type name: new chatter.Member. In Java, you need to use a special syntax, chatter.new Member().

In our network example, you can add a member within its own network, but not across networks.

```
val fred = chatter.join("Fred")
val wilma = chatter.join("Wilma")
fred.contacts += wilma // OK
val barney = myFace.join("Barney") // Has type myFace.Member
fred.contacts += barney
    // No—can't add a myFace.Member to a buffer of chatter.Member elements
```

For networks of people, this behavior probably makes sense. If you don't want it, there are two solutions.

First, you can move the Member type somewhere else. A good place would be the Network companion object. (Companion objects are described in Chapter 6.)

```
object Network {
  class Member(val name: String) {
    val contacts = new ArrayBuffer[Member]
  }
}

class Network {
  private val members = new ArrayBuffer[Network.Member]
  ...
}
```

Alternatively, you can use a *type projection* Network#Member, which means "a Member of *any* Network." For example,

```
class Network {
  class Member(val name: String) {
    val contacts = new ArrayBuffer[Network#Member]
  }
  ...
}
```

You would do that if you want the fine-grained "inner class per object" feature in some places of your program, but not everywhere. See Chapter 19 for more information about type projections.

 NOTE: In a nested class, you can access the this reference of the enclosing class as *EnclosingClass*.this, like in Java. If you like, you can establish an alias for that reference with the following syntax:

```
class Network(val name: String) { outer =>
  class Member(val name: String) {
    ...
    def description = s"$name inside ${outer.name}"
  }
}
```

The class Network { outer => syntax makes the variable outer refer to Network.this. You can choose any name for this variable. The name self is common, but perhaps confusing when used with nested classes.

This syntax is related to the "self type" syntax that you will see in Chapter 19.

Exercises

1. Improve the Counter class in Section 5.1, "Simple Classes and Parameterless Methods," on page 55 so that it doesn't turn negative at Int.MaxValue.

2. Write a class BankAccount with methods deposit and withdraw, and a read-only property balance.

3. Write a class Time with read-only properties hours and minutes and a method before(other: Time): Boolean that checks whether this time comes before the other. A Time object should be constructed as new Time(hrs, min), where hrs is in military time format (between 0 and 23).

4. Reimplement the Time class from the preceding exercise so that the internal representation is the number of minutes since midnight (between 0 and 24 × 60 − 1). *Do not* change the public interface. That is, client code should be unaffected by your change.

5. Make a class Student with read-write JavaBeans properties name (of type String) and id (of type Long). What methods are generated? (Use javap to check.) Can you call the JavaBeans getters and setters in Scala? Should you?

6. In the Person class of Section 5.1, "Simple Classes and Parameterless Methods," on page 55, provide a primary constructor that turns negative ages to 0.

7. Write a class Person with a primary constructor that accepts a string containing a first name, a space, and a last name, such as new Person("Fred Smith"). Supply read-only properties firstName and lastName. Should the primary constructor parameter be a var, a val, or a plain parameter? Why?

8. Make a class Car with read-only properties for manufacturer, model name, and model year, and a read-write property for the license plate. Supply four constructors. All require the manufacturer and model name. Optionally, model year and license plate can also be specified in the constructor. If not, the model year is set to -1 and the license plate to the empty string. Which constructor are you choosing as the primary constructor? Why?

9. Reimplement the class of the preceding exercise in Java, C#, or C++ (your choice). How much shorter is the Scala class?

10. Consider the class

```scala
class Employee(val name: String, var salary: Double) {
  def this() { this("John Q. Public", 0.0) }
}
```

Rewrite it to use explicit fields and a default primary constructor. Which form do you prefer? Why?

Objects

Chapter 6

In this short chapter, you will learn when to use the `object` construct in Scala. Use it when you need a class with a single instance, or when you want to find a home for miscellaneous values or functions.

The key points of this chapter are:

- Use objects for singletons and utility methods.
- A class can have a companion object with the same name.
- Objects can extend classes or traits.
- The `apply` method of an object is usually used for constructing new instances of the companion class.
- To avoid the `main` method, use an object that extends the App trait.
- You can implement enumerations by extending the `Enumeration` object.

6.1 Singletons

Scala has no static methods or fields. Instead, you use the `object` construct. An object defines a single instance of a class with the features that you want. For example,

```
object Accounts {
  private var lastNumber = 0
  def newUniqueNumber() = { lastNumber += 1; lastNumber }
}
```

When you need a new unique account number in your application, call `Accounts.newUniqueNumber()`.

The constructor of an object is executed when the object is first used. In our example, the `Accounts` constructor is executed with the first call to `Accounts.newUniqueNumber()`. If an object is never used, its constructor is not executed.

An object can have essentially all the features of a class—it can even extend other classes or traits (see Section 6.3, "Objects Extending a Class or Trait," on page 73). There is just one exception: You cannot provide constructor parameters.

Use an object in Scala whenever you would have used a singleton object in Java or C++:

- As a home for utility functions or constants
- When a single immutable instance can be shared efficiently
- When a single instance is required to coordinate some service (the singleton design pattern)

 NOTE: Many people view the singleton design pattern with disdain. Scala gives you the tools for both good and bad design, and it is up to you to use them wisely.

6.2 Companion Objects

In Java or C++, you often have a class with both instance methods and static methods. In Scala, you can achieve this by having a class and a "companion" object of the same name. For example,

```scala
class Account {
  val id = Account.newUniqueNumber()
  private var balance = 0.0
  def deposit(amount: Double) { balance += amount }
  ...
}

object Account { // The companion object
  private var lastNumber = 0
  private def newUniqueNumber() = { lastNumber += 1; lastNumber }
}
```

The class and its companion object can access each other's private features. They must be located in the *same source file*.

Note that the companion object's features are not in the scope of the class. For example, the `Account` class has to use `Account.newUniqueNumber()` and not just `newUniqueNumber()` to invoke the method of the companion object.

TIP: In the REPL, you must define the class and the object together in paste mode. Type

:paste

Then type or paste both the class and object definitions, and type Ctrl+D.

NOTE: A companion object contains features that accompany a class. In Chapter 7, you will see how to add features to a package using a *package object*.

6.3 Objects Extending a Class or Trait

An `object` can extend a class and/or one or more traits. The result is an object of a class that extends the given class and/or traits, and in addition has all of the features specified in the object definition.

One useful application is to specify default objects that can be shared. For example, consider a class for undoable actions in a program.

```
abstract class UndoableAction(val description: String) {
  def undo(): Unit
  def redo(): Unit
}
```

A useful default is the "do nothing" action. Of course, we only need one of them.

```
object DoNothingAction extends UndoableAction("Do nothing") {
  override def undo() {}
  override def redo() {}
}
```

The `DoNothingAction` object can be shared across all places that need this default.

```
val actions = Map("open" -> DoNothingAction, "save" -> DoNothingAction, ...)
  // Open and save not yet implemented
```

6.4 The apply Method

It is common to have objects with an `apply` method. The `apply` method is called for expressions of the form

Object(arg1, ..., argN)

Typically, such an apply method returns an object of the companion class.

For example, the Array object defines apply methods that allow array creation with expressions such as

```
Array("Mary", "had", "a", "little", "lamb")
```

Why doesn't one just use a constructor? Not having the new keyword is handy for nested expressions, such as

```
Array(Array(1, 7), Array(2, 9))
```

 CAUTION: It is easy to confuse Array(100) and new Array(100). The first expression calls apply(100), yielding an Array[Int] with a single element, the integer 100. The second expression invokes the constructor this(100). The result is an Array[Nothing] with 100 null elements.

Here is an example of defining an apply method:

```
class Account private (val id: Int, initialBalance: Double) {
  private var balance = initialBalance
  ...
}

object Account { // The companion object
  def apply(initialBalance: Double) =
    new Account(newUniqueNumber(), initialBalance)
  ...
}
```

Now you can construct an account as

```
val acct = Account(1000.0)
```

6.5 Application Objects

Each Scala program must start with an object's main method of type Array[String] => Unit:

```
object Hello {
  def main(args: Array[String]) {
    println("Hello, World!")
  }
}
```

Instead of providing a main method for your application, you can extend the App trait and place the program code into the constructor body:

```
object Hello extends App {
  println("Hello, World!")
}
```

If you need the command-line arguments, you can get them from the args property:

```
object Hello extends App {
  if (args.length > 0)
    println(f"Hello ${args(0)}")
  else
    println("Hello, World!")
}
```

If you invoke the application with the scala.time option set, then the elapsed time is displayed when the program exits.

```
$ scalac Hello.scala
$ scala -Dscala.time Hello Fred
Hello, Fred
[total 4ms]
```

All this involves a bit of magic. The App trait extends another trait, DelayedInit, that gets special handling from the compiler. All initialization code of a class with that trait is moved into a delayedInit method. The main of the App trait method captures the command-line arguments, calls the delayedInit method, and optionally prints the elapsed time.

 NOTE: Older versions of Scala had an Application trait for the same purpose. That trait carried out the program's action in the static initializer, which is not optimized by the just-in-time compiler. Use the App trait instead.

6.6 Enumerations

Unlike Java or C++, Scala does not have enumerated types. However, the standard library provides an Enumeration helper class that you can use to produce enumerations.

Define an object that extends the Enumeration class and initialize each value in your enumeration with a call to the Value method. For example,

```
object TrafficLightColor extends Enumeration {
  val Red, Yellow, Green = Value
}
```

Here we define three fields, Red, Yellow, and Green, and initialize each of them with a call to Value. This is a shortcut for

```
val Red = Value
val Yellow = Value
val Green = Value
```

Each call to the Value method returns a new instance of an inner class, also called Value.

Alternatively, you can pass IDs, names, or both to the Value method:

```
val Red = Value(0, "Stop")
val Yellow = Value(10) // Name "Yellow"
val Green = Value("Go") // ID 11
```

If not specified, the ID is one more than the previously assigned one, starting with zero. The default name is the field name.

You can now refer to the enumeration values as TrafficLightColor.Red, TrafficLightColor.Yellow, and so on. If that gets too tedious, use

```
import TrafficLightColor._
```

(See Chapter 7 for information on importing members of a class or object.)

Remember that the type of the enumeration is TrafficLightColor.Value and *not* TrafficLightColor—that's the type of the object holding the values. Some people recommend that you add a type alias

```
object TrafficLightColor extends Enumeration {
  type TrafficLightColor = Value
  val Red, Yellow, Green = Value
}
```

Now the type of the enumeration is TrafficLightColor.TrafficLightColor, which is only an improvement if you use an import statement. For example,

```
import TrafficLightColor._
def doWhat(color: TrafficLightColor) = {
  if (color == Red) "stop"
  else if (color == Yellow) "hurry up"
  else "go"
}
```

The ID of an enumeration value is returned by the id method, and its name by the toString method.

The call TrafficLightColor.values yields a set of all values:

```
for (c <- TrafficLightColor.values) println(s"${c.id}: $c")
```

Finally, you can look up an enumeration value by its ID or name. Both of the following yield the object TrafficLightColor.Red:

```
TrafficLightColor(0) // Calls Enumeration.apply
TrafficLightColor.withName("Red")
```

Exercises

1. Write an object Conversions with methods inchesToCentimeters, gallonsToLiters, and milesToKilometers.

2. The preceding problem wasn't very object-oriented. Provide a general super-class UnitConversion and define objects InchesToCentimeters, GallonsToLiters, and MilesToKilometers that extend it.

3. Define an Origin object that extends java.awt.Point. Why is this not actually a good idea? (Have a close look at the methods of the Point class.)

4. Define a Point class with a companion object so that you can construct Point instances as Point(3, 4), without using new.

5. Write a Scala application, using the App trait, that prints its command-line arguments in reverse order, separated by spaces. For example, scala Reverse Hello World should print World Hello.

6. Write an enumeration describing the four playing card suits so that the toString method returns ♣, ♦, ♥, or ♠.

7. Implement a function that checks whether a card suit value from the preceding exercise is red.

8. Write an enumeration describing the eight corners of the RGB color cube. As IDs, use the color values (for example, 0xff0000 for Red).

Packages and Imports

Topics in This Chapter A1

Chapter 7

In this chapter, you will learn how packages and import statements work in Scala. Both packages and imports are more regular than in Java; they are also a bit more flexible.

The key points of this chapter are:

- Packages nest just like inner classes.
- Package paths are *not* absolute.
- A chain x.y.z in a package clause leaves the intermediate packages x and x.y invisible.
- Package statements without braces at the top of the file extend to the entire file.
- A package object can hold functions and variables.
- Import statements can import packages, classes, and objects.
- Import statements can be anywhere.
- Import statements can rename and hide members.
- java.lang, scala, and Predef are always imported.

7.1 Packages

Packages in Scala fulfill the same purpose as packages in Java or namespaces in C++: to manage names in a large program. For example, the name Map can occur in the packages scala.collection.immutable and scala.collection.mutable without conflict. To access either name, you can use the fully qualified scala.collection.immutable.Map or scala.collection.mutable.Map. Alternatively, use an import statement to provide a shorter alias—see Section 7.7, "Imports," on page 85.

To add items to a package, you can include them in package statements, such as:

```
package com {
  package horstmann {
    package impatient {
      class Employee
      ...
    }
  }
}
```

Then the class name Employee can be accessed anywhere as com.horstmann. impatient.Employee.

Unlike an object or a class, a package can be defined in multiple files. The preceding code might be in a file Employee.scala, and a file Manager.scala might contain

```
package com {
  package horstmann {
    package impatient {
      class Manager
      ...
    }
  }
}
```

 NOTE: There is no enforced relationship between the directory of the source file and the package. You don't have to put Employee.scala and Manager.scala into a com/horstmann/impatient directory.

Conversely, you can contribute to more than one package in a single file. The file Employee.scala may contain

```
package com {
  package horstmann {
    package impatient {
      class Employee
      ...
    }
  }
}

package net {
  package bigjava {
    class Counter
    ...
  }
}
```

7.2 Scope Rules

In Scala, the scope rules for packages are more consistent than in Java. Scala packages nest just like all other scopes. You can access names from the enclosing scope. For example,

```
package com {
  package horstmann {
    object Utils {
      def percentOf(value: Double, rate: Double) = value * rate / 100
      ...
    }

    package impatient {
      class Employee {
        ...
        def giveRaise(rate: scala.Double) {
          salary += Utils.percentOf(salary, rate)
        }
      }
    }
  }
}
```

Note the Utils.percentOf qualifier. The Utils class was defined in the *parent* package. Everything in the parent package is in scope, and it is not necessary to use com.horstmann.Utils.percentOf. (You could, though, if you prefer—after all, com is also in scope.)

There is a fly in the ointment, however. Consider

```scala
package com {
  package horstmann {
    package impatient {
      class Manager {
        val subordinates = new collection.mutable.ArrayBuffer[Employee]
        ...
      }
    }
  }
}
```

This code takes advantage of the fact that the scala package is always imported. Therefore, the collection package is actually scala.collection.

And now suppose someone introduces the following package, perhaps in a different file:

```scala
package com {
  package horstmann {
    package collection {
      ...
    }
  }
}
```

Now the Manager class no longer compiles. It looks for a mutable member inside the com.horstmann.collection package and doesn't find it. The intent in the Manager class was the collection package in the top-level scala package, not whatever collection subpackage happened to be in some accessible scope.

In Java, this problem can't occur because package names are always *absolute*, starting at the root of the package hierarchy. But in Scala, package names are relative, just like inner class names. With inner classes, one doesn't usually run into problems because all the code is in one file, under control of whoever is in charge of that file. But packages are open-ended. Anyone can contribute to a package at any time.

One solution is to use absolute package names, starting with _root_, for example:

```scala
val subordinates = new _root_.scala.collection.mutable.ArrayBuffer[Employee]
```

Another approach is to use "chained" package clauses, as detailed in the next section.

 NOTE: Most programmers use complete paths for package names, without the _root_ prefix. This is safe as long as everyone avoids names scala, java, com, net, and so on, for nested packages.

7.3 Chained Package Clauses

A package clause can contain a "chain," or path segment, for example:

```
package com.horstmann.impatient {
  // Members of com and com.horstmann are not visible here
  package people {
    class Person
    ...
  }
}
```

Such a clause limits the visible members. Now a com.horstmann.collection package would no longer be accessible as collection.

7.4 Top-of-File Notation

Instead of the nested notation that we have used up to now, you can have package clauses at the top of the file, without braces. For example:

```
package com.horstmann.impatient
package people

class Person
 ...
```

This is equivalent to

```
package com.horstmann.impatient {
  package people {
    class Person
    ...
    // Until the end of the file
  }
}
```

This is the preferred notation if all the code in the file belongs to the same package (which is the usual case).

Note that in the example above, everything in the file belongs to the package com.horstmann.impatient.people, but the package com.horstmann.impatient has also been opened up so you can refer to its contents.

7.5 Package Objects

A package can contain classes, objects, and traits, but not the definitions of functions or variables. That's an unfortunate limitation of the Java virtual machine.

It would make more sense to add utility functions or constants to a package than to some Utils object. Package objects address this limitation.

Every package can have one package object. You define it in the *parent* package, and it has the same name as the child package. For example,

```
package com.horstmann.impatient

package object people {
  val defaultName = "John Q. Public"
}

package people {
  class Person {
    var name = defaultName // A constant from the package
  }
  ...
}
```

Note that the defaultName value didn't need to be qualified because it was in the same package. Elsewhere, it is accessible as com.horstmann.impatient.people.defaultName.

Behind the scenes, the package object gets compiled into a JVM class with static methods and fields, called package.class, inside the package. In our example, that would be a class com.horstmann.impatient.people.package with a static field defaultName. (In the JVM, you can use package as a class name.)

It is a good idea to use the same naming scheme for source files. Put the package object into a file com/horstmann/impatient/people/package.scala. That way, anyone who wants to add functions or variables to a package can find the package object easily.

7.6 Package Visibility

In Java, a class member that isn't declared as public, private, or protected is visible in the package containing the class. In Scala, you can achieve the same effect with qualifiers. The following method is visible in its own package:

```
package com.horstmann.impatient.people

class Person {
  private[people] def description = s"A person with name $name"
  ...
}
```

You can extend the visibility to an enclosing package:

```
private[impatient] def description = s"A person with name $name"
```

7.7 Imports

Imports let you use short names instead of long ones. With the clause

```
import java.awt.Color
```

you can write `Color` in your code instead of `java.awt.Color`.

That is the sole purpose of imports. If you don't mind long names, you'll never need them.

You can import all members of a package as

```
import java.awt._
```

This is the same as the * wildcard in Java. (In Scala, * is a valid character for an identifier. You could define a package `com.horstmann.*.people`, but please don't.)

You can also import all members of a class or object.

```
import java.awt.Color._
val c1 = RED // Color.RED
val c2 = decode("#ff0000") // Color.decode
```

This is like `import static` in Java. Java programmers seem to live in fear of this variant, but in Scala it is commonly used.

Once you import a package, you can access its subpackages with shorter names. For example:

```
import java.awt._

def handler(evt: event.ActionEvent) { // java.awt.event.ActionEvent
    ...
}
```

The event package is a member of `java.awt`, and the import brings it into scope.

7.8 Imports Can Be Anywhere

In Scala, an `import` statement can be anywhere, not just at the top of a file. The scope of the `import` statement extends until the end of the enclosing block. For example,

```
class Manager {
  import scala.collection.mutable._
  val subordinates = new ArrayBuffer[Employee]
  ...
}
```

This is a very useful feature, particularly with wildcard imports. It is always a bit worrisome to import lots of names from different sources. In fact, some Java programmers dislike wildcard imports so much that they never use them but let their IDE generate long lists of imported classes.

By putting the imports where they are needed, you can greatly reduce the potential for conflicts.

7.9 Renaming and Hiding Members

If you want to import more than one member from a package, use a *selector* like this:

```
import java.awt.{Color, Font}
```

The selector syntax lets you rename members:

```
import java.util.{HashMap => JavaHashMap}
import scala.collection.mutable._
```

Now JavaHashMap is a java.util.HashMap and plain HashMap is a scala.collection.mutable.HashMap.

The selector HashMap => _ hides a member instead of renaming it. This is only useful if you import others:

```
import java.util.{HashMap => _, _}
import scala.collection.mutable._
```

Now HashMap unambiguously refers to scala.collection.mutable.HashMap since java.util.HashMap is hidden.

7.10 Implicit Imports

Every Scala program implicitly starts with

```
import java.lang._
import scala._
import Predef._
```

As with Java programs, java.lang is always imported. Next, the scala package is imported, but in a special way. Unlike all other imports, this one is allowed to override the preceding import. For example, scala.StringBuilder overrides java.lang.StringBuilder instead of conflicting with it.

Finally, the Predef object is imported. It contains commonly used types, implicit conversions, and utility methods. (The methods could equally well have been placed into the scala package object, but Predef was introduced before Scala had package objects.)

Since the scala package is imported by default, you never need to write package names that start with scala. For example,

```
collection.mutable.HashMap
```

is just as good as

```
scala.collection.mutable.HashMap
```

Exercises

1. Write an example program to demonstrate that

   ```
   package com.horstmann.impatient
   ```

   is not the same as

   ```
   package com
   package horstmann
   package impatient
   ```

2. Write a puzzler that baffles your Scala friends, using a package com that isn't at the top level.

3. Write a package random with functions nextInt(): Int, nextDouble(): Double, and setSeed(seed: Int): Unit. To generate random numbers, use the linear congruential generator

   $$next = (previous \times a + b) \bmod 2^n,$$

   where $a = 1664525$, $b = 1013904223$, $n = 32$, and the initial value of *previous* is seed.

4. Why do you think the Scala language designers provided the package object syntax instead of simply letting you add functions and variables to a package?

5. What is the meaning of private[com] def giveRaise(rate: Double)? Is it useful?

6. Write a program that copies all elements from a Java hash map into a Scala hash map. Use imports to rename both classes.

7. In the preceding exercise, move all imports into the innermost scope possible.

8. What is the effect of

   ```
   import java._
   import javax._
   ```

   Is this a good idea?

9. Write a program that imports the java.lang.System class, reads the user name from the user.name system property, reads a password from the StdIn object, and prints a message to the standard error stream if the password is not "secret". Otherwise, print a greeting to the standard output stream. Do not use any other imports, and do not use any qualified names (with dots).

10. Apart from StringBuilder, what other members of java.lang does the scala package override?

Inheritance

Topics in This Chapter ▮A1▮

Chapter 8

In this chapter, you will learn the most important ways in which inheritance in Scala differs from inheritance in Java and C++. The highlights are:

- The extends and final keywords are as in Java.
- You must use override when you override a method.
- Only the primary constructor can call the primary superclass constructor.
- You can override fields.

In this chapter, we only discuss the case in which a class inherits from another class. See Chapter 10 for inheriting *traits*—the Scala concept that generalizes Java interfaces.

8.1 Extending a Class

You extend a class in Scala just like you would in Java—with the extends keyword:

```
class Employee extends Person {
  var salary = 0.0
  ...
}
```

As in Java, you specify fields and methods that are new to the subclass or that override methods in the superclass.

As in Java, you can declare a class final so that it cannot be extended. You can also declare individual methods or fields final so that they cannot be overridden. (See Section 8.6, "Overriding Fields," on page 95 for overriding fields.) Note that this is different from Java, where a final field is immutable, similar to val in Scala.

8.2 Overriding Methods

In Scala, you *must* use the override modifier when you override a method that isn't abstract. (See Section 8.8, "Abstract Classes," on page 97 for abstract methods.) For example,

```
class Person {
    ...
    override def toString = s"${getClass.getName}[name=$name]"
}
```

The override modifier can give useful error messages in a number of common situations, such as:

- When you misspell the name of the method that you are overriding

- When you accidentally provide a wrong parameter type in the overriding method

- When you introduce a new method in a superclass that clashes with a subclass method

 NOTE: The last case is an instance of the *fragile base class problem* where a change in the superclass cannot be verified without looking at all the sub-classes. Suppose programmer Alice defines a Person class, and, unbeknownst to Alice, programmer Bob defines a subclass Student with a method id yielding the student ID. Later, Alice also defines a method id that holds the person's national ID. When Bob picks up that change, something may break in Bob's program (but not in Alice's test cases) since Student objects now return unexpected IDs.

In Java, one is often advised to "solve" this problem by declaring all methods as final unless they are explicitly designed to be overridden. That sounds good in theory, but programmers hate it when they can't make even the most innocuous changes to a method (such as adding a logging call). That's why Java eventually introduced an optional @Overrides annotation.

Invoking a superclass method in Scala works exactly like in Java, with the keyword super:

```
class Employee extends Person {
  ...
  override def toString = s"${super.toString}[salary=$salary]"
}
```

The call super.toString invokes the toString method of the superclass—that is, the Person.toString method.

8.3 Type Checks and Casts

To test whether an object belongs to a given class, use the isInstanceOf method. If the test succeeds, you can use the asInstanceOf method to convert a reference to a subclass reference:

```
if (p.isInstanceOf[Employee]) {
  val s = p.asInstanceOf[Employee] // s has type Employee
  ...
}
```

The p.isInstanceOf[Employee] test succeeds if p refers to an object of class Employee or its subclass (such as Manager).

If p is null, then p.isInstanceOf[Employee] returns false and p.asInstanceOf[Employee] returns null.

If p is not an Employee, then p.asInstanceOf[Employee] throws an exception.

If you want to test whether p refers to an Employee object, but not a subclass, use

```
if (p.getClass == classOf[Employee])
```

The classOf method is defined in the scala.Predef object that is always imported.

Table 8–1 shows the correspondence between Scala and Java type checks and casts.

Table 8–1 Type Checks and Casts in Scala and Java

Scala	Java
obj.isInstanceOf[Cl]	obj instanceof Cl
obj.asInstanceOf[Cl]	(Cl) obj
classOf[Cl]	Cl.class

However, pattern matching is usually a better alternative to using type checks and casts. For example,

```
p match {
  case s: Employee => ... // Process s as an Employee
  case _ => ... // p wasn't an Employee
}
```

See Chapter 14 for more information.

8.4 Protected Fields and Methods

As in Java or C++, you can declare a field or method as protected. Such a member is accessible from any subclass, but not from other locations.

Unlike in Java, a protected member is *not* visible throughout the package to which the class belongs. (If you want this visibility, you can use a package modifier—see Chapter 7.)

There is also a protected[this] variant that restricts access to the current object, similar to the private[this] variant discussed in Chapter 5.

8.5 Superclass Construction

Recall from Chapter 5 that a class has one primary constructor and any number of auxiliary constructors, and that all auxiliary constructors must start with a call to a preceding auxiliary constructor or the primary constructor.

As a consequence, an auxiliary constructor can *never* invoke a superclass constructor directly.

The auxiliary constructors of the subclass eventually call the primary constructor of the subclass. Only the primary constructor can call a superclass constructor.

Recall that the primary constructor is intertwined with the class definition. The call to the superclass constructor is similarly intertwined. Here is an example:

```
class Employee(name: String, age: Int, val salary : Double) extends
  Person(name, age)
```

This defines a subclass

```
class Employee(name: String, age: Int, val salary : Double) extends
  Person(name, age)
```

and a primary constructor that calls the superclass constructor

```
class Employee(name: String, age: Int, val salary : Double) extends
  Person(name, age)
```

Intertwining the class and the constructor makes for very concise code. You may find it helpful to think of the primary constructor parameters as parameters of the class. Here, the Employee class has three parameters: name, age, and salary, two of which it "passes" to the superclass.

In Java, the equivalent code is quite a bit more verbose:

```
public class Employee extends Person { // Java
  private double salary;
  public Employee(String name, int age, double salary) {
    super(name, age);
    this.salary = salary;
  }
}
```

 NOTE: In a Scala constructor, you can never call super(params), as you would in Java, to call the superclass constructor.

A Scala class can extend a Java class. Its primary constructor must invoke one of the constructors of the Java superclass. For example,

```
class PathWriter(p: Path, cs: Charset) extends
  java.io.PrintWriter(Files.newBufferedWriter(p, cs))
```

8.6 Overriding Fields

Recall from Chapter 5 that a field in Scala consists of a private field *and* accessor/mutator methods. You can override a val (or a parameterless def) with another val field of the same name. The subclass has a private field and a public getter, and the getter overrides the superclass getter (or method).

For example,

```
class Person(val name: String) {
  override def toString = s"${getClass.getName}[name=$name]"
}

class SecretAgent(codename: String) extends Person(codename) {
  override val name = "secret" // Don't want to reveal name . . .
  override val toString = "secret" // . . . or class name
}
```

This example shows the mechanics, but it is rather artificial. A more common case is to override an abstract def with a val, like this:

```
abstract class Person { // See Section 8.8 for abstract classes
  def id: Int // Each person has an ID that is computed in some way
  ...
}
```

```
class Student(override val id: Int) extends Person
  // A student ID is simply provided in the constructor
```

Note the following restrictions (see also Table 8–2):

- A def can only override another def.
- A val can only override another val or a parameterless def.
- A var can only override an abstract var (see Section 8.8, "Abstract Classes," on page 97).

Table 8–2 Overriding val, def, and var

	with val	with def	with var
Override val	• Subclass has a private field (with the same name as the superclass field—that's OK). • Getter overrides the superclass getter.	Error.	Error.
Override def	• Subclass has a private field. • Getter overrides the superclass method.	Like in Java.	A var can override a getter/setter pair. Overriding just a getter is an error.
Override var	Error.	Error.	Only if the superclass var is abstract (see Section 8.8).

 NOTE: In Chapter 5, I said that it's OK to use a var because you can always change your mind and reimplement it as a getter/setter pair. However, the programmers extending your class do not have that choice. They cannot override a var with a getter/setter pair. In other words, if you provide a var, all subclasses are stuck with it.

8.7 Anonymous Subclasses

As in Java, you make an instance of an *anonymous* subclass if you include a block with definitions or overrides, such as

```
val alien = new Person("Fred") {
  def greeting = "Greetings, Earthling! My name is Fred."
}
```

Technically, this creates an object of a *structural type*—see Chapter 19 for details. The type is denoted as Person{def greeting: String}. You can use this type as a parameter type:

```
def meet(p: Person{def greeting: String}) {
  println(s"${p.name} says: ${p.greeting}")
}
```

8.8 Abstract Classes

As in Java, you can use the abstract keyword to denote a class that cannot be instantiated, usually because one or more of its methods are not defined. For example,

```
abstract class Person(val name: String) {
  def id: Int // No method body—this is an abstract method
}
```

Here we say that every person has an ID, but we don't know how to compute it. Each concrete subclass of Person needs to specify an id method. In Scala, unlike Java, you do not use the abstract keyword for an abstract method. You simply omit its body. As in Java, a class with at least one abstract method must be declared abstract.

In a subclass, you need not use the override keyword when you define a method that was abstract in the superclass.

```
class Employee(name: String) extends Person(name) {
  def id = name.hashCode // override keyword not required
}
```

8.9 Abstract Fields

In addition to abstract methods, a class can also have abstract fields. An abstract field is simply a field without an initial value. For example,

```
abstract class Person {
  val id: Int
    // No initializer—this is an abstract field with an abstract getter method
  var name: String
    // Another abstract field, with abstract getter and setter methods
}
```

This class defines abstract getter methods for the id and name fields, and an abstract setter for the name field. The generated Java class has *no fields*.

Concrete subclasses must provide concrete fields, for example:

```
class Employee(val id: Int) extends Person { // Subclass has concrete id property
  var name = "" // and concrete name property
}
```

As with methods, no override keyword is required in the subclass when you define a field that was abstract in the superclass.

You can always customize an abstract field by using an anonymous type:

```
val fred = new Person {
  val id = 1729
  var name = "Fred"
}
```

8.10 Construction Order and Early Definitions [L3]

When you override a val in a subclass *and* use the value in a superclass constructor, the resulting behavior is unintuitive.

Here is an example. A creature can sense a part of its environment. For simplicity, we assume the creature lives in a one-dimensional world, and the sensory data are represented as integers. A default creature can see ten units ahead.

```
class Creature {
  val range: Int = 10
  val env: Array[Int] = new Array[Int](range)
}
```

Ants, however, are near-sighted:

```
class Ant extends Creature {
  override val range = 2
}
```

Unfortunately, we now have a problem. The range value is used in the superclass constructor, and the superclass constructor runs *before* the subclass constructor. Specifically, here is what happens:

1. The Ant constructor calls the Creature constructor before doing its own construction.

2. The Creature constructor sets *its* range field to 10.

3. The Creature constructor, in order to initialize the env array, calls the range() getter.

4. That method is overridden to yield the (as yet uninitialized) range field of the Ant class.

5. The range method returns 0. (That is the initial value of all integer fields when an object is allocated.)

6. env is set to an array of length 0.

7. The Ant constructor continues, setting its range field to 2.

Even though it appears as if range is either 10 or 2, env has been set to an array of length 0. The moral is that you should not rely on the value of a val in the body of a constructor.

In Java, you have a similar issue when you call a method in a superclass constructor. The method might be overridden in a subclass, and it might not do what you want it to do. (In fact, that is the root cause of our problem—the expression range calls the getter method.)

There are several remedies.

- Declare the val as final. This is safe but not very flexible.

- Declare the val as lazy in the superclass (see Chapter 2). This is safe but a bit inefficient.

- Use the *early definition syntax* in the subclass—see below.

The "early definition" syntax lets you initialize val fields of a subclass *before* the superclass is executed. The syntax is so ugly that only a mother could love it. You place the val fields in a block after the extends keyword, like this:

```
class Ant extends { override val range = 2 } with Creature
```

Note the with keyword before the superclass name. This keyword is normally used with traits—see Chapter 10.

The right-hand side of an early definition can only refer to previous early definitions, not to other fields or methods of the class.

 TIP: You can debug construction order problems with the -Xcheckinit compiler flag. This flag generates code that throws an exception (instead of yielding the default value) when an uninitialized field is accessed.

NOTE: At the root of the construction order problem lies a design decision of the Java language—namely, to allow the invocation of subclass methods in a superclass constructor. In C++, an object's virtual function table pointer is set to the table of the superclass when the superclass constructor executes. Afterwards, the pointer is set to the subclass table. Therefore, in C++, it is not possible to modify constructor behavior through overriding. The Java designers felt that this subtlety was unnecessary, and the Java virtual machine does not adjust the virtual function table during construction.

8.11 The Scala Inheritance Hierarchy

Figure 8–1 shows the inheritance hierarchy of Scala classes. The classes that correspond to the primitive types in Java, as well as the type Unit, extend AnyVal. You can also define your own *value classes*—see Section 8.13, "Value Classes," on page 103.

All other classes are subclasses of the AnyRef class. When compiling to the Java virtual machine, this is a synonym for the java.lang.Object class.

Both AnyVal and AnyRef extend the Any class, the root of the hierarchy.

The Any class defines methods isInstanceOf, asInstanceOf, and the methods for equality and hash codes that we will look at in Section 8.12, "Object Equality," on page 102.

AnyVal does not add any methods. It is just a marker for value types.

The AnyRef class adds the monitor methods wait and notify/notifyAll from the Object class. It also provides a synchronized method with a function parameter. That method is the equivalent of a synchronized block in Java. For example,

```
account.synchronized { account.balance += amount }
```

 NOTE: Just like in Java, I suggest you stay away from wait, notify, and synchronized unless you have a good reason to use them instead of higher-level concurrency constructs.

All Scala classes implement the marker interface ScalaObject, which has no methods.

At the other end of the hierarchy are the Nothing and Null types.

Null is the type whose sole instance is the value null. You can assign null to any reference, but not to one of the value types. For example, setting an Int to null is not possible. This is better than in Java, where it would be possible to set an Integer wrapper to null.

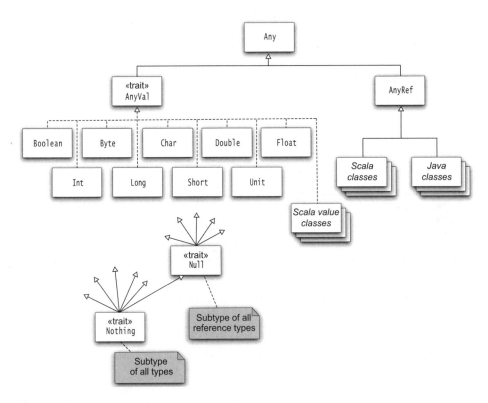

Figure 8–1   The inheritance hierarchy of Scala classes

The Nothing type has no instances. It is occasionally useful for generic constructs. For example, the empty list Nil has type List[Nothing], which is a subtype of List[T] for any T.

The ??? method is declared with return type Nothing. It never returns but instead throws a NotImplementedError when invoked. You can use it for methods that you still need to implement:

```scala
class Person(val name: String) {
  def description = ???
}
```

The Person class compiles since Nothing is a subtype of every type. You can start using the class, so long as you don't call the description method.

CAUTION: The Nothing type is not at all the same as void in Java or C++. In Scala, void is represented by the Unit type, the type with the sole value (). Note that Unit is not a supertype of any other type. However, the compiler still allows any value to be *replaced* by a (). Consider

```scala
def printAny(x: Any) { println(x) }
def printUnit(x: Unit) { println(x) }
printAny("Hello") // Prints Hello
printUnit("Hello")
  // Replaces "Hello" with () and calls printUnit(()), which prints ()
```

 CAUTION: When a method has a parameter of type Any or AnyRef, and it is called with multiple arguments, then they are placed in a tuple:

```scala
def show(o: Any) { println(s"${o.getClass}: $o") }
show(3) // Prints class java.lang.Integer: 3
show(3, 4, 5) // Prints class scala.Tuple3: (3,4,5)
```

If you call show() with no parameters, a Unit value is passed. However, that behavior is deprecated.

8.12 Object Equality L1

In Scala, the eq method of the AnyRef class checks whether two references refer to the same object. The equals method in AnyRef calls eq. When you implement a class, you should consider overriding the equals method to provide a natural notion of equality for your situation.

For example, if you define a class Item(val description: String, val price: Double), you might want to consider two items equal if they have the same description and price. Here is an appropriate equals method:

```scala
final override def equals(other: Any) = {
  other.isInstanceOf[Item] && {
    val that = other.asInstanceOf[Item]
    description == that.description && price == that.price
  }
}
```

Or better, use pattern matching:

```scala
final override def equals(other: Any) = other match {
  case that: Item => description == that.description && price == that.price
  case _ => false
}
```

NOTE: We defined the method as final because it is generally very difficult to correctly extend equality in a subclass. The problem is symmetry. You want a.equals(b) to have the same result as b.equals(a), even when b belongs to a subclass.

 CAUTION: Be sure to define the equals method with parameter type Any. The following would be wrong:

```
final def equals(other: Item) = { ... } // Don't!
```

This is a different method which does not override the equals method of AnyRef.

Also, don't supply an == method. You can't override the == method defined in AnyRef, but you could accidentally supply a different one with an Item argument:

```
final def ==(other: Item) = { ... } // Don't!
```

When you define equals, remember to define hashCode as well. The hash code should be computed only from the fields that you use in the equality check, so that equal objects have the same hash code. In the Item example, combine the hash codes of the fields.

```
final override def hashCode = (description, price).##
```

The ## method is a null-safe version of the hashCode method that yields 0 for null instead of throwing an exception.

 TIP: You are not compelled to override equals and hashCode. For many classes, it is appropriate to consider distinct objects unequal. For example, if you have two distinct input streams or radio buttons, you will never consider them equal.

In an application program, you don't generally call eq or equals. Simply use the == operator. For reference types, it calls equals after doing the appropriate check for null operands.

8.13 Value Classes

Some classes have a single field, such as the wrapper classes for primitive types, and the "rich" or "ops" wrappers that Scala uses to add methods to existing types. It is inefficient to allocate a new object that holds just one value. *Value classes* allow you to define classes that are "inlined," so that the single field is used directly.

A value class has these properties:

1. The class extends AnyVal.

2. Its primary constructor has exactly one parameter, which is a val, and no body.

3. The class has no other fields or constructors.

4. The automatically provided equals and hashCode methods compare and hash the underlying value.

As an example, let us define a value class that wraps a "military time" value:

```
class MilTime(val time: Int) extends AnyVal {
  def minutes = time % 100
  def hours = time / 100
  override def toString = f"$time04d"
}
```

When you construct a new MilTime(1230), the compiler doesn't allocate a new object. Instead, it uses the underlying value, the integer 1230. You can invoke the minutes and hours methods on the value but, just as importantly, you cannot invoke Int methods.

```
MilTime lunch = new MilTime(1230)
println(lunch.hours) // OK
println(lunch * 2) // Error
```

To guarantee proper initialization, make the primary constructor private and provide a factory method in the companion object:

```
class MilTime private(val time: Int) extends AnyVal ...
object MilTime {
  def apply(t: Int) =
    if (0 <= t && t < 2400 && t % 100 < 60) new MilTime(t)
    else throw new IllegalArgumentException
}
```

 CAUTION: In some programming languages, value types are any types that are allocated on the runtime stack, including structured types with multiple fields. In Scala, a value class can only have one field.

 NOTE: If you want a value class to implement a trait (see Chapter 10), the trait must explicitly extend Any, and it may not have fields. Such traits are called *universal traits*.

TIP: Value types were designed to make implicit conversions efficient, but you can use them for your own overhead-free "tiny types." For example, instead of a class Book(val author: String, val title: String), you can wrap each string into a separate value class Author and Title. When the class is defined as class Book(val author: Author, val title: Title), programmers who construct Book objects can't accidentally switch the author and the title.

Exercises

1. Extend the following BankAccount class to a CheckingAccount class that charges $1 for every deposit and withdrawal.

```
class BankAccount(initialBalance: Double) {
  private var balance = initialBalance
  def currentBalance = balance
  def deposit(amount: Double) = { balance += amount; balance }
  def withdraw(amount: Double) = { balance -= amount; balance }
}
```

2. Extend the BankAccount class of the preceding exercise into a class SavingsAccount that earns interest every month (when a method earnMonthlyInterest is called) and has three free deposits or withdrawals every month. Reset the transaction count in the earnMonthlyInterest method.

3. Consult your favorite Java or C++ textbook which is sure to have an example of a toy inheritance hierarchy, perhaps involving employees, pets, graphical shapes, or the like. Implement the example in Scala.

4. Define an abstract class Item with methods price and description. A SimpleItem is an item whose price and description are specified in the constructor. Take advantage of the fact that a val can override a def. A Bundle is an item that contains other items. Its price is the sum of the prices in the bundle. Also provide a mechanism for adding items to the bundle and a suitable description method.

5. Design a class Point whose x and y coordinate values can be provided in a constructor. Provide a subclass LabeledPoint whose constructor takes a label value and x and y coordinates, such as

```
new LabeledPoint("Black Thursday", 1929, 230.07)
```

6. Define an abstract class Shape with an abstract method centerPoint and subclasses Rectangle and Circle. Provide appropriate constructors for the subclasses and override the centerPoint method in each subclass.

7. Provide a class Square that extends java.awt.Rectangle and has three constructors: one that constructs a square with a given corner point and width, one that constructs a square with corner (0, 0) and a given width, and one that constructs a square with corner (0, 0) and width 0.

8. Compile the Person and SecretAgent classes in Section 8.6, "Overriding Fields," on page 95 and analyze the class files with javap. How many name fields are there? How many name getter methods are there? What do they get? (Hint: Use the -c and -private options.)

9. In the Creature class of Section 8.10, "Construction Order and Early Definitions," on page 98, replace val range with a def. What happens when you also use a def in the Ant subclass? What happens when you use a val in the subclass? Why?

10. The file scala/collection/immutable/Stack.scala contains the definition

    ```
    class Stack[A] protected (protected val elems: List[A])
    ```

    Explain the meanings of the protected keywords. (Hint: Review the discussion of private constructors in Chapter 5.)

11. Define a value class Point that packs integer x and y coordinates into a Long (which you should make private).

Files and Regular Expressions

Chapter 9

In this chapter, you will learn how to carry out common file processing tasks, such as reading all lines or words from a file or reading a file containing numbers.

Chapter highlights:

- `Source.fromFile(...).getLines.toArray` yields all lines of a file.
- `Source.fromFile(...).mkString` yields the file contents as a string.
- To convert a string into a number, use the `toInt` or `toDouble` method.
- Use the Java `PrintWriter` to write text files.
- *"regex"*`.r` is a `Regex` object.
- Use `"""`...`"""` if your regular expression contains backslashes or quotes.
- If a regex pattern has groups, you can extract their contents using the syntax `for (regex(`*var₁*`, ...,`*varₙ*`) <- `*string*`)`.

9.1 Reading Lines

To read all lines from a file, call the `getLines` method on a `scala.io.Source` object:

```
import scala.io.Source
val source = Source.fromFile("myfile.txt", "UTF-8")
  // The first argument can be a string or a java.io.File
  // You can omit the encoding if you know that the file uses
```

```
// the default platform encoding
val lineIterator = source.getLines
```

The result is an iterator (see Chapter 13). You can use it to process the lines one at a time:

```
for (l <- lineIterator) process l
```

Or you can put the lines into an array or array buffer by applying the toArray or toBuffer method to the iterator:

```
val lines = source.getLines.toArray
```

Sometimes, you just want to read an entire file into a string. That's even simpler:

```
val contents = source.mkString
```

 CAUTION: Call close when you are done using the Source object.

9.2 Reading Characters

To read individual characters from a file, you can use a Source object directly as an iterator since the Source class extends Iterator[Char]:

```
for (c <- source) process c
```

If you want to be able to peek at a character without consuming it (like istream::peek in C++ or a PushbackInputStreamReader in Java), call the buffered method on the source object. Then you can peek at the next input character with the head method without consuming it.

```
val source = Source.fromFile("myfile.txt", "UTF-8")
val iter = source.buffered
while (iter.hasNext) {
  if (iter.head is nice)
    process iter.next
  else
    ...
}
source.close()
```

Alternatively, if your file isn't large, you can just read it into a string and process that:

```
val contents = source.mkString
```

9.3 Reading Tokens and Numbers

Here is a quick-and-dirty way of reading all whitespace-separated tokens in a source:

```
val tokens = source.mkString.split("\\s+")
```

To convert a string into a number, use the toInt or toDouble method. For example, if you have a file containing floating-point numbers, you can read them all into an array by

```
val numbers = for (w <- tokens) yield w.toDouble
```

or

```
val numbers = tokens.map(_.toDouble)
```

 TIP: Remember—you can always use the java.util.Scanner class to process a file that contains a mixture of text and numbers.

Finally, note that you can read numbers from scala.io.StdIn:

```
print("How old are you? ")
val age = Scala.io.readInt()
  // Or use readDouble or readLong
```

 CAUTION: These methods assume that the next input line contains a single number, without leading or trailing whitespace. Otherwise, a NumberFormatException occurs.

9.4 Reading from URLs and Other Sources

The Source object has methods to read from sources other than files:

```
val source1 = Source.fromURL("http://horstmann.com", "UTF-8")
val source2 = Source.fromString("Hello, World!")
  // Reads from the given string—useful for debugging
val source3 = Source.stdin
  // Reads from standard input
```

 CAUTION: When you read from a URL, you need to know the character set in advance, perhaps from an HTTP header. See www.w3.org/International/0-charset for more information.

9.5 Reading Binary Files

Scala has no provision for reading binary files. You'll need to use the Java library. Here is how you can read a file into a byte array:

```
val file = new File(filename)
val in = new FileInputStream(file)
val bytes = new Array[Byte](file.length.toInt)
in.read(bytes)
in.close()
```

9.6 Writing Text Files

Scala has no built-in support for writing files. To write a text file, use a java.io.PrintWriter, for example:

```
val out = new PrintWriter("numbers.txt")
for (i <- 1 to 100) out.println(i)
out.close()
```

Everything works as expected, except for the printf method. When you pass a number to printf, the compiler will complain that you need to convert it to an AnyRef:

```
out.printf("%6d %10.2f",
    quantity.asInstanceOf[AnyRef], price.asInstanceOf[AnyRef]) // Ugh
```

Instead, use the f interpolator:

```
out.print(f"$quantity%6d $price%10.2f")
```

9.7 Visiting Directories

There are no "official" Scala classes for visiting all files in a directory, or for recursively traversing directories.

The simplest approach is to use the Files.list and Files.walk methods of the java.nio.file package. The list method only visits the children of a directory, and the walk method visits all descendants. These methods yield Java streams of Path objects. You can visit them as follows:

```
import java.nio.file._
String dirname = "/home/cay/scala-impatient/code"
val entries = Files.walk(Paths.get(dirname)) // or Files.list
```

```
try {
  entries.forEach(p => Process the path p)
} finally {
  entries.close()
}
```

9.8 Serialization

In Java, serialization is used to transmit objects to other virtual machines or for short-term storage. (For long-term storage, serialization can be awkward—it is tedious to deal with different object versions as classes evolve over time.)

Here is how you declare a serializable class in Java and Scala.

Java:

```
public class Person implements java.io.Serializable {
  private static final long serialVersionUID = 42L;
  ...
}
```

Scala:

```
@SerialVersionUID(42L) class Person extends Serializable
```

The Serializable trait is defined in the scala package and does not require an import.

 NOTE: You can omit the @SerialVersionUID annotation if you are OK with the default ID.

Serialize and deserialize objects in the usual way:

```
val fred = new Person(...)
import java.io._
val out = new ObjectOutputStream(new FileOutputStream("/tmp/test.obj"))
out.writeObject(fred)
out.close()
val in = new ObjectInputStream(new FileInputStream("/tmp/test.obj"))
val savedFred = in.readObject().asInstanceOf[Person]
```

The Scala collections are serializable, so you can have them as members of your serializable classes:

```
class Person extends Serializable {
  private val friends = new ArrayBuffer[Person] // OK—ArrayBuffer is serializable
  ...
}
```

9.9 Process Control A2

Traditionally, programmers use shell scripts to carry out mundane processing tasks, such as moving files from one place to another, or combining a set of files. The shell language makes it easy to specify subsets of files and to pipe the output of one program into the input of another. However, as programming languages, most shell languages leave much to be desired.

Scala was designed to scale from humble scripting tasks to massive programs. The scala.sys.process package provides utilities to interact with shell programs. You can write your shell scripts in Scala, with all the power that the Scala language puts at your disposal.

Here is a simple example:

```
import scala.sys.process._
"ls -al ..".!
```

As a result, the ls -al .. command is executed, showing all files in the parent directory. The result is printed to standard output.

The scala.sys.process package contains an implicit conversion from strings to ProcessBuilder objects. The ! method *executes* the ProcessBuilder object.

The result of the ! method is the exit code of the executed program: 0 if the program was successful, or a nonzero failure indicator otherwise.

If you use !! instead of !, the output is returned as a string:

```
val result = "ls -al /".!!
```

 NOTE: The ! and !! operators were originally intended to be used as postfix operators without the method invocation syntax:

```
"ls -al /" !!
```

However, as you will see in Chapter 11, the postfix syntax is being deprecated since it can lead to parsing errors.

You can pipe the output of one program into the input of another, using the #| method:

```
("ls -al /" #| "grep u").!
```

 NOTE: As you can see, the process library uses the commands of the underlying operating system. Here, I use bash commands because bash is available on Linux, Mac OS X, and Windows.

To redirect the output to a file, use the #> method:

```
("ls -al /" #> new File("filelist.txt")).!
```

To append to a file, use #>> instead:

```
("ls -al /etc" #>> new File("filelist.txt")).!
```

To redirect input from a file, use #<:

```
("grep u" #< new File("filelist.txt")).!
```

You can also redirect input from a URL:

```
("grep Scala" #< new URL("http://horstmann.com/index.html")).!
```

You can combine processes with p #&& q (execute q if p was successful) and p #|| q (execute q if p was unsuccessful). But frankly, Scala is better at control flow than the shell, so why not implement the control flow in Scala?

 NOTE: The process library uses the familiar shell operators | > >> < && ||, but it prefixes them with a # so that they all have the same precedence.

If you need to run a process in a different directory, or with different environment variables, construct a ProcessBuilder with the apply method of the Process object. Supply the command, the starting directory, and a sequence of (*name*, *value*) pairs for environment settings:

```
val p = Process(cmd, new File(dirName), ("LANG", "en_US"))
```

Then execute it with the ! method:

```
("echo 42" #| p).!
```

 NOTE: If you want to use Scala for shell scripts in a UNIX/Linux/MacOS environment, start your script files like this:

```
#!/bin/sh
exec scala "$0" "$@"
!#
```
Scala commands

 NOTE: You can also run Scala scripts from Java programs with the scripting integration of the javax.script package. To get a script engine, call

```
ScriptEngine engine =
    new ScriptEngineManager().getScriptEngineByName("scala")
```

9.10 Regular Expressions

When you process input, you often want to use regular expressions to analyze it. The scala.util.matching.Regex class makes this simple. To construct a Regex object, use the r method of the String class:

```
val numPattern = "[0-9]+".r
```

If the regular expression contains backslashes or quotation marks, then it is a good idea to use the "raw" string syntax, """...""". For example:

```
val wsnumwsPattern = """\s+[0-9]+\s+""".r
    // A bit easier to read than "\\s+[0-9]+\\s+".r
```

The findAllIn method returns an Iterator[String] through all matches. You can use it in a for loop:

```
for (matchString <- numPattern.findAllIn("99 bottles, 98 bottles"))
    println(matchString)
```

Alternatively, turn the iterator into an array:

```
val matches = numPattern.findAllIn("99 bottles, 98 bottles").toArray
    // Array("99", "98")
```

To find the first match in a string, use findFirstIn. You get an Option[String]. (See Chapter 14 for the Option class.)

```
val firstMatch = wsnumwsPattern.findFirstIn("99 bottles, 98 bottles")
    // Some(" 98 ")
```

 NOTE: There is no method to test whether a string matches the regex in its entirety, but you can add anchors:

```
val anchoredPattern = "^[0-9]+$".r
if (anchoredPattern.findFirstIn(str) != None) ...
```

Alternatively, use the String.matches method:

```
if (str.matches("[0-9]+")) ...
```

You can replace the first match, all matches, or some matches. In the latter case, supply a function Match => Option[String]. The Match class has information about the match (see the next section for details). If the function returns Some(str), the match is replaced with str.

```
numPattern.replaceFirstIn("99 bottles, 98 bottles", "XX")
    // "XX bottles, 98 bottles"
```

```
numPattern.replaceAllIn("99 bottles, 98 bottles", "XX")
  // "XX bottles, XX bottles"
numPattern.replaceSomeIn("99 bottles, 98 bottles",
  m => if (m.matched.toInt % 2 == 0) Some("XX") else None)
  // "99 bottles, XX bottles"
```

Here is a more useful application of the replaceSomeIn method. We want to replace placeholders $0, $1, and so on, in a message string with values from an argument sequence. Make a pattern for the variable with a group for the index, and then map the group to the sequence element.

```
val varPattern = """\$[0-9]+""".r
def format(message: String, vars: String*) =
  varPattern.replaceSomeIn(message, m => vars.lift(
    m.matched.tail.toInt))
format("At $1, there was $2 on $0.",
  "planet 7", "12:30 pm", "a disturbance of the force")
  // At 12:30 pm, there was a disturbance of the force on planet 7.
```

The lift method turns a Seq[String] into a function. The expression vars.lift(i) is Some(vars(i)) if i is a valid index or None if it is not.

9.11 Regular Expression Groups

Groups are useful to get subexpressions of regular expressions. Add parentheses around the subexpressions that you want to extract, for example:

```
val numitemPattern = "([0-9]+) ([a-z]+)".r
```

You can get the group contents from a Match object. The methods findAllMatchIn and findFirstMatchIn are analogs of the findAllIn and findFirstIn methods that return an Iterator[Match] or Option[Match].

If m is a Match object, then m.matched is the entire match string and m.group(i) is the ith group. The start and end indices of these substrings in the original string are m.start, m.end, m.start(i), and m.end(i).

```
for (m <- numitemPattern.findAllMatchIn("99 bottles, 98 bottles"))
  println(m.group(1)) // Prints 99 and 98
```

 CAUTION: The Match class has methods for retrieving groups by name. However, this does *not* work with group names inside regular expressions, such as "(?<num>[0-9]+) (?<item>[a-z]+)".r. Instead, one needs to supply names to the r method: "([0-9]+) ([a-z]+)".r("num", "item")

There is another convenient way of extracting matches. Use a regular expression variable as an "extractor" (see Chapter 14), like this:

```
val numitemPattern(num, item) = "99 bottles"
  // Sets num to "99", item to "bottles"
```

When you use a pattern as an extractor, it must match the string from which you extract the matches, and there must be a group for each variable.

To extract groups from multiple matches, you can use a for statement like this:

```
for (numitemPattern(num, item) <- numitemPattern.findAllIn("99 bottles, 98 bottles"))
  process num and item
```

Exercises

1. Write a Scala code snippet that reverses the lines in a file (making the last line the first one, and so on).

2. Write a Scala program that reads a file with tabs, replaces each tab with spaces so that tab stops are at *n*-column boundaries, and writes the result to the same file.

3. Write a Scala code snippet that reads a file and prints all words with more than 12 characters to the console. Extra credit if you can do this in a single line.

4. Write a Scala program that reads a text file containing only floating-point numbers. Print the sum, average, maximum, and minimum of the numbers in the file.

5. Write a Scala program that writes the powers of 2 and their reciprocals to a file, with the exponent ranging from 0 to 20. Line up the columns:

```
1            1
2            0.5
4            0.25
...          ...
```

6. Make a regular expression searching for quoted strings "like this, maybe with \" or \\" in a Java or C++ program. Write a Scala program that prints out all such strings in a source file.

7. Write a Scala program that reads a text file and prints all tokens in the file that are *not* floating-point numbers. Use a regular expression.

8. Write a Scala program that prints the src attributes of all img tags of a web page. Use regular expressions and groups.

9. Write a Scala program that counts how many files with .class extension are in a given directory and its subdirectories.

10. Expand the example in Section 9.8, "Serialization," on page 113. Construct a few Person objects, make some of them friends of others, and save an Array[Person] to a file. Read the array back in and verify that the friend relations are intact.

Traits

Chapter 10

In this chapter, you will learn how to work with traits. A class extends one or more traits in order to take advantage of the services that the traits provide. A trait may require implementing classes to support certain features. However, unlike Java interfaces, Scala traits can supply state and behavior for these features, which makes them far more useful.

Key points of this chapter:

- A class can implement any number of traits.

- Traits can require implementing classes to have certain fields, methods, or superclasses.

- Unlike Java interfaces, a Scala trait can provide implementations of methods and fields.

- When you layer multiple traits, the order matters—the trait whose methods execute *first* goes to the back.

10.1 Why No Multiple Inheritance?

Scala, like Java, does not allow a class to inherit from multiple superclasses. At first, this seems like an unfortunate restriction. Why shouldn't a class extend multiple classes? Some programming languages, in particular C++, allow multiple inheritance—but at a surprisingly high cost.

Multiple inheritance works fine when you combine classes that have *nothing in common*. But if these classes have common methods or fields, thorny issues come up. Here is a typical example. A teaching assistant is a student and also an employee:

```
class Student {
  def id: String = ...
  ...
}

class Employee {
  def id: String = ...
  ...
}
```

Suppose we could have

```
class TeachingAssistant extends Student, Employee {  // Not actual Scala code
  ...
}
```

Unfortunately, this `TeachingAssistant` class inherits *two* id methods. What should `myTA.id` return? The student ID? The employee ID? Both? (In C++, you need to redefine the id method to clarify what you want.)

Next, suppose that both `Student` and `Employee` extend a common superclass `Person`:

```
class Person {
  var name: String = _
}

class Student extends Person { ... }
class Employee extends Person { ... }
```

This leads to the *diamond inheritance* problem (see Figure 10–1). We only want one `name` field inside a `TeachingAssistant`, not two. How do the fields get merged? How does the field get constructed? In C++, you use "virtual base classes," a complex and brittle feature, to address this issue.

Java designers were so afraid of these complexities that they took a very restrictive approach. A class can extend only one superclass; it can implement any number of *interfaces*, but interfaces can have only abstract, static, or default methods, and no fields.

Java default methods are very restricted. They can call other interface methods, but they cannot make use of object state. It is therefore common in Java to provide both an interface and an abstract base class, but that just kicks the can down the road. What if you need to extend two of those abstract base classes?

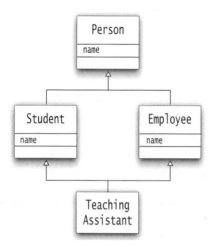

Figure 10–1   Diamond inheritance must merge common fields.

Scala has *traits* instead of interfaces. A trait can have abstract and concrete methods, as well as state, and a class can implement multiple traits. This neatly solves the problem of Java interfaces. You will see in the following sections how Scala deals with the perils of conflicting features from multiple traits.

10.2 Traits as Interfaces

Let's start with something familiar. A Scala trait can work exactly like a Java interface. For example:

```
trait Logger {
  def log(msg: String) // An abstract method
}
```

Note that you need not declare the method as abstract—an unimplemented method in a trait is automatically abstract.

A subclass can provide an implementation:

```
class ConsoleLogger extends Logger { // Use extends, not implements
  def log(msg: String) { println(msg) } // No override needed
}
```

You need not supply the override keyword when overriding an abstract method of a trait.

NOTE: Scala doesn't have a special keyword for implementing a trait. As you will see throughout this chapter, traits can be much more similar to classes than Java interfaces.

If you need more than one trait, add the others using the `with` keyword:

```
class ConsoleLogger extends Logger with Cloneable with Serializable
```

Here we use the `Cloneable` and `Serializable` interfaces from the Java library, just for the sake of showing the syntax. All Java interfaces can be used as Scala traits.

As in Java, a Scala class can have only one superclass but any number of traits.

 NOTE: It may seem odd that you use the extends keyword before the first trait but `with` before all the others. But that's not the way that Scala thinks about it. In Scala, `Logger with Cloneable with Serializable` is the entity that the class extends.

10.3 Traits with Concrete Implementations

In Scala, the methods of a trait need not be abstract. For example, we can make our `ConsoleLogger` into a trait:

```
trait ConsoleLogger {
  def log(msg: String) { println(msg) }
}
```

The `ConsoleLogger` trait provides a method *with an implementation*—in this case, one that prints the logging message on the console.

Here is an example of using this trait:

```
class SavingsAccount extends Account with ConsoleLogger {
  def withdraw(amount: Double) {
    if (amount > balance) log("Insufficient funds")
    else balance -= amount
  }
  ...
}
```

Note how the `SavingsAccount` picks up a concrete implementation from the `ConsoleLogger` trait. In Java, this is also possible by using default methods in interfaces. However, as you will see shortly, traits can also have state, which would not be possible with a Java interface.

In Scala (and other programming languages that allow this), we say that the `ConsoleLogger` functionality is "mixed in" with the `SavingsAccount` class.

NOTE: Supposedly, the "mix in" term comes from the world of ice cream. In the ice cream parlor parlance, a "mix in" is an additive that is kneaded into a scoop of ice cream before dispensing it to the customer—a practice that may be delicious or disgusting depending on your point of view.

10.4 Objects with Traits

You can add a trait to an individual object when you construct it. Let's first define this class:

```
abstract class SavingsAccount extends Account with Logger {
  def withdraw(amount: Double) {
    if (amount > balance) log("Insufficient funds")
    else ...
  }
  ...
}
```

This class is abstract since it can't yet do any logging, which might seem pointless. But you can "mix in" a concrete logger when constructing an object.

```
trait ConsoleLogger extends Logger {
  def log(msg: String) { println(msg) }
}
```

```
val acct = new SavingsAccount with ConsoleLogger
```

When calling log on the acct object, the log method of the ConsoleLogger trait executes.

Of course, another object can add in a different trait:

```
val acct2 = new SavingsAccount with FileLogger
```

10.5 Layered Traits

You can add, to a class or an object, multiple traits that invoke each other starting with the *last one*. This is useful when you need to transform a value in stages.

Here is a simple example. We may want to add a timestamp to all logging messages.

```
trait TimestampLogger extends ConsoleLogger {
  override def log(msg: String) {
    super.log(s"${java.time.Instant.now()} $msg")
  }
}
```

Also, suppose we want to truncate overly chatty log messages like this:

```
trait ShortLogger extends ConsoleLogger {
  override def log(msg: String) {
    super.log(
      if (msg.length <= 15) msg else s"${msg.substring(0, 12)}...")
  }
}
```

Note that each of the log methods passes a modified message to super.log.

With traits, super.log does *not* have the same meaning as it does with classes. Instead, super.log calls the log method of another trait, which depends on the order in which the traits are added.

To see how the order matters, compare the following two examples:

```
val acct1 - new SavingsAccount with TimestampLogger with ShortLogger
val acct2 = new SavingsAccount with ShortLogger with TimestampLogger
```

If we overdraw acct1, we get a message

```
Sun Feb 06 17:45:45 ICT 2011 Insufficient...
```

As you can see, the ShortLogger's log method was called first, and its call to super.log called the TimestampLogger.

However, overdrawing acct2 yields

```
Sun Feb 06 1...
```

Here, the TimestampLogger appeared last in the list of traits. Its log message was called first, and the result was subsequently shortened.

For simple mixin sequences, the "back to front" rule will give you the right intuition. See Section 10.10, "Trait Construction Order," on page 130 for the gory details that arise when the traits form an arbitrary tree and not just a chain.

NOTE: With traits, you cannot tell from the source code which method is invoked by super.*someMethod*. The exact method depends on the ordering of the traits in the object or class that uses them. This makes super far more flexible than in plain old inheritance.

NOTE: If you want to control which trait's method is invoked, you can specify it in brackets: super[ConsoleLogger].log(...). The specified type must be an immediate supertype; you can't access traits or classes that are further away in the inheritance hierarchy.

10.6 Overriding Abstract Methods in Traits

In the preceding section, the `TimestampLogger` and `ShortLogger` traits extended `ConsoleLogger`. Let's make them extend our `Logger` trait instead, where we provide *no implementation* to the `log` method.

```
trait Logger {
  def log(msg: String) // This method is abstract
}
```

Then, the `TimestampLogger` class no longer compiles.

```
trait TimestampLogger extends Logger {
  override def log(msg: String) { // Overrides an abstract method
    super.log(s"${java.time.Instant.now()} $msg") // Is super.log defined?
  }
}
```

The compiler flags the call to `super.log` as an error.

Under normal inheritance rules, this call could never be correct—the `Logger.log` method has no implementation. But actually, as you saw in the preceding section, there is no way of knowing which `log` method is actually being called—it depends on the order in which traits are mixed in.

Scala takes the position that `TimestampLogger.log` is still abstract—it requires a concrete `log` method to be mixed in. You therefore need to tag the method with the abstract keyword *and* the `override` keyword, like this:

```
abstract override def log(msg: String) {
  super.log(s"${java.time.Instant.now()} $msg")
}
```

10.7 Traits for Rich Interfaces

A trait can have many utility methods that depend on a few abstract ones. One example is the Scala `Iterator` trait that defines dozens of methods in terms of the abstract `next` and `hasNext` methods.

Let us enrich our rather anemic logging API. Usually, a logging API lets you specify a level for each log message to distinguish informational messages from warnings or errors. We can easily add this capability without forcing any policy for the destination of logging messages.

```
trait Logger {
  def log(msg: String)
  def info(msg: String) { log(s"INFO: $msg") }
  def warn(msg: String) { log(s"WARN: $msg") }
  def severe(msg: String) { log(s"SEVERE: $msg") }
}
```

Note the combination of abstract and concrete methods.

A class that uses the Logger trait can now call any of these logging messages, for example:

```
abstract class SavingsAccount extends Account with Logger {
  def withdraw(amount: Double) {
    if (amount > balance) severe("Insufficient funds")
    else ...
  }
  ...
}
```

This use of concrete and abstract methods in a trait is very common in Scala. In Java, you can achieve the same with default methods.

10.8 Concrete Fields in Traits

A field in a trait can be concrete or abstract. If you supply an initial value, the field is concrete.

```
trait ShortLogger extends Logger {
  val maxLength = 15 // A concrete field
  abstract override def log(msg: String) {
    super.log(
      if (msg.length <= maxLength) msg
      else s"${msg.substring(0, maxLength - 3)}...")
  }
}
```

A class that mixes in this trait acquires a maxLength field. In general, a class gets a field for each concrete field in one of its traits. These fields are not inherited; they are simply added to the subclass. This may seem a subtle distinction, but it is important. Let us look at the process more closely, with this version of the SavingsAccount class:

```
class SavingsAccount extends Account with ConsoleLogger with ShortLogger {
  var interest = 0.0
  def withdraw(amount: Double) {
    if (amount > balance) log("Insufficient funds")
    else ...
  }
}
```

Note that our subclass has a field interest. That's a plain old field in the subclass.

Suppose Account has a field.

```
class Account {
  var balance = 0.0
}
```

The SavingsAccount class *inherits* that field in the usual way. A SavingsAccount object is made up of all the fields of its superclasses, together with any fields in the subclass. You can think of a SavingsAcccount object as "starting out" with a superclass object (see Figure 10–2).

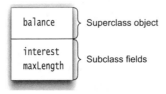

Figure 10–2 Fields from a trait are placed in the subclass.

In the JVM, a class can only extend one superclass, so the trait fields can't be inherited in the same way. Instead, the Scala compiler adds the maxLength field to the SavingsAccount class, next to the interest field.

 CAUTION: When you extend a class and then change the superclass, the subclass doesn't have to be recompiled because the virtual machine understands inheritance. But when a trait changes, all classes that mix in that trait must be recompiled.

You can think of concrete trait fields as "assembly instructions" for the classes that use the trait. Any such fields become fields of the class.

10.9 Abstract Fields in Traits

An uninitialized field in a trait is abstract and must be overridden in a concrete subclass.

For example, the following maxLength field is abstract:

```
trait ShortLogger extends Logger {
  val maxLength: Int // An abstract field
  abstract override def log(msg: String) { ... }
    super.log(
      if (msg.length <= maxLength) msg
      else s"${msg.substring(0, maxLength - 3)}...")
        // The maxLength field is used in the implementation
  }
  ...
}
```

When you use this trait in a concrete class, you must supply the maxLength field:

```
class SavingsAccount extends Account with ConsoleLogger with ShortLogger {
  val maxLength = 20 // No override necessary
  ...
}
```

Now all logging messages are truncated after 20 characters.

This way of supplying values for trait parameters is particularly handy when you construct objects on the fly. Let's go back to our original savings account:

```
class SavingsAccount extends Account with Logger { ... }
```

Now, we can truncate the messages in an instance as follows:

```
val acct = new SavingsAccount with ConsoleLogger with ShortLogger {
  val maxLength = 20
}
```

10.10 Trait Construction Order

Just like classes, traits can have constructors, made up of field initializations and other statements in the trait's body. For example,

```
trait FileLogger extends Logger {
  val out = new PrintWriter("app.log") // Part of the trait's constructor
  out.println(s"# ${java.time.Instant.now()}") // Also part of the constructor

  def log(msg: String) { out.println(msg); out.flush() }
}
```

These statements are executed during construction of any object incorporating the trait.

Constructors execute in the following order:

1. The superclass constructor is called first.

2. Trait constructors are executed after the superclass constructor but before the class constructor.

3. Traits are constructed left-to-right.

4. Within each trait, the parents get constructed first.

5. If multiple traits share a common parent, and that parent has already been constructed, it is not constructed again.

6. After all traits are constructed, the subclass is constructed.

For example, consider this class:

```
class SavingsAccount extends Account with FileLogger with ShortLogger
```

The constructors execute in the following order:

1. `Account` (the superclass).

2. `Logger` (the parent of the first trait).

3. `FileLogger` (the first trait).

4. `ShortLogger` (the second trait). Note that its `Logger` parent has already been constructed.

5. `SavingsAccount` (the class).

NOTE: The constructor ordering is the reverse of the *linearization* of the class. The linearization is a technical specification of all supertypes of a type. It is defined by the rule:

If C extends C_1 with C_2 with ... with C_n, then $lin(C) = C$ » $lin(C_n)$ » ... » $lin(C_2)$ » $lin(C_1)$

Here, » means "concatenate and remove duplicates, with the right winning out." For example,

lin(SavingsAccount)

= SavingsAccount » lin(ShortLogger) » lin(FileLogger) » lin(Account)

= SavingsAccount » (ShortLogger » Logger) » (FileLogger » Logger) » lin(Account)

= SavingsAccount » ShortLogger » FileLogger » Logger » Account.

(For simplicity, I omitted the types ScalaObject, AnyRef, and Any that are at the end of any linearization.)

The linearization gives the order in which super is resolved in a trait. For example, calling super in a ShortLogger invokes the FileLogger method, and calling super in a FileLogger invokes the Logger method.

10.11 Initializing Trait Fields

Traits cannot have constructor parameters. Every trait has a single parameterless constructor.

 NOTE: Interestingly, the absence of constructor parameters is the *only* technical difference between traits and classes. Otherwise, traits can have all the features of classes, such as concrete and abstract fields and superclasses.

This limitation can be a problem for traits that need some customization to be useful. Consider a file logger. We would like to specify the log file, but we can't use a construction parameter:

```
val acct = new SavingsAccount with FileLogger("myapp.log")
  // Error: Can't have constructor parameters for traits
```

You saw one possible approach in the preceding section. The FileLogger can have an abstract field for the file name.

```
trait FileLogger extends Logger {
  val filename: String
  val out = new PrintStream(filename)
  def log(msg: String) { out.println(msg); out.flush() }
}
```

A class using this trait can override the filename field. Unfortunately, there is a pitfall. The straightforward approach does *not* work:

```
val acct = new SavingsAccount with FileLogger {
  val filename = "myapp.log" // Does *not* work
}
```

The problem is the construction order. The FileLogger constructor runs *before* the subclass constructor. Here, the subclass is a bit hard to see. The new statement constructs an instance of an anonymous class extending SavingsAccount (the superclass) with the FileLogger trait. The initialization of filename only happens in the anonymous subclass. Actually, it doesn't happen at all—before the subclass gets its turn, a null pointer exception is thrown in the FileLogger constructor.

One remedy is an obscure feature that we described in Chapter 8: *early definition*. Here is the correct version:

```
val acct = new { // Early definition block after new
  val filename = "myapp.log"
} with SavingsAccount with FileLogger
```

It's not pretty, but it solves our problem. The early definition happens before the regular construction sequence. When the FileLogger is constructed, the filename field is initialized.

If you need to do the same in a class, the syntax looks like this:

```
class SavingsAccount extends { // Early definition block after extends
  val filename = "savings.log"
} with Account with FileLogger {
  ... // SavingsAccount implementation
}
```

Another alternative is to use a *lazy value* in the FileLogger constructor, like this:

```
trait FileLogger extends Logger {
  val filename: String
  lazy val out = new PrintStream(filename)
  def log(msg: String) { out.println(msg) } // No override needed
}
```

Then the out field is initialized when it is first used. At that time, the filename field will have been set. However, lazy values are somewhat inefficient because they are checked for initialization before every use.

10.12 Traits Extending Classes

As you have seen, a trait can extend another trait, and it is common to have a hierarchy of traits. Less commonly, a trait can also extend a class. That class becomes a superclass of any class mixing in the trait.

Here is an example. The LoggedException trait extends the Exception class:

```
trait LoggedException extends Exception with ConsoleLogger {
  def log() { log(getMessage()) }
}
```

A LoggedException has a log method to log the exception's message. Note that the log method calls the getMessage method that is inherited from the Exception superclass.

Now let's form a class that mixes in this trait:

```
class UnhappyException extends LoggedException { // This class extends a trait
  override def getMessage() = "arggh!"
}
```

The superclass of the trait becomes the superclass of our class (see Figure 10–3).

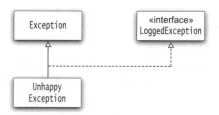

Figure 10–3   The Superclass of a trait becomes the superclass of any class mixing in the trait.

What if our class already extends another class? That's OK, as long as it's a subclass of the trait's superclass. For example,

```
class UnhappyException extends IOException with LoggedException
```

Here UnhappyException extends IOException, which already extends Exception. When mixing in the trait, its superclass is already present, and there is no need to add it.

However, if our class extends an unrelated class, then it is not possible to mix in the trait. For example, you cannot form the following class:

```
class UnhappyFrame extends JFrame with LoggedException
  // Error: Unrelated superclasses
```

It would be impossible to add both JFrame and Exception as superclasses.

10.13 Self Types L2

When a trait extends a class, there is a guarantee that the superclass is present in any class mixing in the trait. Scala has an alternate mechanism for guaranteeing this: *self types.*

When a trait starts out with

```
this: Type =>
```

then it can only be mixed into a subclass of the given type.

Let's use this feature for our LoggedException:

```
trait LoggedException extends ConsoleLogger {
  this: Exception =>
    def log() { log(getMessage()) }
}
```

Note that the trait does *not* extend the Exception class. Instead, it has a self type of Exception. That means it can only be mixed into subclasses of Exception.

In the trait's methods, we can call any methods of the self type. For example, the call to getMessage() in the log method is valid, since we know that this must be an Exception.

If you try to mix the trait into a class that doesn't conform to the self type, an error occurs.

```
val f = new JFrame with LoggedException
  // Error: JFrame isn't a subtype of Exception, the self type of LoggedException
```

A trait with a self type is similar to a trait with a supertype. In both cases, it is ensured that a type is present in a class that mixes in the trait.

There are a few situations where the self type notation is more flexible than traits with supertypes. Self types can handle circular dependencies between traits. This can happen if you have two traits that need each other.

Self types can also handle *structural types*—types that merely specify the methods that a class must have, without naming the class. Here is the LoggedException using a structural type:

```
trait LoggedException extends ConsoleLogger {
  this: { def getMessage() : String } =>
    def log() { log(getMessage()) }
}
```

The trait can be mixed into any class that has a getMessage method.

We discuss self types and structural types in more detail in Chapter 19.

10.14 What Happens under the Hood

Scala needs to translate traits into classes and interfaces of the JVM. You are not required to know how this is done, but you may find it helpful for understanding how traits work.

A trait that has only abstract methods is simply turned into a Java interface. For example,

```
trait Logger {
  def log(msg: String)
}
```

turns into

```
public interface Logger { // Generated Java interface
  void log(String msg);
}
```

Trait methods become default methods. For example,

```
trait ConsoleLogger {
  def log(msg: String) { println(msg) }
}
```

becomes

```
public interface ConsoleLogger {
  default void log(String msg) { ... }
}
```

If the trait has fields, the Java interface has getter and setter methods.

```
trait ShortLogger extends Logger {
  val maxLength = 15 // A concrete field
  ...
}
```

is translated to

```
public interface ShortLogger extends Logger {
  int maxLength();
  void weird_prefix$maxLength_$eq(int);
  default void log(String msg) { ... } // Calls maxLength()
  default void $init$() { weird_prefix$maxLength_$eq(15); }
}
```

Of course, the interface can't have any fields, and the getter and setter methods are unimplemented. But the getter is called when the field value is needed.

The weird setter is needed to initialize the field. This happens in the $init$ method.

When the trait is mixed into a class, the class gets a maxLength field, and the getter and setter are defined to get and set the field. The constructors of that class invokes the $init$ method of the trait. For example,

```
class SavingsAccount extends Account with ConsoleLogger with ShortLogger
```

turns into

```
public class SavingsAccount extends Account
    implements ConsoleLogger, ShortLogger {
  private int maxLength;
  public int maxLength() { return maxLength; }
  public void weird_prefix$maxLength_$eq(int arg) { maxLength = arg; }
  public SavingsAccount() {
    super();
    ConsoleLogger.$init$();
    ShortLogger.$init$();
  }
  ...
}
```

If a trait extends a superclass, the trait still turns into an interface. Of course, a class mixing in the trait extends the superclass.

Exercises

1. The `java.awt.Rectangle` class has useful methods `translate` and `grow` that are unfortunately absent from classes such as `java.awt.geom.Ellipse2D`. In Scala, you can fix this problem. Define a trait `RectangleLike` with concrete methods `translate` and `grow`. Provide any abstract methods that you need for the implementation, so that you can mix in the trait like this:

   ```
   val egg = new java.awt.geom.Ellipse2D.Double(5, 10, 20, 30) with RectangleLike
   egg.translate(10, -10)
   egg.grow(10, 20)
   ```

2. Define a class `OrderedPoint` by mixing `scala.math.Ordered[Point]` into `java.awt.Point`. Use lexicographic ordering, i.e. $(x, y) < (x', y')$ if $x < x'$ or $x = x'$ and $y < y'$.

3. Look at the `BitSet` class, and make a diagram of all its superclasses and traits. Ignore the type parameters (everything inside the [...]). Then give the linearization of the traits.

4. Provide a `CryptoLogger` trait that encrypts the log messages with the Caesar cipher. The key should be 3 by default, but it should be overridable by the user. Provide usage examples with the default key and a key of –3.

5. The JavaBeans specification has the notion of a *property change listener*, a standardized way for beans to communicate changes in their properties. The `PropertyChangeSupport` class is provided as a convenience superclass for any bean that wishes to support property change listeners. Unfortunately, a class that already has another superclass—such as `JComponent`—must reimplement the methods. Reimplement `PropertyChangeSupport` as a trait, and mix it into the `java.awt.Point` class.

6. In the Java AWT library, we have a class `Container`, a subclass of `Component` that collects multiple components. For example, a `Button` is a `Component`, but a `Panel` is a `Container`. That's the composite pattern at work. Swing has `JComponent` and `JButton`, but if you look closely, you will notice something strange. `JComponent` extends `Container`, even though it makes no sense to add other components to, say, a `JButton`. Ideally, the Swing designers would have preferred the design in Figure 10–4.

   But that's not possible in Java. Explain why not. How could the design be executed in Scala with traits?

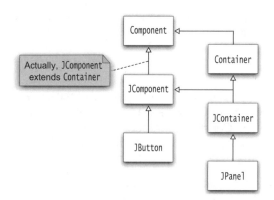

Figure 10–4   A better design for Swing containers

7. Construct an example where a class needs to be recompiled when one of the mixins changes. Start with `class SavingsAccount extends Account with ConsoleLogger`. Put each class and trait in a separate source file. Add a field to `Account`. In `Main` (also in a separate source file), construct a `SavingsAccount` and access the new field. Recompile all files *except for* `SavingsAccount` and verify that the program works. Now add a field to `ConsoleLogger` and access it in `Main`. Again, recompile all files *except for* `SavingsAccount`. What happens? Why?

8. There are dozens of Scala trait tutorials with silly examples of barking dogs or philosophizing frogs. Reading through contrived hierarchies can be tedious and not very helpful, but designing your own is very illuminating. Make your own silly trait hierarchy example that demonstrates layered traits, concrete and abstract methods, and concrete and abstract fields.

9. In the `java.io` library, you add buffering to an input stream with a `BufferedInputStream` decorator. Reimplement buffering as a trait. For simplicity, override the `read` method.

10. Using the logger traits from this chapter, add logging to the solution of the preceding problem that demonstrates buffering.

11. Implement a class `IterableInputStream` that extends `java.io.InputStream` with the trait `Iterable[Byte]`.

12. Using `javap -c -private`, analyze how the call `super.log(msg)` is translated to Java. How does the same call invoke two different methods, depending on the mixin order?

Operators

Chapter 11

This chapter covers in detail implementing your own *operators*—methods with the same syntax as the familiar mathematical operators. Operators are often used to build *domain-specific languages*—minilanguages embedded inside Scala. *Implicit conversions* (type conversion functions that are applied automatically) are another tool facilitating the creation of domain-specific languages. This chapter also discusses the special methods `apply`, `update`, and `unapply`. We end the chapter with a discussion of *dynamic invocations*—method calls that can be intercepted at runtime, so that arbitrary actions can occur depending on the method names and arguments.

The key points of this chapter are:

- Identifiers contain either alphanumeric or operator characters.

- Unary and binary operators are method calls.

- Operator precedence depends on the first character, associativity on the last.

- The `apply` and `update` methods are called when evaluating *expr*(*args*).

- Extractors extract tuples or sequences of values from an input **L2**.

- Types extending the `Dynamic` trait can inspect the names of methods and arguments at runtime. **L2**

11.1 Identifiers

The names of variables, functions, classes, and so on are collectively called *identifiers*. In Scala, you have more choices for forming identifiers than in Java. Of course, you can follow the time-honored pattern: sequences of alphanumeric characters, starting with an alphabetic character or an underscore, such as `input1` or `next_token`.

As in Java, Unicode characters are allowed. For example, `quantité` or `ποσό` are valid identifiers.

In addition, you can use *operator characters* in identifiers:

- The ASCII characters ! # % & * + - / : < = > ? @ \ ^ | ~ that are not letters, digits, underscore, the .,; punctuation marks, parentheses () [] {}, or quotation marks ' ` ".

- Unicode mathematical symbols or other symbols from the Unicode categories Sm and So.

For example, `**` and `√` are valid identifiers. With the definition

```
val √ = scala.math.sqrt _
```

you can write `√(2)` to compute a square root. This may be a good idea, provided one's programming environment makes it easy to type the symbol.

 NOTE: The identifiers @ # : = _ => <- <: <% >: ⇒ ← are reserved in the specification, and you cannot redefine them.

You can also form identifiers from alphanumerical characters, followed by an underscore, and then a sequence of operator characters, such as

```
val happy_birthday_!!! = "Bonne anniversaire!!!"
```

This is probably not a good idea.

Finally, you can include just about any sequence of characters in backquotes. For example,

```
val `val` = 42
```

That example is silly, but backquotes can sometimes be an "escape hatch." For example, in Scala, `yield` is a reserved word, but you may need to access a Java method of the same name. Backquotes to the rescue: `Thread.`yield`()`.

11.2 Infix Operators

You can write

    a *identifier* b

where *identifier* denotes a method with two parameters (one implicit, one explicit). For example, the expression

    1 to 10

is actually a method call

    1.to(10)

This is called an *infix* expression because the operator is between the arguments. The operator can contain letters, as in to, or it can contain operator characters—for example,

    1 -> 10

is a method call

    1 .->(10)

To define an operator in your own class, simply define a method whose name is that of the desired operator. For example, here is a Fraction class that multiplies two fractions according to the law

$$(n_1 \mathbin{/} d_1) \times (n_2 \mathbin{/} d_2) = (n_1 n_2 \mathbin{/} d_1 d_2)$$

```
class Fraction(n: Int, d: Int) {
  private val num = ...
  private val den = ...
  ...
  def *(other: Fraction) = new Fraction(num * other.num, den * other.den)
}
```

11.3 Unary Operators

Infix operators are binary operators—they have two parameters. An operator with one parameter is called a unary operator.

The four operators +, -, !, ~ are allowed as *prefix* operators, appearing before their arguments. They are converted into calls to methods with the name unary_*operator*. For example,

    -a

means the same as a.unary_-.

If a unary operator follows its argument, it is a *postfix* operator. The expression

a *identifier*

is the same as the method call a.*identifier*(). For example,

```
42 toString
```

is the same as

```
42.toString()
```

 CAUTION: Postfix operators can lead to parsing errors. For example, the code

```
val result = 42 toString
println(result)
```

yields the error message "too many arguments for method toString." Since parsing precedes type inference and overload resolution, the compiler does not yet know that toString is a unary method. Instead, the code is parsed as val result = 42.toString(println(result)).

For that reason, the compiler warns you if you use postfix operators. You can turn the warning off with the compiler option -language:postfixOps, or by adding the clause

```
import scala.language.postfixOps
```

11.4 Assignment Operators

An assignment operator has the form *operator=*, and the expression

a *operator=* b

means the same as

a = a *operator* b

For example, a += b is equivalent to a = a + b.

There are a few technical details.

- <=, >=, and != are not assignment operators.
- An operator starting with an = is never an assignment operator (==, ===, =/=, and so on).
- If a has a method called *operator=*, then that method is called directly.

11.5 Precedence

When you have two or more operators in a row without parentheses, the ones with higher *precedence* are executed first. For example, in the expression

```
1 + 2 * 3
```

the * operator is evaluated first. Languages such as Java and C++ have a fixed number of operators, and the language standard decrees which have precedence over which. Scala can have arbitrary operators, so it uses a scheme that works for all operators, while also giving the familiar precedence order to the standard ones.

Except for assignment operators, the precedence is determined by the *first character* of the operator.

Highest precedence: An operator character other than those below
* / %
+ -
:
< >
! =
&
^
|
A character that is not an operator character
Lowest precedence: Assignment operators

Characters in the same row yield operators with the same precedence. For example, + and -> have the same precedence.

Postfix operators have lower precedence than infix operators:

a *infixOp* b*postfixOp*

is the same as

(a *infixOp* b)*postfixOp*

11.6 Associativity

When you have a sequence of operators of the same precedence, the *associativity* determines whether they are evaluated left-to-right or right-to-left. For example, in the expression 17 − 2 − 9, one computes (17 − 2) − 9. The − operator is *left-associative*.

In Scala, all operators are left-associative except for

- operators that end in a colon (:)
- assignment operators

In particular, the :: operator for constructing lists is right-associative. For example,

```
1 :: 2 :: Nil
```

means

```
1 :: (2 :: Nil)
```

This is as it should be—we first need to form the list containing 2, and that list becomes the tail of the list whose head is 1.

A right-associative binary operator is a method of its second argument. For example,

```
2 :: Nil
```

means

```
Nil.::(2)
```

11.7 The apply and update Methods

Scala lets you extend the function call syntax

```
f(arg1, arg2, ...)
```

to values other than functions. If f is not a function or method, then this expression is equivalent to the call

```
f.apply(arg1, arg2, ...)
```

unless it occurs to the left of an assignment. The expression

```
f(arg1, arg2, ...) = value
```

corresponds to the call

```
f.update(arg1, arg2, ..., value)
```

This mechanism is used in arrays and maps. For example,

```
val scores = new scala.collection.mutable.HashMap[String, Int]
scores("Bob") = 100 // Calls scores.update("Bob", 100)
val bobsScore = scores("Bob") // Calls scores.apply("Bob")
```

The apply method is also commonly used in companion objects to construct objects without calling new. For example, consider a Fraction class.

```
class Fraction(n: Int, d: Int) {
  ...
}

object Fraction {
  def apply(n: Int, d: Int) = new Fraction(n, d)
}
```

Because of the apply method, we can construct a fraction as Fraction(3, 4) instead of new Fraction(3, 4). That sounds like a small thing, but if you have many Fraction values, it is a welcome improvement:

```
val result = Fraction(3, 4) * Fraction(2, 5)
```

11.8 Extractors L2

An extractor is an object with an unapply method. You can think of the unapply method as the opposite of the apply method of a companion object. An apply method takes construction parameters and turns them into an object. An unapply method takes an object and extracts values from it—usually the values from which the object was constructed.

Consider the Fraction class from the preceding section. The apply method makes a fraction from a numerator and denominator. An unapply method retrieves the numerator and denominator. You can use it in a variable definition

```
var Fraction(a, b) = Fraction(3, 4) * Fraction(2, 5)
  // a, b are initialized with the numerator and denominator of the result
```

or a pattern match

```
case Fraction(a, b) => ... // a, b are bound to the numerator and denominator
```

(See Chapter 14 for more information about pattern matching.)

In general, a pattern match can fail. Therefore, the unapply method returns an Option. It contains a tuple with one value for each matched variable. In our case, we return an Option[(Int, Int)].

```
object Fraction {
  def unapply(input: Fraction) =
    if (input.den == 0) None else Some((input.num, input.den))
}
```

Just to show the possibility, this method returns None when the denominator is zero, indicating no match.

A declaration

```
val Fraction(a, b) = f;
```

becomes

```
val tupleOption = Fraction.unapply(f)
if (tupleOption == None) throw new MatchError
// tupleOption is Some((t1, t2))
val a = t1
val b = t1
```

NOTE: Note that in the declaration

```
val Fraction(a, b) = f;
```

neither the `Fraction.apply` method nor the `Fraction` constructor are called. Instead, the statement means: "Initialize a and b so that if they would be passed to `Fraction.apply`, the result would be f."

In the preceding example, the `apply` and `unapply` methods are inverses of one another. However, that is not a requirement. You can use extractors to extract information from an object of any type.

For example, suppose you want to extract first and last names from a string:

```
val author = "Cay Horstmann"
val Name(first, last) = author // Calls Name.unapply(author)
```

Provide an object `Name` with an unapply method that returns an `Option[(String, String)]`. If the match succeeds, return a pair with the first and last name. The components of the pair will be bound to the variables in the pattern. Otherwise, return `None`.

```
object Name {
  def unapply(input: String) = {
    val pos = input.indexOf(" ")
    if (pos == -1) None
    else Some((input.substring(0, pos), input.substring(pos + 1)))
  }
}
```

NOTE: In this example, there is no `Name` class. The `Name` object is an extractor for `String` objects.

Every case class automatically has `apply` and `unapply` methods. (Case classes are discussed in Chapter 14.) For example, consider

```
case class Currency(value: Double, unit: String)
```

You can construct a `Currency` instance as

```
Currency(29.95, "EUR") // Calls Currency.apply
```

You can extract values from a Currency object:

```
case Currency(amount, "USD") => println(s"$$$amount") // Calls Currency.unapply
```

11.9 Extractors with One or No Arguments L2

In Scala, there are no tuples with one component. If the unapply method extracts a single value, it should just return an Option of the target type. For example,

```
object Number {
  def unapply(input: String): Option[Int] =
    try {
      Some(input.trim.toInt)
    } catch {
      case ex: NumberFormatException => None
    }
}
```

With this extractor, you can extract a number from a string:

```
val Number(n) = "1729"
```

An extractor can just test its input without extracting any value. In that case, the unapply method should return a Boolean. For example,

```
object IsCompound {
  def unapply(input: String) = input.contains(" ")
}
```

You can use this extractor to add a test to a pattern, for example

```
author match {
  case Name(first, IsCompound()) => ...
    // Matches if the last name is compound, such as van der Linden
  case Name(first, last) => ...
}
```

11.10 The unapplySeq Method L2

To extract an arbitrary sequence of values, the method needs to be called unapplySeq. It returns an Option[Seq[A]], where A is the type of the extracted values. For example, a Name extractor can produce a sequence of the name's components:

```
object Name {
  def unapplySeq(input: String): Option[Seq[String]] =
    if (input.trim == "") None else Some(input.trim.split("\\s+"))
}
```

Now you can match for any number of variables:

```
author match {
  case Name(first, last) => ...
  case Name(first, middle, last) => ...
  case Name(first, "van", "der", last) => ...
  ...
}
```

 CAUTION: Do not supply both an unapply and an unapplySeq methods with the same argument types.

11.11 Dynamic Invocation

Scala is a strongly typed language that reports type errors at compile time rather than at runtime. If you have an expression x.f(args), and your program compiles, then you know for sure that x has a method f that can accept the given arguments. However, there are situations where it is desirable to define methods in a running program. This is common with object-relational mappers in dynamic languages such as Ruby or JavaScript. Objects that represent database tables have methods findByName, findById, and so on, with the method names matching the table columns. For database entities, the column names can be used to get and set fields, such as person.lastName = "Doe".

In Scala, you can do this too. If a type extends the trait scala.Dynamic, then method calls, getters, and setters are rewritten as calls to special methods that can inspect the name of the original call and the parameters, and then take arbitrary actions.

NOTE: Dynamic types are an "exotic" feature, and the compiler wants your explicit consent when you implement such a type. You do that by adding the import statement

```
import scala.language.dynamics
```

Users of such types do not need to provide the import statement.

Here are the details of the rewriting. Consider obj.name, where obj belongs to a class that's a subtype of Dynamic. Here is what the Scala compiler does with it.

1. If name is a known method or field of obj, it is processed in the usual way.

2. If obj.name is followed by (arg1, arg2, ...),

    a. If none of the arguments are named (of the form *name=arg*), pass the arguments on to applyDynamic:

    ```
    obj.applyDynamic("name")(arg1, arg2, ...)
    ```

b. If at least one of the arguments is named, pass the name/value pairs on to `applyDynamicNamed`:

```
obj.applyDynamicNamed("name")((name1, arg1), (name2, arg2), ...)
```

Here, `name1`, `name2`, and so on are strings with the argument names, or `""` for unnamed arguments.

3. If `obj.name` is to the left of an `=`, call

```
obj.updateDynamic("name")(rightHandSide)
```

4. Otherwise call

```
obj.selectDynamic("sel")
```

NOTE: The calls to `updateDynamic`, `applyDynamic`, and `applyDynamicNamed` have two sets of parentheses, one for the selector name and one for the arguments. This construct is explained in Chapter 12.

Let's look at a few examples. Suppose `person` is an instance of a type extending `Dynamic`. A statement

```
person.lastName = "Doe"
```

is replaced with a call

```
person.updateDynamic("lastName")("Doe")
```

The `Person` class must have such a method:

```
class Person {
  ...
  def updateDynamic(field: String)(newValue: String) { ... }
}
```

It is then up to you to implement the `updateDynamic` method. For example, if you are implementing an object-relational mapper, you might update the cached entity and mark it as changed, so that it can be persisted in the database.

Conversely, a statement

```
val name = person.lastName
```

turns into

```
val name = name.selectDynamic("lastName")
```

The `selectDynamic` method would simply look up the field value.

Method calls that don't involve named parameters are translated to `applyDynamic` calls. For example,

```
val does = people.findByLastName("Doe")
```

becomes

```
val does = people.applyDynamic("findByLastName")("Doe")
```

and

```
val johnDoes = people.find(lastName = "Doe", firstName = "John")
```

becomes

```
val johnDoes = people.applyDynamicNamed("find")
  (("lastName", "Doe"), ("firstName", "John"))
```

It is then up to you to implement applyDynamic and applyDynamicNamed as calls that retrieve the matching objects.

Here is a concrete example. Suppose we want to be able to dynamically look up and set elements of a java.util.Properties instance, using the dot notation:

```
val sysProps = new DynamicProps(System.getProperties)
sysProps.username = "Fred" // Sets the "username" property to "Fred"
val home = sysProps.java_home // Gets the "java.home" property
```

For simplicity, we replace periods in the property name with underscores. (Exercise 11 on page 154 shows how to keep the periods.)

The DynamicProps class extends the Dynamic trait and implements the updateDynamic and selectDynamic methods:

```
class DynamicProps(val props: java.util.Properties) extends Dynamic {
  def updateDynamic(name: String)(value: String) {
    props.setProperty(name.replaceAll("_", "."), value)
  }
  def selectDynamic(name: String) =
    props.getProperty(name.replaceAll("_", "."))
}
```

As an additional enhancement, let us use the add method to add key/value pairs in bulk, using named arguments:

```
sysProps.add(username="Fred", password="Secret")
```

Then we need to supply the applyDynamicNamed method in the DynamicProps class. Note that the name of the method is fixed. We are only interested in arbitrary parameter names.

```
class DynamicProps(val props: java.util.Properties) extends Dynamic {
  ...
  def applyDynamicNamed(name: String)(args: (String, String)*) {
    if (name != "add") throw new IllegalArgumentException
    for ((k, v) <- args)
      props.setProperty(k.replaceAll("_", "."), v)
  }
}
```

These examples are only meant to illustrate the mechanism—I don't think that it is a good idea to use the dot notation for map access. Like operator overloading, dynamic invocation is a feature that is best used with restraint.

Exercises

1. According to the precedence rules, how are 3 + 4 -> 5 and 3 -> 4 + 5 evaluated?

2. The BigInt class has a pow method, not an operator. Why didn't the Scala library designers choose ** (as in Fortran) or ^ (as in Pascal) for a power operator?

3. Implement the Fraction class with operations + - * /. Normalize fractions, for example, turning 15/–6 into –5/2. Divide by the greatest common divisor, like this:

```
class Fraction(n: Int, d: Int) {
  private val num: Int = if (d == 0) 1 else n * sign(d) / gcd(n, d);
  private val den: Int = if (d == 0) 0 else d * sign(d) / gcd(n, d);
  override def toString = s"$num/$den"
  def sign(a: Int) = if (a > 0) 1 else if (a < 0) -1 else 0
  def gcd(a: Int, b: Int): Int = if (b == 0) abs(a) else gcd(b, a % b)
  ...
}
```

4. Implement a class Money with fields for dollars and cents. Supply +, - operators as well as comparison operators == and <. For example, Money(1, 75) + Money(0, 50) == Money(2, 25) should be true. Should you also supply * and / operators? Why or why not?

5. Provide operators that construct an HTML table. For example,

```
Table() | "Java" | "Scala" || "Gosling" | "Odersky" || "JVM" | "JVM, .NET"
```

should produce

```
<table><tr><td>Java</td><td>Scala</td></tr><tr><td>Gosling...
```

6. Provide a class `ASCIIArt` whose objects contain figures such as

```
 /\_/\
( ' ' )
(  -  )
 | | |
(__|__)
```

Supply operators for combining two `ASCIIArt` figures horizontally

```
 /\_/\    -----
( ' ' )  / Hello \
(  -  ) <  Scala |
 | | |   \ Coder /
(__|__)    -----
```

or vertically. Choose operators with appropriate precedence.

7. Implement a class `BitSequence` that stores a sequence of 64 bits packed in a `Long` value. Supply `apply` and `update` operators to get and set an individual bit.

8. Provide a class `Matrix`. Choose whether you want to implement 2 × 2 matrices, square matrices of any size, or $m \times n$ matrices. Supply operations + and *. The latter should also work with scalars, for example, `mat` * 2. A single element should be accessible as `mat(row, col)`.

9. Define an object `PathComponents` with an `unapply` operation class that extracts the directory path and file name from an `java.nio.file.Path`. For example, the file /home/cay/readme.txt has directory path /home/cay and file name `readme.txt`.

10. Modify the `PathComponents` object of the preceding exercise to instead define an `unapplySeq` operation that extracts all path segments. For example, for the file /home/cay/readme.txt, you should produce a sequence of three segments: home, cay, and `readme.txt`.

11. Improve the dynamic property selector in Section 11.11, "Dynamic Invocation," on page 150 so that one doesn't have to use underscores. For example, `sysProps.java.home` should select the property with key "java.home". Use a helper class, also extending `Dynamic`, that contains partially completed paths.

12. Define a class `XMLElement` that models an XML element with a name, attributes, and child elements. Using dynamic selection and method calls, make it possible to select paths such as `rootElement.html.body.ul(id="42").li`, which should return all `li` elements inside `ul` with `id` attribute 42 inside `body` inside `html`.

13. Provide an `XMLBuilder` class for dynamically building XML elements, as `builder.ul(id="42", style="list-style: lower-alpha;")`, where the method name becomes the element name and the named arguments become the attributes. Come up with a convenient way of building nested elements.

Higher-Order Functions

Topics in This Chapter ⬛

Chapter

Scala mixes object orientation with functional features. In a functional programming language, functions are first-class citizens that can be passed around and manipulated just like any other data types. This is very useful whenever you want to pass some action detail to an algorithm. In a functional language, you just wrap that detail into a function that you pass as a parameter. In this chapter, you will see how to be productive with functions that use or return functions.

Highlights of the chapter include:

- Functions are "first-class citizens" in Scala, just like numbers.

- You can create anonymous functions, usually to give them to other functions.

- A function argument specifies behavior that should be executed later.

- Many collection methods take function parameters, applying a function to the values of the collection.

- There are syntax shortcuts that allow you to express function parameters in a way that is short and easy to read.

- You can create functions that operate on blocks of code and look much like the built-in control statements.

12.1 Functions as Values

In Scala, a function is a first-class citizen, just like a number. You can store a function in a variable:

```
import scala.math._
val num = 3.14
val fun = ceil _
```

This code sets num to 3.14 and fun to the ceil function.

The _ behind the ceil function indicates that you really meant the function, and you didn't just forget to supply the arguments.

When you try this code in the REPL, the type of num is, not surprisingly, Double. The type of fun is reported as (Double) => Double—that is, a function receiving and returning a Double.

 NOTE: Technically, the _ turns the ceil *method* into a function. In Scala, you cannot manipulate methods, only functions. The type of the function is (Double) => Double, with an arrow. In contrast, the type of the ceil method is (Double)Double, without an arrow. There is no way for you to work with such a type, but you will find it in compiler and REPL messages.

The _ suffix is not necessary when you use a method name in a context where a function is expected. For example, the following is legal:

```
val f: (Double) => Double = ceil // No underscore needed
```

 NOTE: The ceil method is a method of the scala.math package object. If you have a method from a class, the syntax for turning it into a function is slightly different:

```
val f = (_: String).charAt(_: Int)
   // A function (String, Int) => Char
```

Alternatively, you can specify the type of the function instead of the parameter types:

```
val f: (String, Int) => Char = _.charAt(_)
```

What can you do with a function? Two things:

- Call it.

- Pass it around, by storing it in a variable or giving it to a function as a parameter.

Here is how to call the function stored in fun:

```
fun(num) // 4.0
```

As you can see, the normal function call syntax is used. The only difference is that fun is a *variable containing a function*, not a fixed function.

Here is how you can give fun to another function:

```
Array(3.14, 1.42, 2.0).map(fun) // Array(4.0, 2.0, 2.0)
```

The map method accepts a function, applies it to all values in an array, and returns an array with the function values. In this chapter, you will see many other methods that accept functions as parameters.

12.2 Anonymous Functions

In Scala, you don't have to give a name to each function, just like you don't have to give a name to each number. Here is an *anonymous function*:

```
(x: Double) => 3 * x
```

This function multiplies its argument by 3.

Of course, you can store this function in a variable:

```
val triple = (x: Double) => 3 * x
```

That's just as if you had used a def:

```
def triple(x: Double) = 3 * x
```

But you don't have to name the function. You can just pass it to another function:

```
Array(3.14, 1.42, 2.0).map((x: Double) => 3 * x)
  // Array(9.42, 4.26, 6.0)
```

Here, we tell the map method: "Multiply each element by 3."

 NOTE: If you prefer, you can enclose the function argument in braces instead of parentheses, for example:

```
Array(3.14, 1.42, 2.0).map{ (x: Double) => 3 * x }
```

This is more common when a method is used in infix notation (without the dot).

```
Array(3.14, 1.42, 2.0) map { (x: Double) => 3 * x }
```

 NOTE: Anything defined with def (in the REPL or a class or object) is a method, not a function:

```
scala> def triple(x: Double) = 3 * x
triple: (x: Double)Double
```

Note the method type (x: Double)Double. In contrast, a function definition has a function type:

```
scala> val triple = (x: Double) => 3 * x
triple: Double => Double
```

12.3 Functions with Function Parameters

In this section, you will see how to implement a function that takes another function as a parameter. Here is an example:

```
def valueAtOneQuarter(f: (Double) => Double) = f(0.25)
```

Note that the parameter can be *any* function receiving and returning a Double. The valueAtOneQuarter function computes the value of that function at 0.25.

For example,

```
valueAtOneQuarter(ceil _) // 1.0
valueAtOneQuarter(sqrt _) // 0.5 (because 0.5 × 0.5 = 0.25)
```

What is the type of valueAtOneQuarter? It is a function with one parameter, so its type is written as

(parameterType) => *resultType*

The *resultType* is clearly Double, and the *parameterType* is already given in the function header as (Double) => Double. Therefore, the type of valueAtOneQuarter is

```
((Double) => Double) => Double
```

Since valueAtOneQuarter is a function that receives a function, it is called a *higher-order function*.

A higher-order function can also *produce a function*. Here is a simple example:

```
def mulBy(factor : Double) = (x : Double) => factor * x
```

For example, mulBy(3) returns the function (x : Double) => 3 * x which you have seen in the preceding section. The power of mulBy is that it can deliver functions that multiply by any amount:

```
val quintuple = mulBy(5)
quintuple(20) // 100
```

The mulBy function has a parameter of type Double, and it returns a function of type (Double) => Double. Therefore, its type is

```
(Double) => ((Double) => Double)
```

12.4 Parameter Inference

When you pass an anonymous function to another function or method, Scala helps you out by deducing types when possible. For example, you don't have to write

```
valueAtOneQuarter((x: Double) => 3 * x) // 0.75
```

Since the `valueAtOneQuarter` method knows that you will pass in a `(Double) => Double` function, you can just write

```
valueAtOneQuarter((x) => 3 * x)
```

As a special bonus, for a function that has just one parameter, you can omit the () around the parameter:

```
valueAtOneQuarter(x => 3 * x)
```

It gets better. If a parameter occurs only once on the right-hand side of the =>, you can replace it with an underscore:

```
valueAtOneQuarter(3 * _)
```

This is the ultimate in comfort, and it is also pretty easy to read: a function that multiplies something by 3.

Keep in mind that these shortcuts only work when the parameter types are known.

```
val fun = 3 * _ // Error: Can't infer types
val fun = 3 * (_: Double) // OK
val fun: (Double) => Double = 3 * _ // OK because we specified the type for fun
```

Of course, the last definition is contrived. But it shows what happens when a function is passed to a parameter (which has just such a type).

 NOTE: Specifying the type of _ is useful for turning methods into functions. For example, `(_: String).length` is a function `String => Int`, and `(_: String).substring(_:Int, _: Int)` is a function `(String, Int, Int) => String`.

12.5 Useful Higher-Order Functions

A good way of becoming comfortable with higher-order functions is to practice with some common (and obviously useful) methods in the Scala collections library that take function parameters.

You have seen `map`, which applies a function to all elements of a collection and returns the result. Here is a quick way of producing a collection containing 0.1, 0.2, ... , 0.9:

```
(1 to 9).map(0.1 * _)
```

 NOTE: There is a general principle at work. If you want a sequence of values, see if you can transform it from a simpler one.

Try this to print a triangle:

```
(1 to 9).map("*" * _).foreach(println _)
```

The result is

```
*
**
***
****
*****
******
*******
********
*********
```

Here, we also use foreach, which is like map except that its function doesn't return a value. The foreach method simply applies the function to each argument.

The filter method yields all elements that match a particular condition. For example, here's how to get only the even numbers in a sequence:

```
(1 to 9).filter(_ % 2 == 0) // 2, 4, 6, 8
```

Of course, that's not the most efficient way of getting this result ☺.

The reduceLeft method takes a *binary* function—that is, a function with two parameters—and applies it to all elements of a sequence, going from left to right. For example,

```
(1 to 9).reduceLeft(_ * _)
```

is

```
1 * 2 * 3 * 4 * 5 * 6 * 7 * 8 * 9
```

or, strictly speaking,

```
(...((1 * 2) * 3) * ... * 9)
```

Note the compact form of the multiplication function: _ * _. Each underscore denotes a separate parameter.

You also need a binary function for sorting. For example,

```
"Mary had a little lamb".split(" ").sortWith(_.length < _.length)
```

yields an array that is sorted by increasing length: Array("a", "had", "Mary", "lamb", "little").

12.6 Closures

In Scala, you can define a function inside any scope: in a package, in a class, or even inside another function or method. In the body of a function, you can access any variables from an enclosing scope. That may not sound so remarkable, but note that your function may be called when the variable is *no longer in scope*.

Here is an example: the mulBy function from Section 12.3, "Functions with Function Parameters," on page 160.

```
def mulBy(factor : Double) = (x : Double) => factor * x
```

Consider these calls:

```
val triple = mulBy(3)
val half = mulBy(0.5)
println(s"${triple(14)} ${half(14)}") // Prints 42 7
```

Let's look at them in slow motion.

1. The first call to mulBy sets the parameter variable factor to 3. That variable is referenced in the body of the function (x : Double) => factor * x, which is stored in triple. Then the parameter variable factor is popped off the runtime stack.

2. Next, mulBy is called again, now with factor set to 0.5. That variable is referenced in the body of the function (x : Double) => factor * x, which is stored in half.

Each of the returned functions has its own setting for factor.

Such a function is called a *closure*. A closure consists of code together with the definitions of any nonlocal variables that the code uses.

These functions are actually implemented as objects of a class, with an instance variable factor and an apply method that contains the body of the function.

It doesn't really matter how a closure is implemented. It is the job of the Scala compiler to ensure that your functions can access nonlocal variables.

 NOTE: Closures aren't difficult or surprising if they are a natural part of the language. Many modern languages, such as JavaScript, Ruby, and Python, support closures. Java, as of version 8, has closures in the form of lambda expressions.

12.7 SAM Conversions

In Scala, you pass a function as a parameter whenever you want to tell another function what action to carry out. Prior to Java 8, this was not possible in Java without defining a class and a method for the action. For example, to implement a button callback, one had to use this Scala code (or its Java equivalent):

```
var counter = 0

val button = new JButton("Increment")
button.addActionListener(new ActionListener {
  override def actionPerformed(event: ActionEvent) {
    counter += 1
  }
})
```

In Java 8, it is possible to specify such actions with lambda expressions, which are closely related to functions in Scala. Fortunately, that means that as of Scala 2.12, one can pass Scala functions to Java code expecting a "SAM interface"—that is, any Java interface with a single abstract method. (Such interfaces are officially called *functional interfaces* in Java.)

Simply pass the function to the addActionListener method, like this:

```
button.addActionListener(event => counter += 1)
```

Note that the conversion from a Scala function to a Java SAM interface only works for *function literals*, not for variables holding functions. The following does not work:

```
val listener = (event: ActionListener) => println(counter)
button.addActionListener(listener)
  // Cannot convert a nonliteral function to a Java SAM interface
```

The simplest remedy is to declare the variable holding the function as a Java SAM interface:

```
val listener: ActionListener = event => println(counter)
button.addActionListener(listener) // Ok
```

Alternatively, you can turn a function variable into a literal expression:

```
val exit = (event: ActionEvent) => if (counter > 9) System.exit(0)
button.addActionListener(exit(_))
```

12.8 Currying

Currying (named after logician Haskell Brooks Curry) is the process of turning a function that takes two arguments into a function that takes one argument. That function returns a function that consumes the second argument.

Huh? Let's look at an example. This function takes two arguments:

```
val mul = (x: Int, y: Int) => x * y
```

This function takes one argument, yielding a function that takes one argument:

```
val mulOneAtATime = (x: Int) => ((y: Int) => x * y)
```

To multiply two numbers, you call

```
mulOneAtATime(6)(7)
```

Strictly speaking, the result of `mulOneAtATime(6)` is the function `(y: Int) => 6 * y`. That function is applied to 7, yielding 42.

When you use `def`, there is a shortcut for defining such curried methods in Scala:

```
def mulOneAtATime(x: Int)(y: Int) = x * y
```

NOTE: Recall that anything defined with `def` (in the REPL or a class or object) is a method, not a function. When defining curried methods with `def`, you can use multiple parentheses:

```
scala> def mulOneAtATime(x: Int)(y: Int) = x * y
mulOneAtATime: (x: Int)(y: Int)Int
```

Note the method type `(x: Int)(y: Int)Int`. In contrast, when you define a function, you must use multiple arrows, not multiple parentheses:

```
scala> val mulOneAtATime = (x: Int) => (y: Int) => x * y
mulOneAtATime: Int => (Int => Int)
```

As you can see, multiple parameters are just a frill, not an essential feature of a programming language. That's an amusing theoretical insight, but it has one practical use in Scala. Sometimes, you can use currying for a method parameter so that the type inferencer has more information.

Here is a typical example. The `corresponds` method can compare whether two sequences are the same under some comparison criterion. For example,

```
val a = Array("Hello", "World")
val b = Array("hello", "world")
a.corresponds(b)(_.equalsIgnoreCase(_))
```

Note that the function `_.equalsIgnoreCase(_)` is passed as a curried parameter, in a separate set of (...). When you look into the Scaladoc, you will see that `corresponds` is declared as

```
def corresponds[B](that: Seq[B])(p: (A, B) => Boolean): Boolean
```

The `that` sequence and the predicate function `p` are separate curried parameters. The type inferencer can figure out what `B` is from the type of `that`, and then it can use that information when analyzing the function that is passed for `p`.

In our example, `that` is a `String` sequence. Therefore, the predicate is expected to have type `(String, String) => Boolean`. With that information, the compiler can accept `_.equalsIgnoreCase(_)` as a shortcut for `(a: String, b: String) => a.equalsIgnoreCase(b)`.

12.9 Control Abstractions

In Scala, one can model a sequence of statements as a function with no parameters or return value. For example, here is a function that runs some code in a thread:

```
def runInThread(block: () => Unit) {
  new Thread {
    override def run() { block() }
  }.start()
}
```

The code is given as a function of type () => Unit. However, when you call this function, you need to supply an unsightly () =>:

```
runInThread { () => println("Hi"); Thread.sleep(10000); println("Bye") }
```

To avoid the () => in the call, use the *call by name* notation: Omit the (), but not the =>, in the parameter declaration and in the call to the parameter function:

```
def runInThread(block: => Unit) {
  new Thread {
    override def run() { block }
  }.start()
}
```

Then the call becomes simply

```
runInThread { println("Hi"); Thread.sleep(10000); println("Bye") }
```

This looks pretty nice. Scala programmers can build *control abstractions*: functions that look like language keywords. For example, we can implement a function that is used *exactly* as a while statement. Or, we can innovate a bit and define an until statement that works like while, but with an inverted condition:

```
def until(condition: => Boolean)(block: => Unit) {
  if (!condition) {
    block
    until(condition)(block)
  }
}
```

Here is how you use until:

```
var x = 10
until (x == 0) {
  x -= 1
  println(x)
}
```

The technical term for such a function parameter is a *call-by-name* parameter. Unlike a regular (or call-by-value) parameter, the parameter expression is *not* evaluated when the function is called. After all, we don't want x == 0 to evaluate to false in the call to until. Instead, the expression becomes the body of a function with no arguments. That function is passed as a parameter.

Look carefully at the until function definition. Note that it is curried: It first consumes the condition, then the block as a second parameter. Without currying, the call would look like this:

```
until(x == 0, { ... })
```

which wouldn't be as pretty.

12.10 The return Expression

In Scala, you don't use a return statement to return function values. The return value of a function is simply the value of the function body.

However, you can use return to return a value from an anonymous function to an enclosing named function. This is useful in control abstractions. For example, consider this function:

```
def indexOf(str: String, ch: Char): Int = {
  var i = 0
  until (i == str.length) {
    if (str(i) == ch) return i
    i += 1
  }
  return -1
}
```

Here, the anonymous function { if (str(i) == ch) return i; i += 1 } is passed to until. When the return expression is executed, the enclosing named function indexOf terminates and returns the given value.

If you use return inside a named function, you need to specify its return type. For example, in the indexOf function above, the compiler was not able to infer that it returns an Int.

The control flow is achieved with a special exception that is thrown by the return expression in the anonymous function, passed out of the until function, and caught in the indexOf function.

 CAUTION: If the exception is caught in a try block, before it is delivered to the named function, then the value will not be returned.

Exercises

1. Write a function values(fun: (Int) => Int, low: Int, high: Int) that yields a collection of function inputs and outputs in a given range. For example, values(x => x * x, -5, 5) should produce a collection of pairs (-5, 25), (-4, 16), (-3, 9), ..., (5, 25).

2. How do you get the largest element of an array with reduceLeft?

3. Implement the factorial function using to and reduceLeft, without a loop or recursion.

4. The previous implementation needed a special case when $n < 1$. Show how you can avoid this with foldLeft. (Look at the Scaladoc for foldLeft. It's like reduceLeft, except that the first value in the chain of combined values is supplied in the call.)

5. Write a function largest(fun: (Int) => Int, inputs: Seq[Int]) that yields the largest value of a function within a given sequence of inputs. For example, largest(x => 10 * x - x * x, 1 to 10) should return 25. Don't use a loop or recursion.

6. Modify the previous function to return the *input* at which the output is largest. For example, largestAt(x => 10 * x - x * x, 1 to 10) should return 5. Don't use a loop or recursion.

7. It's easy to get a sequence of pairs, for example:

   ```
   val pairs = (1 to 10) zip (11 to 20)
   ```

   Now, suppose you want to do something with such a sequence—say, add up the values. But you can't do

   ```
   pairs.map(_ + _)
   ```

   The function _ + _ takes two Int parameters, not an (Int, Int) pair. Write a function adjustToPair that receives a function of type (Int, Int) => Int and returns the equivalent function that operates on a pair. For example, adjustToPair(_ * _)((6, 7)) is 42.

   Then use this function in conjunction with map to compute the sums of the elements in pairs.

8. In Section 12.8, "Currying," on page 164, you saw the corresponds method used with two arrays of strings. Make a call to corresponds that checks whether the elements in an array of strings have the lengths given in an array of integers.

9. Implement corresponds without currying. Then try the call from the preceding exercise. What problem do you encounter?

10. Implement an unless control abstraction that works just like if, but with an inverted condition. Does the first parameter need to be a call-by-name parameter? Do you need currying?

Collections

Chapter 13

In this chapter, you will learn about the Scala collections library from a library user's point of view. In addition to arrays and maps, which you have already encountered, you will see other useful collection types. There are many methods that can be applied to collections, and this chapter presents them in an orderly way.

The key points of this chapter are:

- All collections extend the Iterable trait.

- The three major categories of collections are sequences, sets, and maps.

- Scala has mutable and immutable versions of most collections.

- A Scala list is either empty, or it has a head and a tail which is again a list.

- Sets are unordered collections.

- Use a LinkedHashSet to retain the insertion order or a SortedSet to iterate in sorted order.

- + adds an element to an unordered collection; +: and :+ prepend or append to a sequence; ++ concatenates two collections; - and -- remove elements.

- The Iterable and Seq traits have dozens of useful methods for common operations. Check them out before writing tedious loops.

- Mapping, folding, and zipping are useful techniques for applying a function or operation to the elements of a collection.

13.1 The Main Collections Traits

Figure 13–1 shows the most important traits that make up the Scala collections hierarchy.

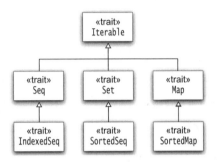

Figure 13–1   Key traits in the Scala collections hierarchy

An Iterable is any collection that can yield an Iterator with which you can access all elements in the collection:

```
val coll = ... // some Iterable
val iter = coll.iterator
while (iter.hasNext)
    do something with iter.next()
```

This is the most basic way of traversing a collection. However, as you will see throughout this chapter, usually there are more convenient ways.

A Seq is an ordered sequence of values, such as an array or list. An IndexedSeq allows fast random access through an integer index. For example, an ArrayBuffer is indexed but a linked list is not.

A Set is an unordered collection of values. In a SortedSet, elements are always visited in sorted order.

A Map is a set of (*key*, *value*) pairs. A SortedMap visits the entries as sorted by the keys. See Chapter 4 for more information.

This hierarchy is similar to that in Java, with a couple of welcome improvements:

1. Maps are a part of the hierarchy and not a separate hierarchy.

2. IndexedSeq is the supertype of arrays but not of lists, allowing you to tell the two apart.

NOTE: In Java, both `ArrayList` and `LinkedList` implement a common `List` interface, making it difficult to write efficient code when random access is preferred, for example when searching in a sorted sequence. This was a flawed design decision in the original Java collections framework. In a later version, a marker interface `RandomAccess` was added to deal with this problem.

Each Scala collection trait or class has a companion object with an `apply` method for constructing an instance of the collection. For example,

```
Iterable(0xFF, 0xFF00, 0xFF0000)
Set(Color.RED, Color.GREEN, Color.BLUE)
Map(Color.RED -> 0xFF0000, Color.GREEN -> 0xFF00, Color.BLUE -> 0xFF)
SortedSet("Hello", "World")
```

This is called the "uniform creation principle."

There are methods `toSeq`, `toSet`, `toMap`, and so on, as well as a generic `to[C]` method, that you can use to translate between collection types.

```
val coll = Seq(1, 1, 2, 3, 5, 8, 13)
val set = coll.toSet
val buffer = coll.to[ArrayBuffer]
```

 NOTE: You can use the `==` operator to compare any sequence, set, or map with another collection of the same kind. For example, `Seq(1, 2, 3) == (1 to 3)` yields `true`. But comparing different kinds, for example, `Seq(1, 2, 3) == Set(1, 2, 3)` always yields `false`. In that case, use the `sameElements` method.

13.2 Mutable and Immutable Collections

Scala supports both mutable and immutable collections. An immutable collection can never change, so you can safely share a reference to it, even in a multi-threaded program. For example, there is a `scala.collection.mutable.Map` and a `scala.collection.immutable.Map`. Both have a common supertype `scala.collection.Map` (which, of course, contains no mutation operations).

 NOTE: When you have a reference to a `scala.collection.immutable.Map`, you know that *nobody* can change the map. If you have a `scala.collection.Map`, then *you* can't change it, but someone else might.

Scala gives a preference to immutable collections. The companion objects in the `scala.collection` package produce immutable collections. For example, `scala.collection.Map("Hello" -> 42)` is an immutable map.

Moreover, the scala package and the Predef object, which are always imported, have type aliases List, Set, and Map that refer to the immutable traits. For example, Predef.Map is the same as scala.collection.immutable.Map.

 TIP: With the statement

```
import scala.collection.mutable
```

you can get an immutable map as Map and a mutable one as mutable.Map.

If you had no prior experience with immutable collections, you may wonder how you can do useful work with them. The key is that you can create new collections out of old ones. For example, if numbers is an immutable set, then

```
numbers + 9
```

is a new set containing the numbers together with 9. If 9 was already in the set, you just get a reference to the old set. This is particularly natural in recursive computations. For example, here we compute the set of all digits of an integer:

```
def digits(n: Int): Set[Int] =
  if (n < 0) digits(-n)
  else if (n < 10) Set(n)
  else digits(n / 10) + (n % 10)
```

This method starts out with a set containing a single digit. At each step, another digit is added. However, adding the digit doesn't mutate a set. Instead, in each step, a new set is constructed.

13.3 Sequences

Figure 13–2 shows the most important immutable sequences.

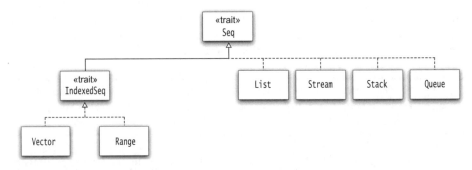

Figure 13–2   Immutable sequences

A Vector is the immutable equivalent of an ArrayBuffer: an indexed sequence with fast random access. Vectors are implemented as trees where each node has up to 32 children. For a vector with one million elements, one needs four layers of nodes. (Since $10^3 \approx 2^{10}$, $10^6 \approx 32^4$.) Accessing an element in such a list will take 4 hops, whereas in a linked list it would take an average of 500,000.

A Range represents an integer sequence, such as 0,1,2,3,4,5,6,7,8,9 or 10,20,30. Of course a Range object doesn't store all sequence values but only the start, end, and increment. You construct Range objects with the to and until methods, as described in Chapter 2.

We discuss lists in the next section, and streams in Section 13.12, "Streams," on page 189.

See Figure 13–3 for the most useful mutable sequences.

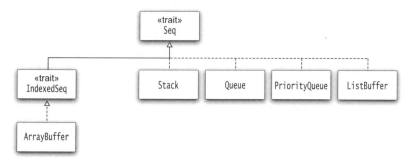

Figure 13–3   Mutable sequences

We discussed array buffers in Chapter 3. Stacks, queues, and priority queues are standard data structures that are useful for implementing certain algorithms. If you are familiar with these structures, the Scala implementations won't surprise you.

13.4 Lists

In Scala, a list is either Nil (that is, empty) or an object with a head element and a tail that is again a list. For example, consider the list

```
val digits = List(4, 2)
```

The value of digits.head is 4, and digits.tail is List(2). Moreover, digits.tail.head is 2 and digits.tail.tail is Nil.

The :: operator makes a new list from a given head and tail. For example,

```
9 :: List(4, 2)
```

is List(9, 4, 2). You can also write that list as

```
9 :: 4 :: 2 :: Nil
```

Note that :: is right-associative. With the :: operator, lists are constructed from the end:

```
9 :: (4 :: (2 :: Nil))
```

In Java or C++, one uses an iterator to traverse a linked list. You can do this in Scala as well, but it is often more natural to use recursion. For example, the following function computes the sum of all elements in a linked list of integers:

```
def sum(lst: List[Int]): Int =
  if (lst == Nil) 0 else lst.head + sum(lst.tail)
```

Or, if you prefer, you can use pattern matching:

```
def sum(lst: List[Int]): Int = lst match {
  case Nil => 0
  case h :: t => h + sum(t) // h is lst.head, t is lst.tail
}
```

Note the :: operator in the second pattern. It "destructures" the list into head and tail.

 NOTE: Recursion works so naturally because the tail of a list is again a list.

Of course, for this particular example, you do not need to use recursion at all. The Scala library already has a sum method:

```
List(9, 4, 2).sum // Yields 15
```

If you want to mutate list elements in place, you can use a ListBuffer, a data structure that is backed by a linked list with a reference to the last node. This makes it efficient to add or remove elements at either end of the list.

However, adding or removing elements in the middle is not efficient. For example, suppose you want to remove every second element of a mutable list. With a Java LinkedList, you use an iterator and call remove after every second call to next. There is no analogous operation on a ListBuffer. Of course, removing multiple elements by their index positions is very inefficient in a linked list. Your best bet is to generate a new list with the result (see Exercise 3 on page 194).

 NOTE: There are deprecated LinkedList and DoubleLinkedList classes and an internal MutableList class that you should not be using.

13.5 Sets

A set is a collection of distinct elements. Trying to add an existing element has no effect. For example,

```
Set(2, 0, 1) + 1
```

is the same as Set(2, 0, 1).

Unlike lists, sets do not retain the order in which elements are inserted. By default, sets are implemented as *hash sets* in which elements are organized by the value of the hashCode method. (In Scala, as in Java, every object has a hashCode method.)

For example, if you iterate over

```
Set(1, 2, 3, 4, 5, 6)
```

the elements are visited in the order

```
5 1 6 2 3 4
```

You may wonder why sets don't retain the element order. It turns out that you can find elements much faster if you allow sets to reorder their elements. Finding an element in a hash set is *much* faster than in an array or list.

A *linked hash set* remembers the order in which elements were inserted. It keeps a linked list for this purpose. For example,

```
val weekdays = scala.collection.mutable.LinkedHashSet("Mo", "Tu", "We", "Th", "Fr")
```

If you want to iterate over elements in sorted order, use a *sorted set*:

```
val numbers = scala.collection.mutable.SortedSet(1, 2, 3, 4, 5)
```

A *bit set* is an implementation of a set of non-negative integers as a sequence of bits. The *i*th bit is 1 if *i* is present in the set. This is an efficient implementation as long as the maximum element is not too large. Scala provides both mutable and immutable BitSet classes.

The contains method checks whether a set contains a given value. The subsetOf method checks whether all elements of a set are contained in another set.

```
val digits = Set(1, 7, 2, 9)
digits contains 0 // false
Set(1, 2) subsetOf digits // true
```

The union, intersect, and diff methods carry out the usual set operations. If you prefer, you can write them as |, &, and &~. You can also write union as ++ and difference as --. For example, if we have the set

```
val primes = Set(2, 3, 5, 7)
```

then digits union primes is Set(1, 2, 3, 5, 7, 9), digits & primes is Set(2, 7), and digits -- primes is Set(1, 9).

13.6 Operators for Adding or Removing Elements

When you want to add or remove an element, or a number of elements, the operators to use depend on the collection type. Table 13–1 provides a summary.

Table 13–1 Operators for Adding and Removing Elements

Operator	Description	Collection Type
coll(k) (i.e., coll.apply(k))	The kth sequence element or the map value for key k.	Seq, Map
coll :+ elem elem +: coll	A collection of the same type as coll to which elem has been appended or prepended.	Seq
coll + elem coll + (e1, e2, ...)	A collection of the same type as coll to which the given elements have been added.	Set, Map
coll - elem coll - (e1, e2, ...)	A collection of the same type as coll from which the given elements have been removed.	Set, Map, ArrayBuffer
coll ++ coll2 coll2 ++: coll	A collection of the same type as coll, containing the elements of both collections.	Iterable
coll -- coll2	A collection of the same type as coll from which the elements of coll2 have been removed. (For sequences, use diff.)	Set, Map, ArrayBuffer
elem :: lst lst2 ::: lst	A list with the element or given list prepended to lst. Same as +: and ++:.	List
list ::: list2	Same as list ++: list2.	List
set | set2 set & set2 set &~ set2	Set union, intersection, difference. | is the same as ++, and &~ is the same as --.	Set
coll += elem coll += (e1, e2, ...) coll ++= coll2 coll -= elem coll -= (e1, e2, ...) coll --= coll2	Modifies coll by adding or removing the given elements.	Mutable collections
elem +=: coll coll2 ++=: coll	Modifies coll by prepending the given element or collection.	ArrayBuffer

Generally, + is used for adding an element to an unordered collection, while +: and :+ add an element to the beginning or end of an ordered collection.

```
Vector(1, 2, 3) :+ 5 // Yields Vector(1, 2, 3, 5)
1 +: Vector(1, 2, 3) // Yields Vector(1, 1, 2, 3)
```

Note that +:, like all operators ending in a colon, is right-associative, and that it is a method of the right operand.

These operators return new collections (of the same type as the original ones) without modifying the original. Mutable collections have a += operator that mutates the left-hand side. For example,

```
val numbers = ArrayBuffer(1, 2, 3)
numbers += 5 // Adds 5 to numbers
```

With an immutable collection, you can use += or :+= with a var, like this:

```
var numbers = Set(1, 2, 3)
numbers += 5 // Sets numbers to the immutable set numbers + 5
var numberVector = Vector(1, 2, 3)
numberVector :+= 5 // += does not work since vectors don't have a + operator
```

To remove an element, use the - operator:

```
Set(1, 2, 3) - 2 // Yields Set(1, 3)
```

You can add multiple elements with the ++ operator:

```
coll ++ coll2
```

yields a collection of the same type as coll that contains both coll and coll2. Similarly, the -- operator removes multiple elements.

 TIP: As you can see, Scala provides many operators for adding and removing elements. Here is a summary:

1. Append (:+) or prepend (+:) to a sequence.

2. Add (+) to an unordered collection.

3. Remove with the - operator.

4. Use ++ and -- for bulk add and remove.

5. Mutations are += ++= -= --=.

6. For lists, many Scala programmers prefer the :: and ::: operators.

7. Stay away from ++: +=: ++=:.

 NOTE: For lists, you can use +: instead of :: for consistency, with one exception: Pattern matching (case h::t) does *not* work with the +: operator.

13.7 Common Methods

Table 13–2 gives a brief overview of the most important methods of the Iterable trait, sorted by functionality.

Table 13–2 Important Methods of the Iterable Trait

Methods	Description
head, last, headOption, lastOption	Returns the first or last element; or, that element as an Option.
tail, init	Returns everything but the first or last element.
length, isEmpty	Returns the length, or true if the length is zero.
map(f), flatMap(f), foreach(f), transform(f)collect(pf)	Applies a function to all elements; see Section 13.8.
reduceLeft(op), reduceRight(op), foldLeft(init)(op), foldRight(init)(op)	Applies a binary operation to all elements in a given order; see Section 13.9.
reduce(op), fold(init)(op), aggregate(init)(op, combineOp)	Applies a binary operation to all elements in arbitrary order; see Section 13.15.
sum, product, max, min	Returns the sum or product (provided the element type can be implicitly converted to the Numeric trait), or the maximum or minimum (provided the element type can be converted to the Ordered trait).
count(pred), forall(pred), exists(pred)	Returns the count of elements fulfilling the predicate; true if all elements do, or at least one element does.
filter(pred), filterNot(pred), partition(pred)	Returns all elements fulfilling or not fulfilling the predicate; the pair of both.
takeWhile(pred), dropWhile(pred), span(pred)	Returns the first elements fulfilling pred; all but those elements; the pair of both.
take(n), drop(n), splitAt(n)	Returns the first n elements; everything but the first n elements; the pair of both.
takeRight(n), dropRight(n)	Returns the last n elements; everything but the last n elements.
slice(from, to), view(from, to)	Returns the elements in the range from until to, or a view thereto; see Section 13.13.

(Continues)

Table 13–2 Important Methods of the Iterable Trait *(Continued)*

Methods	Description
`zip(coll2)`, `zipAll(coll2, fill, fill2)`, `zipWithIndex`	Returns pairs of elements from this collection and another; see Section 13.10.
`grouped(n)`, `sliding(n)`	Returns iterators of subcollections of length n; grouped yields elements with index 0 until n, then with index n until 2 * n, and so on; sliding yields elements with index 0 until n, then with index 1 until n + 1, and so on.
`groupBy(k)`	Yields a map whose keys are k(x) for all elements x. The value for each key is the collection of elements with that key.
`mkString(before, between, after)`, `addString(sb, before, between, after)`	Makes a string of all elements, adding the given strings before the first, between each, and after the last element. The second method appends that string to a string builder.
`toIterable, toSeq, toIndexedSeq, toArray, toBuffer, toList, toStream, toSet, toVector, toMap, to[C]`	Converts the collection to a collection of the specified type.

The Seq trait adds several methods to the Iterable trait. Table 13–3 shows the most important ones.

Table 13–3 Important Methods of the Seq Trait

Methods	Description
`contains(elem)`, `containsSlice(seq)`, `startsWith(seq)`, `endsWith(seq)`	Returns true if this sequence contains the given element or sequence; if it starts or ends with the given sequence.
`indexOf(elem)`, `lastIndexOf(elem)`, `indexOfSlice(seq)`, `lastIndexOfSlice(seq)`	Returns the index of the first or last occurrence of the given element or element sequence.
`indexWhere(pred)`	Returns the index of the first element fulfilling pred.
`prefixLength(pred)`, `segmentLength(pred, n)`	Returns the length of the longest sequence of elements fulfilling pred, starting with 0 or n.

(Continues)

Table 13–3 Important Methods of the Seq Trait *(Continued)*

Methods	Description
`padTo(n, fill)`	Returns a copy of this sequence, with `fill` appended until the length is `n`.
`intersect(seq), diff(seq)`	Returns the "multiset" intersection or difference of the sequences. For example, if a contains five 1s and b contains two, then a `intersect` b contains two (the smaller count), and a `diff` b contains three (the difference).
`reverse`	The reverse of this sequence.
`sorted, sortWith(less), sortBy(f)`	The sequence sorted using the element ordering, the binary `less` function, or a function f that maps each element to an ordered type.
`permutations, combinations(n)`	Returns an iterator over all permutations or combinations (subsequences of length n).

 NOTE: Note that these methods never mutate a collection. They return a collection of the same type as the original. This is sometimes called the "uniform return type" principle.

13.8 Mapping a Function

You may want to transform all elements of a collection. The `map` method applies a function to a collection and yields a collection of the results. For example, given a list of strings

```
val names = List("Peter", "Paul", "Mary")
```

you get a list of the uppercased strings as

```
names.map(_.toUpperCase) // List("PETER", "PAUL", "MARY")
```

This is exactly the same as

```
for (n <- names) yield n.toUpperCase
```

If the function yields a collection instead of a single value, you may want to concatenate all results. In that case, use `flatMap`. For example, consider

```
def ulcase(s: String) = Vector(s.toUpperCase(), s.toLowerCase())
```

Then names.map(ulcase) is

```
List(Vector("PETER", "peter"), Vector("PAUL", "paul"), Vector("MARY", "mary"))
```

but `names.flatMap(ulcase)` is

    List("PETER", "peter", "PAUL", "paul", "MARY", "mary")

 TIP: If you use `flatMap` with a function that returns an `Option`, the resulting collection contains all values v for which the function returns `Some(v)`.

 NOTE: The `map` and `flatMap` methods are important because they are used for translating `for` expressions. For example, the expression

    for (i <- 1 to 10) yield i * i

is translated to

    (1 to 10).map(i => i * i)

and

    for (i <- 1 to 10; j <- 1 to i) yield i * j

becomes

    (1 to 10).flatMap(i => (1 to i).map(j => i * j))

Why `flatMap`? See Exercise 9 on page 195.

The `transform` method is the in-place equivalent of `map`. It applies to mutable collections, and replaces each element with the result of a function. For example, the following code changes all buffer elements to uppercase:

    val buffer = ArrayBuffer("Peter", "Paul", "Mary")
    buffer.transform(_.toUpperCase)

If you just want to apply a function for its side effect and don't care about the function values, use `foreach`:

    names.foreach(println)

The `collect` method works with *partial functions*—functions that may not be defined for all inputs. It yields a collection of all function values of the arguments on which it is defined. For example,

    "-3+4".collect { case '+' => 1 ; case '-' => -1 } // Vector(-1, 1)

The `groupBy` method yields a map whose keys are the function values, and whose values are the collections of elements whose function value is the given key. For example,

    val words = ...
    val map = words.groupBy(_.substring(0, 1).toUpper)

builds a map that maps "A" to all words starting with A, and so on.

13.9 Reducing, Folding, and Scanning A3

The map method applies a unary function to all elements of a collection. The methods that we discuss in this section combine elements with a *binary* function. The call c.reduceLeft(op) applies op to successive elements, like this:

```
        .
       .
      .
    op
   / \
  op   coll(3)
 / \
op    coll(2)
/ \
coll(0)  coll(1)
```

For example,

```
List(1, 7, 2, 9).reduceLeft(_ - _)
```

is

```
        -
       / \
      -   9
     / \
    -   2
   / \
  1   7
```

or

```
((1 - 7) - 2) - 9 = 1 - 7 - 2 - 9 = -17
```

The reduceRight method does the same, but it starts at the end of the collection. For example,

```
List(1, 7, 2, 9).reduceRight(_ - _)
```

is

```
1 - (7 - (2 - 9)) = 1 - 7 + 2 - 9 = -13
```

Often, it is useful to start the computation with an initial element other than the initial element of a collection. The call coll.foldLeft(init)(op) computes

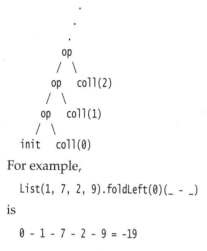

```
        op
       /  \
     op   coll(2)
     / \
   op   coll(1)
   / \
init   coll(0)
```

For example,

```
List(1, 7, 2, 9).foldLeft(0)(_ - _)
```

is

```
0 - 1 - 7 - 2 - 9 = -19
```

 NOTE: The initial value and the operator are separate "curried" parameters so that Scala can use the type of the initial value for type inference in the operator. For example, in `List(1, 7, 2, 9).foldLeft("")(_ + _)`, the initial value is a string, so the operator must be a function `(String, Int) => String`.

You can also write the `foldLeft` operation with the `/:` operator, like this:

```
(0 /: List(1, 7, 2, 9))(_ - _)
```

The `/:` is supposed to remind you of the shape of the tree.

 NOTE: With the `/:` operator, the initial value is the first operand. Note that, since the operator ends with a colon, it is a method of the second operand.

There is a `foldRight` or `:\` variant as well, computing

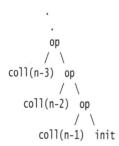

```
           op
          /  \
   coll(n-3)  op
             /  \
      coll(n-2)  op
                /  \
         coll(n-1)  init
```

These examples don't seem to be very useful. Of course, `coll.reduceLeft(_ + _)` or `coll.foldLeft(0)(_ + _)` computes the sum, but you can get that directly with `coll.sum`.

Folding is sometimes attractive as a replacement for a loop. Suppose, for example, we want to count the frequencies of the letters in a string. One way is to visit each letter and update a mutable map.

```
val freq = scala.collection.mutable.Map[Char, Int]()
for (c <- "Mississippi") freq(c) = freq.getOrElse(c, 0) + 1
// Now freq is Map('i' -> 4, 'M' -> 1, 's' -> 4, 'p' -> 2)
```

Here is another way of thinking about this process. At each step, combine the frequency map and the newly encountered letter, yielding a new frequency map. That's a fold:

```
           .
          .
         .
        op
       /  \
      op   's'
     /  \
    op   'i'
   /  \
empty map 'M'
```

What is `op`? The left operand is the partially filled map, and the right operand is the new letter. The result is the augmented map. It becomes the input to the next call to `op`, and at the end, the result is a map with all counts. The code is

```
(Map[Char, Int]() /: "Mississippi") {
  (m, c) => m + (c -> (m.getOrElse(c, 0) + 1))
}
```

Note that this is an immutable map. We compute a new map at each step.

 NOTE: It is possible to replace any `while` loop with a fold. Build a data structure that combines all variables updated in the loop, and define an operation that implements one step through the loop. I am not saying that this is always a good idea, but you may find it interesting that loops and mutations can be eliminated in this way.

Finally, the `scanLeft` and `scanRight` methods combine folding and mapping. You get a collection of all intermediate results. For example,

```
(1 to 10).scanLeft(0)(_ + _)
```

yields all partial sums:

```
Vector(0, 1, 3, 6, 10, 15, 21, 28, 36, 45, 55)
```

13.10 Zipping

The methods of the preceding section apply an operation to adjacent elements in the same collection. Sometimes, you have two collections, and you want to combine corresponding elements. For example, suppose you have a list of product prices and corresponding quantities:

```
val prices = List(5.0, 20.0, 9.95)
val quantities = List(10, 2, 1)
```

The zip method lets you combine them into a list of pairs. For example,

```
prices zip quantities
```

is a List[(Double, Int)]:

```
List[(Double, Int)] = List((5.0, 10), (20.0, 2), (9.95, 1))
```

The method is called "zip" because it combines the two collections like the teeth of a zipper.

Now it is easy to apply a function to each pair.

```
(prices zip quantities) map { p => p._1 * p._2 }
```

The result is a list of prices:

```
List(50.0, 40.0, 9.95)
```

The total price of all items is then

```
((prices zip quantities) map { p => p._1 * p._2 }) sum
```

If one collection is shorter than the other, the result has as many pairs as the shorter collection. For example,

```
List(5.0, 20.0, 9.95) zip List(10, 2)
```

is

```
List((5.0, 10), (20.0, 2))
```

The zipAll method lets you specify defaults for the shorter list:

```
List(5.0, 20.0, 9.95).zipAll(List(10, 2), 0.0, 1)
```

is

```
List((5.0, 10), (20.0, 2), (9.95, 1))
```

The zipWithIndex method returns a list of pairs where the second component is the index of each element. For example,

```
"Scala".zipWithIndex
```

is

```
Vector(('S', 0), ('c', 1), ('a', 2), ('l', 3), ('a', 4))
```

This can be useful if you want to compute the index of an element with a certain property. For example,

```
"Scala".zipWithIndex.max
```

is ('l', 3). The index of the value with the largest encoding is

```
"Scala".zipWithIndex.max._2
```

13.11 Iterators

You can obtain an iterator from a collection with the iterator method. This isn't as common as in Java or C++ because you can usually get what you need more easily with one of the methods from the preceding sections.

However, iterators are useful for collections that are expensive to construct fully. For example, Source.fromFile yields an iterator because it might not be efficient to read an entire file into memory. There are a few Iterable methods that yield an iterator, such as grouped or sliding.

When you have an iterator, you can iterate over the elements with the next and hasNext methods.

```
while (iter.hasNext)
    do something with iter.next()
```

If you prefer, you can use a for loop instead:

```
for (elem <- iter)
    do something with elem
```

Both loops end up moving the iterator to the end of the collection, after which it is no longer usable.

Sometimes, you want to be able to look at the next element before deciding whether to consume it. In that case, use the buffered method to turn an Iterator into a BufferedIterator. The head method yields the next element without advancing the iterator.

```
val iter = scala.io.Source.fromFile(filename).buffered
while (iter.hasNext && iter.head.isWhitespace) iter.next
    // Now iter points to the first non-whitespace character
```

The Iterator class defines a number of methods that work identically to the methods on collections. In particular, all Iterable methods listed in Section 13.7, "Common Methods," on page 180 are available, except for head, headOption, last, lastOption, tail, init, takeRight, and dropRight. After calling a method such as map, filter, count, sum, or even length, the iterator is at the end of the collection, and you can't use it again. With other methods, such as find or take, the iterator is past the found element or the taken ones.

If you find it too tedious to work with an iterator, you can use a method such as toArray, toIterable, toSeq, toSet, or toMap to copy the values into a collection.

13.12 Streams A3

In the preceding sections, you saw that an iterator is a "lazy" alternative to a collection. You get the elements as you need them. If you don't need any more elements, you don't pay for the expense of computing the remaining ones.

However, iterators are fragile. Each call to next mutates the iterator. *Streams* offer an immutable alternative. A stream is an immutable list in which the tail is computed lazily—that is, only when you ask for it.

Here is a typical example:

```
def numsFrom(n: BigInt): Stream[BigInt] = n #:: numsFrom(n + 1)
```

The #:: operator is like the :: operator for lists, but it constructs a stream.

When you call

```
val tenOrMore = numsFrom(10)
```

you get a stream object that is displayed as

```
Stream(10, ?)
```

The tail is unevaluated. If you call

```
tenOrMore.tail.tail.tail
```

you get

```
Stream(13, ?)
```

Stream methods are executed lazily. For example,

```
val squares = numsFrom(1).map(x => x * x)
```

yields

```
Stream(1, ?)
```

You have to call squares.tail to force evaluation of the next entry.

If you want to get more than one answer, you can invoke take followed by force, which forces evaluation of all values. For example,

```
squares.take(5).force
```

produces Stream(1, 4, 9, 16, 25).

Of course, you don't want to call

```
squares.force // No!
```

That call would attempt to evaluate all members of an infinite stream, causing an OutOfMemoryError.

You can construct a stream from an iterator. For example, the Source.getLines method returns an Iterator[String]. With that iterator, you can only visit the lines once. A stream caches the visited lines so you can revisit them:

```
val words = Source.fromFile("/usr/share/dict/words").getLines.toStream
words // Stream(A, ?)
words(5) // Aachen
words // Stream(A, A's, AOL, AOL's, Aachen, ?)
```

> **NOTE:** Scala streams are quite different from streams in Java 8. However, lazy views, covered in the next section, are conceptually equivalent to Java 8 streams.

13.13 Lazy Views A3

In the preceding section, you saw that stream methods are computed lazily, delivering results only when they are needed. You can get a similar effect with other collections by applying the view method. This method yields a collection on which methods are applied lazily. For example,

```
val palindromicSquares = (1 to 1000000).view
  .map(x => x * x)
  .filter(x => x.toString == x.toString.reverse)
```

yields a collection that is unevaluated. (Unlike a stream, not even the first element is evaluated.) When you call

```
palindromicSquares.take(10).mkString(",")
```

then enough squares are generated until ten palindromes have been found, and then the computation stops. Unlike streams, views do not cache any values. If you call palindromicSquares.take(10).mkString(",") again, the computation starts over.

As with streams, use the force method to force evaluation of a lazy view. You get back a collection of the same type as the original.

CAUTION: The apply method forces evaluation of the entire view. Instead of calling `lazyView(i)`, call `lazyView.take(i).last`.

When you obtain a view into a slice of a mutable collection, any mutations affect the original collection. For example,

```
ArrayBuffer buffer = ...
buffer.view(10, 20).transform(x => 0)
```

clears the given slice and leaves the other elements unchanged.

13.14 Interoperability with Java Collections

At times you may need to use a Java collection, and you will likely miss the rich set of methods that you get with Scala collections. Conversely, you may want to build up a Scala collection and then pass it to Java code. The JavaConversions object provides a set of conversions between Scala and Java collections.

Give the target value an explicit type to trigger the conversion. For example,

```
import scala.collection.JavaConversions._
val props: scala.collection.mutable.Map[String, String] = System.getProperties()
```

If you are worried about unwanted implicit conversions, just import the ones you need, for example:

```
import scala.collection.JavaConversions.propertiesAsScalaMap
```

Table 13–4 shows the conversions from Scala to Java collections.

And Table 13–5 shows the opposite conversions from Java to Scala collections.

Note that the conversions yield wrappers that let you use the target interface to access the original type. For example, if you use

```
val props: scala.collection.mutable.Map[String, String] = System.getProperties()
```

then props is a wrapper whose methods call the methods of the underlying Java object. If you call

```
props("com.horstmann.scala") = "impatient"
```

then the wrapper calls `put("com.horstmann.scala", "impatient")` on the underlying Properties object.

Table 13–4 Conversions from Scala Collections to Java Collections

Implicit Function	From Type in scala.collection	To Type in java.util
asJavaCollection	Iterable	Collection
asJavaIterable	Iterable	Iterable
asJavaIterator	Iterator	Iterator
asJavaEnumeration	Iterator	Enumeration
seqAsJavaList	Seq	List
mutableSeqAsJavaList	mutable.Seq	List
bufferAsJavaList	mutable.Buffer	List
setAsJavaSet	Set	Set
mutableSetAsJavaSet	mutable.Set	Set
mapAsJavaMap	Map	Map
mutableMapAsJavaMap	mutable.Map	Map
asJavaDictionary	Map	Dictionary
asJavaConcurrentMap	mutable.ConcurrentMap	concurrent.ConcurrentMap

Table 13–5 Conversions from Java Collections to Scala Collections

Implicit Function	From Type in java.util	To Type in scala.collection
collectionAsScalaIterable	Collection	Iterable
iterableAsScalaIterable	Iterable	Iterable
asScalaIterator	Iterator	Iterator
enumerationAsScalaIterator	Enumeration	Iterator
asScalaBuffer	List	mutable.Buffer
asScalaSet	Set	mutable.Set
mapAsScalaMap	Map	mutable.Map
dictionaryAsScalaMap	Dictionary	mutable.Map
propertiesAsScalaMap	Properties	mutable.Map
asScalaConcurrentMap	concurrent.ConcurrentMap	mutable.ConcurrentMap

13.15 Parallel Collections

It is hard to write correct concurrent programs, yet concurrency is often required nowadays to keep all processors of a computer busy. Scala offers a particularly attractive solution for manipulating large collections. Such tasks often parallelize naturally. For example, to compute the sum of all elements, multiple threads can concurrently compute the sums of different sections; in the end, these partial results are summed up. Of course it is troublesome to schedule these concurrent activities—but with Scala, you don't have to. If `coll` is a large collection, then

```
coll.par.sum
```

computes the sum concurrently. The par method produces a *parallel implementation* of the collection. That implementation parallelizes the collection methods whenever possible. For example,

```
coll.par.count(_ % 2 == 0)
```

counts the even numbers in `coll` by evaluating the predicate on subcollections in parallel and combining the results.

You can parallelize a `for` loop by applying `.par` to the collection over which you iterate, like this:

```
for (i <- (0 until 100000).par) print(s" $i")
```

Try it out—the numbers are printed in the order they are produced by the threads working on the task.

In a `for/yield` loop, the results are assembled in order. Try this:

```
(for (i <- (0 until 100000).par) yield i) == (0 until 100000)
```

 CAUTION: If parallel computations mutate shared variables, the result is unpredictable. For example, do not update a shared counter:

```
var count = 0
for (c <- coll.par) { if (c % 2 == 0) count += 1 } // Error!
```

The parallel collections returned by the par method belong to types that extend the `ParSeq`, `ParSet`, or `ParMap` traits. These are *not* subtypes of `Seq`, `Set`, or `Map`, and you cannot pass a parallel collection to a method that expects a sequential collection.

You can convert a parallel collection back to a sequential one with the seq method.

```
val result = coll.par.filter(p).seq
```

Not all methods can be parallelized. For example, `reduceLeft` and `reduceRight` require that each operator is applied in sequence. There is an alternate method, `reduce`, that operates on parts of the collection and combines the results. For this to work, the operator must be *associative*—it must fulfill $(a\ \text{op}\ b)\ \text{op}\ c = a\ \text{op}\ (b\ \text{op}\ c)$. For example, addition is associative but subtraction is not: $(a - b) - c \ne a - (b - c)$.

Similarly, there is a fold method that operates on parts of the collection. Unfortunately, it is not as flexible as foldLeft or foldRight—both arguments of the operator must be elements. That is, you can do coll.par.fold(0)(_ + _), but you cannot do a more complex fold such as the one at the end of Section 13.9, "Reducing, Folding, and Scanning," on page 184.

To solve this problem, there is an even more general aggregate that applies an operator to parts of the collection, and then uses another operator to combine the results. For example, str.par.aggregate(Set[Char]())(_ + _, _ ++ _) is the equivalent of str.foldLeft(Set[Char]())(_ + _), forming a set of all distinct characters in str.

 NOTE: By default, parallel collections use a global fork-join pool, which is well suited for processor-intensive calculations. If you carry out parallel computation steps that block, you should choose a different "execution context"—see Chapter 17.

Exercises

1. Write a function that, given a string, produces a map of the indexes of all characters. For example, indexes("Mississippi") should return a map associating 'M' with the set {0}, 'i' with the set {1, 4, 7, 10}, and so on. Use a mutable map of characters to mutable sets. How can you ensure that the set is sorted?

2. Repeat the preceding exercise, using an immutable map of characters to lists.

3. Write a function that removes every second element from a ListBuffer. Try it two ways. Call remove(i) for all even i starting at the end of the list. Copy every second element to a new list. Compare the performance.

4. Write a function that receives a collection of strings and a map from strings to integers. Return a collection of integers that are values of the map corresponding to one of the strings in the collection. For example, given Array("Tom", "Fred", "Harry") and Map("Tom" -> 3, "Dick" -> 4, "Harry" -> 5), return Array(3, 5). Hint: Use flatMap to combine the Option values returned by get.

5. Implement a function that works just like mkString, using reduceLeft.

6. Given a list of integers lst, what is (lst :\ List[Int]())(_ :: _)? (List[Int]() /: lst)(_ :+ _)? How can you modify one of them to reverse the list?

7. In Section 13.10, "Zipping," on page 187, the expression (prices zip quantities) map { p => p._1 * p._2 } is a bit inelegant. We can't do (prices zip quantities) map { _ * _ } because _ * _ is a function with two arguments, and we need a function with one argument that is a tuple. The tupled method of the Function

object changes a function with two arguments to one that takes a tuple. Apply `tupled` to the multiplication function so you can map it over the list of pairs.

8. Write a function that turns an array of `Double` values into a two-dimensional array. Pass the number of columns as a parameter. For example, with `Array(1, 2, 3, 4, 5, 6)` and three columns, return `Array(Array(1, 2, 3), Array(4, 5, 6))`. Use the `grouped` method.

9. The Scala compiler transforms a `for/yield` expression

   ```
   for (i <- 1 to 10; j <- 1 to i) yield i * j
   ```

   to invocations of `flatMap` and `map`, like this:

   ```
   (1 to 10).flatMap(i => (1 to i).map(j => i * j))
   ```

   Explain the use of `flatMap`. Hint: What is `(1 to i).map(j => i * j)` when i is 1, 2, 3?

   What happens when there are three generators in the `for/yield` expression?

10. The method `java.util.TimeZone.getAvailableIDs` yields time zones such as `Africa/Cairo` and `Asia/Chungking`. Which continent has the most time zones? Hint: `groupBy`.

11. Harry Hacker reads a file into a string and wants to use a parallel collection to update the letter frequencies concurrently on portions of the string. He uses the following code:

    ```
    val frequencies = new scala.collection.mutable.HashMap[Char, Int]
    for (c <- str.par) frequencies(c) = frequencies.getOrElse(c, 0) + 1
    ```

    Why is this a terrible idea? How can he really parallelize the computation? (Hint: Use `aggregate`.)

Pattern Matching and Case Classes

Chapter 14

Pattern matching is a powerful mechanism that has a number of applications: switch statements, type inquiry, and "destructuring" (getting at the parts of complex expressions). Case classes are optimized to work with pattern matching.

The key points of this chapter are:

- The match expression is a better switch, without fall-through.
- If no pattern matches, a MatchError is thrown. Use the case _ pattern to avoid that.
- A pattern can include an arbitrary condition, called a guard.
- You can match on the type of an expression; prefer this over isInstanceOf/asInstanceOf.
- You can match patterns of arrays, tuples, and case classes, and bind parts of the pattern to variables.
- In a for expression, nonmatches are silently skipped.
- A case class is a class for which the compiler automatically produces the methods that are needed for pattern matching.
- The common superclass in a case class hierarchy should be sealed.
- Use the Option type for values that may or may not be present—it is safer than using null.

14.1 A Better Switch

Here is the equivalent of the C-style `switch` statement in Scala:

```
var sign = ...
val ch: Char = ...

ch match {
  case '+' => sign = 1
  case '-' => sign = -1
  case _ => sign = 0
}
```

The equivalent of `default` is the catch-all `case _` pattern. It is a good idea to have such a catch-all pattern. If no pattern matches, a `MatchError` is thrown.

Unlike the `switch` statement, Scala pattern matching does not suffer from the "fall-through" problem. (In C and its derivatives, you must use explicit `break` statements to exit a `switch` at the end of each branch, or you will fall through to the next branch. This is annoying and error-prone.)

 NOTE: In his entertaining book *Deep C Secrets*, Peter van der Linden reports a study of a large body of C code in which the fall-through behavior was unwanted in 97% of the cases.

Similar to `if`, `match` is an expression, not a statement. The preceding code can be simplified to

```
sign = ch match {
  case '+' => 1
  case '-' => -1
  case _  => 0
}
```

Use | to separate multiple alternatives:

```
prefix match {
  case "0" | "0x" | "0X"  => ...
  ...
}
```

You can use the `match` statement with any types. For example:

```
color match {
  case Color.RED => ...
  case Color.BLACK => ...
  ...
}
```

14.2 Guards

Suppose we want to extend our example to match all digits. In a C-style `switch` statement, you would simply add multiple case labels, for example case `'0':` case `'1':` ... case `'9':`. (Except that, of course, you can't use ... but must write out all ten cases explicitly.) In Scala, you add a *guard clause* to a pattern, like this:

```
ch match {
  case _ if Character.isDigit(ch) => digit = Character.digit(ch, 10)
  case '+' => sign = 1
  case '-' => sign = -1
  case _ => sign = 0
}
```

The guard clause can be any Boolean condition.

Patterns are always matched top-to-bottom. If the pattern with the guard clause doesn't match, the case `'+'` pattern is attempted next.

14.3 Variables in Patterns

If the case keyword is followed by a variable name, then the match expression is assigned to that variable. For example:

```
str(i) match {
  case '+' => sign = 1
  case '-' => sign = -1
  case ch => digit = Character.digit(ch, 10)
}
```

You can think of case _ as a special case of this feature, where the variable name is _.

You can use the variable name in a guard:

```
str(i) match {
  case ch if Character.isDigit(ch) => digit = Character.digit(ch, 10)
  ...
}
```

CAUTION: Unfortunately, variable patterns can conflict with constants, for example:

```
import scala.math._
0.5 * c / r match {
  case Pi => ... // If 0.5 * c / r equals Pi ...
  case x => ... // Otherwise set x to 0.5 * c / r ...
}
```

How does Scala know that `Pi` is a constant, not a variable? The rule is that a variable must start with a *lowercase* letter.

If you have an expression that starts with a lowercase letter, enclose it in backquotes:

```
import java.io.File._ // Imports java.io.File.pathSeparator
str match {
  case `pathSeparator` => ... // If str == pathSeparator ...
  case pathSeparator => ...
    // Caution—declares a new variable pathSeparator
}
```

14.4 Type Patterns

You can match on the type of an expression, for example:

```
obj match {
  case x: Int => x
  case s: String => Integer.parseInt(s)
  case _: BigInt => Int.MaxValue
  case _ => 0
}
```

In Scala, this form is preferred to using the `isInstanceOf` operator.

Note the variable names in the patterns. In the first pattern, the match is bound to *x as an* Int, and in the second pattern, it is bound to *s as a* String. No asInstanceOf casts are needed!

CAUTION: When you match against a type, you must supply a variable name. Otherwise, you match the *object*:

```
obj match {
  case _: BigInt => Int.MaxValue // Matches any object of type BigInt
  case BigInt => -1 // Matches the BigInt object of type Class
}
```

CAUTION: Matches occur at runtime, and generic types are erased in the Java virtual machine. For that reason, you cannot make a type match for a specific Map type.

```
case m: Map[String, Int] => ... // Don't
```

You can match a generic map:

```
case m: Map[_, _] => ... // OK
```

However, arrays are not erased. You can match an Array[Int].

14.5 Matching Arrays, Lists, and Tuples

To match an array against its contents, use Array expressions in the patterns, like this:

```
arr match {
  case Array(0) => "0"
  case Array(x, y) => s"$x $y"
  case Array(0, _*) => "0 ..."
  case _ => "something else"
}
```

The first pattern matches the array containing 0. The second pattern matches any array with two elements, and it binds the variables x and y to the elements. The third pattern matches any array starting with zero.

If you want to bind a variable argument match _* to a variable, use the @ notation like this:

```
case Array(x, rest @ _*) => rest.min
```

You can match lists in the same way, with List expressions. Alternatively, you can use the :: operator:

```
1st match {
  case 0 :: Nil => "0"
  case x :: y :: Nil => s"$x $y"
  case 0 :: tail => "0 ..."
  case _ => "something else"
}
```

With tuples, use the tuple notation in the pattern:

```
pair match {
  case (0, _) => "0 ..."
  case (y, 0) => s"$y 0"
  case _ => "neither is 0"
}
```

Again, note how the variables are bound to parts of the list or tuple. Since these bindings give you easy access to parts of a complex structure, this operation is called *destructuring*.

 CAUTION: The same warning applies as in Section 14.3, "Variables in Patterns," on page 199. The variable names that you use in the pattern must start with a *lowercase* letter. In a match against case Array(X, Y), X and Y are deemed constants, not variables.

 NOTE: If a pattern has alternatives, you cannot use variables other than an underscore. For example,

```
pair match {
    case (_, 0) | (0, _) => ... // OK, matches if one component is zero
    case (x, 0) | (0, x) => ... // Error—cannot bind with alternatives
}
```

14.6 Extractors

In the preceding section, you have seen how patterns can match arrays, lists, and tuples. These capabilities are provided by *extractors*—objects with an unapply or unapplySeq method that extract values from an object. The implementation of these methods is covered in Chapter 11. The unapply method is provided to extract a fixed number of objects, while unapplySeq extracts a sequence whose length can vary.

For example, consider the expression

```
arr match {
  case Array(x, 0) => x
  case Array(x, rest @ _*) => rest.min
  ...
}
```

The Array companion object is an extractor—it defines an unapplySeq method. That method is called *with the expression that is being matched*, not with what appear to be the parameters in the pattern. The call Array.unapplySeq(arr), when successful, results in a sequence of values, namely the two values in the array. In the first case, the match succeeds if the array has length 2 and the second element is zero. In that case, the initial array element is assigned to x.

Regular expressions provide another good use of extractors. When a regular expression has groups, you can match each group with an extractor pattern. For example:

```
val pattern = "([0-9]+) ([a-z]+)".r
"99 bottles" match {
  case pattern(num, item) => ...
    // Sets num to "99", item to "bottles"
}
```

The call `pattern.unapplySeq("99 bottles")` yields a sequence of strings that match the groups. These are assigned to the variables `num` and `item`.

Note that here the extractor isn't a companion object but a regular expression object.

14.7 Patterns in Variable Declarations

In the preceding sections, you have seen how patterns can contain variables. You can use these patterns inside variable declarations. For example,

```
val (x, y) = (1, 2)
```

simultaneously defines x as 1 and y as 2. That is useful for functions that return a pair, for example:

```
val (q, r) = BigInt(10) /% 3
```

The /% method returns a pair containing the quotient and the remainder, which are captured in the variables q and r.

The same syntax works for any patterns with variable names. For example,

```
val Array(first, second, rest @ _*) = arr
```

assigns the first and second element of the array arr to the variables first and second and rest to a Seq of the remaining elements.

 CAUTION: The same warning applies as in Section 14.3, "Variables in Patterns," on page 199. The variable names that you use in the pattern must start with a *lowercase* letter. In a declaration val Array(E, x) = arr, E is deemed a constant and x a variable that becomes arr(1) if arr has length 2 and arr(0) == E.

NOTE: The expression

$$\text{val } p(x_1, \ldots, x_n) = e$$

is, by definition, exactly the same as

```
val $result = e match { case p(x1, ..., xn) => (x1, ..., xn) }
val x1 = $result._1
...
val xn = $result._n
```

where $x_1, \ldots, x_n$ are the free variables in the pattern p.

This definition holds even when there are no free variables in the pattern. For example,

```
val 2 = x
```

is perfectly legal Scala code, provided x has been defined elsewhere. When you apply the definition, you get

```
val $result = x match { case 2 => () }
```

followed by no assignments. In other words, it is equivalent to

```
if (!(2 == x)) throw new MatchError
```

14.8 Patterns in for Expressions

You can use patterns with variables in for expressions. For each traversed value, the variables are bound. This makes it possible to traverse a map:

```
import scala.collection.JavaConversions.propertiesAsScalaMap
// Converts Java Properties to a Scala map—just to get an interesting example
for ((k, v) <- System.getProperties())
  println(s"$k -> $v")
```

For each (*key*, *value*) pair in the map, k is bound to the key and v to the value.

In a for expression, match failures are silently ignored. For example, the following loop prints all keys with empty value, skipping over all others:

```
for ((k, "") <- System.getProperties())
  println(k)
```

You can also use a guard. Note that the if goes after the <- symbol:

```
for ((k, v) <- System.getProperties() if v == "")
  println(k)
```

14.9 Case Classes

Case classes are a special kind of classes that are optimized for use in pattern matching. In this example, we have two case classes that extend a regular (noncase) class:

```
abstract class Amount
case class Dollar(value: Double) extends Amount
case class Currency(value: Double, unit: String) extends Amount
```

You can also have case objects for singletons:

```
case object Nothing extends Amount
```

When we have an object of type Amount, we can use pattern matching to match the amount type and bind the property values to variables:

```
amt match {
  case Dollar(v) => s"$$$v"
  case Currency(_, u) => s"Oh noes, I got $u"
  case Nothing => ""
}
```

 NOTE: Use () with case class instances, no parentheses with case objects.

When you declare a case class, several things happen automatically.

- Each of the constructor parameters becomes a val unless it is explicitly declared as a var (which is not recommended).

- An apply method is provided for the companion object that lets you construct objects without new, such as Dollar(29.95) or Currency(29.95, "EUR").

- An unapply method is provided that makes pattern matching work—see Chapter 11 for the details. (You don't really need to know these details to use case classes for pattern matching.)

- Methods toString, equals, hashCode, and copy are generated unless they are explicitly provided.

Otherwise, case classes are just like any other classes. You can add methods and fields to them, extend them, and so on.

14.10 The copy Method and Named Parameters

The copy method of a case class makes a new object with the same values as an existing one. For example,

```
val amt = Currency(29.95, "EUR")
val price = amt.copy()
```

By itself, that isn't very useful—after all, a Currency object is immutable, and one can just share the object reference. However, you can use named parameters to modify some of the properties:

```
val price = amt.copy(value = 19.95) // Currency(19.95, "EUR")
```

or

```
val price = amt.copy(unit = "CHF") // Currency(29.95, "CHF")
```

14.11 Infix Notation in case Clauses

When an unapply method yields a pair, you can use infix notation in the case clause. In particular, you can use infix notation with a case class that has two parameters. For example:

```
amt match { case a Currency u => ... } // Same as case Currency(a, u)
```

Of course, that is a silly example. The feature is meant for matching sequences. For example, every List object is either Nil or an object of the case class ::, defined as

```
case class ::[E](head: E, tail: List[E]) extends List[E]
```

Therefore, you can write

```
lst match { case h :: t => ... }
  // Same as case ::(h, t), which calls ::.unapply(lst)
```

In Chapter 20, you will encounter the ~ case class for combining pairs of parse results. It is also intended for use as an infix expression in case clauses:

```
result match { case p ~ q => ... } // Same as case ~(p, q)
```

These infix expressions are easier to read when you have more than one. For example,

```
result match { case p ~ q ~ r => ... }
```

is nicer than ~(~(p, q), r).

If the operator ends in a colon, it associates right-to-left. For example,

```
case first :: second :: rest
```

means

```
case ::(first, ::(second, rest))
```

NOTE: Infix notation works with any unapply method that returns a pair. Here is an example:

```
case object +: {
  def unapply[T](input: List[T]) =
    if (input.isEmpty) None else Some((input.head, input.tail))
}
```

Now you can destructure lists using +:.

```
1 +: 7 +: 2 +: 9 +: Nil match {
  case first +: second +: rest => first + second + rest.length
}
```

14.12 Matching Nested Structures

Case classes are often used for nested structures. Consider, for example, items that a store sells. Sometimes, we bundle items together for a discount.

```
abstract class Item
case class Article(description: String, price: Double) extends Item
case class Bundle(description: String, discount: Double, items: Item*) extends Item
```

Not having to use new makes it easy to specify nested objects:

```
Bundle("Father's day special", 20.0,
  Article("Scala for the Impatient", 39.95),
  Bundle("Anchor Distillery Sampler", 10.0,
    Article("Old Potrero Straight Rye Whiskey", 79.95),
    Article("Junípero Gin", 32.95)))
```

Patterns can match specific nestings, for example

```
case Bundle(_, _, Article(descr, _), _*) => ...
```

binds descr to the description of the first article in a bundle.

You can bind a nested value to a variable with the @ notation:

```
case Bundle(_, _, art @ Article(_, _), rest @ _*) => ...
```

Now art is the first article in a bundle and rest is the sequence of the other items.

Note that the _* is required in this example. The pattern

```
case Bundle(_, _, art @ Article(_, _), rest) => ...
```

would match a bundle with an article and exactly one additional item, bound to rest.

As an application, here is a function that computes the price of an item:

```
def price(it: Item): Double = it match {
  case Article(_, p) => p
  case Bundle(_, disc, its @ _*) => its.map(price _).sum - disc
}
```

14.13 Are Case Classes Evil?

The example in the preceding section can enrage OO purists. Shouldn't price be a method of the superclass? Shouldn't each subclass override it? Isn't polymorphism better than making a switch on each type?

In many situations, this is true. If someone comes up with another kind of Item, you'll need to revisit all those match clauses. In such a situation, case classes are not the right solution.

Case classes work well for structures whose makeup doesn't change. For example, the Scala List is implemented with case classes. Simplifying things a bit, a list is essentially

```
abstract class List
case object Nil extends List
case class ::(head: Any, tail: List) extends List
```

A list is either empty, or it has a head and a tail (which may be empty or not). Nobody is ever going to add a third case. (You'll see in the next section how to stop anyone from trying.)

When they are appropriate, case classes are quite convenient, for the following reasons:

- Pattern matching often leads to more concise code than inheritance.
- It is easier to read compound objects that are constructed without new.
- You get toString, equals, hashCode, and copy for free.

Those automatically generated methods do what you think they do—print, compare, hash, and copy each field. See Section 14.10, "The copy Method and Named Parameters," on page 205 for more information about the copy method.

For certain kinds of classes, case classes give you exactly the right semantics. Some people call them *value classes*. For example, consider the Currency class:

```
case class Currency(value: Double, unit: String)
```

A Currency(10, "EUR") is the same as any other Currency(10, "EUR"), and that's how equals and hashCode are implemented. Typically, such classes are immutable.

Case classes with variable fields are somewhat suspect, at least with respect to the hash code. With mutable classes, one should always derive the hash code from fields that are never mutated, such as an ID.

CAUTION: The toString, equals, hashCode, and copy methods are *not* generated for case classes that extend other case classes. You get a compiler warning if one case class inherits from another. A future version of Scala may outlaw such inheritance altogether. If you need multiple levels of inheritance to factor out common behavior of case classes, make only the leaves of the inheritance tree into case classes.

14.14 Sealed Classes

When you use pattern matching with case classes, you would like the compiler to check that you exhausted all alternatives. To achieve this, declare the common superclass as *sealed*:

```
sealed abstract class Amount
case class Dollar(value: Double) extends Amount
case class Currency(value: Double, unit: String) extends Amount
```

All subclasses of a sealed class must be defined in the same file as the class itself. For example, if someone wants to add another class for euros,

```
case class Euro(value: Double) extends Amount
```

they must do so in the file in which Amount is declared.

When a class is sealed, all of its subclasses are known at compile time, enabling the compiler to check pattern clauses for completeness. It is a good idea for all case classes to extend a sealed class or trait.

14.15 Simulating Enumerations

Case classes let you simulate enumerated types in Scala.

```
sealed abstract class TrafficLightColor
case object Red extends TrafficLightColor
case object Yellow extends TrafficLightColor
case object Green extends TrafficLightColor

color match {
  case Red => "stop"
  case Yellow => "hurry up"
  case Green => "go"
}
```

Note that the superclass was declared as sealed, enabling the compiler to check that the match clause is complete.

If you find this a bit heavyweight, you may prefer the Enumeration helper class that was described in Chapter 6.

14.16 The Option Type

The Option type in the standard library uses case classes to express values that might or might not be present. The case subclass Some wraps a value, for example Some("Fred"). The case object None indicates that there is no value.

This is less ambiguous than using an empty string and safer than using null for a missing value.

Option is a generic type. For example, Some("Fred") is an Option[String].

The get method of the Map class returns an Option. If there is no value for a given key, get returns None. Otherwise, it wraps the value inside Some.

You can use pattern matching to analyze such a value.

```
val alicesScore = scores.get("Alice")
alicesScore match {
  case Some(score) => println(score)
  case None => println("No score")
}
```

But frankly, that is tedious. Alternatively, you can use the isEmpty and get:

```
if (alicesScore.isEmpty) println("No score")
else println(alicesScore.get)
```

That's tedious too. It is better to use the getOrElse method:

```
println(alicesScore.getOrElse("No score"))
```

If alicesScore is None, then getOrElse returns "No score".

A more powerful way of working with options is to consider them as collections that have zero or one element. You can visit the element with a for loop:

```
for (score <- alicesScore) println(score)
```

If alicesScore is None, nothing happens. If it is a Some, then the loop executes once, with score bound to the contents of the option.

You can also use methods such as map, filter, or foreach. For example,

```
val biggerScore = alicesScore.map(_ + 1) // Some(score + 1) or None
val acceptableScore = alicesScore.filter(_ > 5) // Some(score) if score > 5 or None
alicesScore.foreach(println _) // Prints the score if it exists
```

 TIP: When you create an Option from a value that may be null, you can simply use Option(value). The result is None if value is null and Some(value) otherwise.

14.17 Partial Functions

A set of case clauses enclosed in braces is a *partial function*—a function which may not be defined for all inputs. It is an instance of a class PartialFunction[A, B]. (A is the parameter type, B the return type.) That class has two methods: apply, which computes the function value from the matching pattern, and isDefinedAt, which returns true if the input matches at least one of the patterns.

For example,

```
val f: PartialFunction[Char, Int] = { case '+' => 1 ; case '-' => -1 }
f('-') // Calls f.apply('-'), returns -1
f.isDefinedAt('0') // false
f('0') // Throws MatchError
```

Some methods accept a PartialFunction as a parameter. For example, the collect method of the GenTraversable trait applies a partial function to all elements where it is defined, and returns a sequence of the results.

```
"-3+4".collect { case '+' => 1 ; case '-' => -1 } // Vector(-1, 1)
```

The partial function expression must be in a context where the compiler can infer the return type. This is the case when you assign it to a typed variable or pass it as an argument.

NOTE: An exhaustive set of case clauses defines a Function1, not just a PartialFunction, that you can pass whenever a function is expected.

```
"-3+4".map { case '+' => 1 ; case '-' => -1; case _ => 0 }
// Vector(-1, 0, 1, 0)
```

A Seq[A] is a PartialFunction[Int, A], and a Map[K, V] is a PartialFunction[K, V]. For example, you can pass a map to collect:

```
val names = Array("Alice", "Bob", "Carmen")
val scores = Map("Alice" -> 10, "Carmen" -> 7)
names.collect(scores) // Yields Array(10, 7)
```

The lift method turns a PartialFunction[T, R] into a regular function with return type Option[R].

```
val f: PartialFunction[Char, Int] = { case '+' => 1 ; case '-' => -1 }
val g = f.lift // A function with type Char => Option[Int]
```

Now g('-') is Some(-1) and g('*') is None.

In Chapter 9, you saw that the Regex.replaceSomeIn method requires a function String => Option[String] for the replacement. If you have a map (or some other PartialFunction), you can use lift to produce such a function:

```
val varPattern = """\{([0-9]+)\}""".r
val message = "At {1}, there was {2} on {0}"
val vars = Map("{0}" -> "planet 7", "{1}" -> "12:30 pm",
  "{2}" -> "a disturbance of the force.")
val result = varPattern.replaceSomeIn(message, m => vars.lift(m.matched))
```

Conversely, you can turn a function returning Option[R] into a partial function by calling Function.unlift.

 NOTE: The catch clause of the try statement is a partial function. You can even use a variable holding a function:

```
def tryCatch[T](b: => T, catcher: PartialFunction[Throwable, T]) =
  try { b } catch catcher
```

Then you can supply a custom catch clause like this:

```
val result = tryCatch(str.toInt,
  { case _: NumberFormatException => -1 })
```

Exercises

1. Your Java Development Kit distribution has the source code for much of the JDK in the src.zip file. Unzip and search for case labels (regular expression case [^:]+:). Then look for comments starting with // and containing [Ff]alls? thr to catch comments such as // Falls through or // just fall thru. Assuming the JDK programmers follow the Java code convention, which requires such a comment, what percentage of cases falls through?

2. Using pattern matching, write a function swap that receives a pair of integers and returns the pair with the components swapped.

3. Using pattern matching, write a function swap that swaps the first two elements of an array provided its length is at least two.

4. Add a case class Multiple that is a subclass of the Item class. For example, Multiple(10, Article("Blackwell Toaster", 29.95)) describes ten toasters. Of course, you should be able to handle any items, such as bundles or multiples, in the second argument. Extend the price function to handle this new case.

5. One can use lists to model trees that store values only in the leaves. For example, the list ((3 8) 2 (5)) describes the tree

However, some of the list elements are numbers and others are lists. In Scala, you cannot have heterogeneous lists, so you have to use a `List[Any]`. Write a `leafSum` function to compute the sum of all elements in the leaves, using pattern matching to differentiate between numbers and lists.

6. A better way of modeling such trees is with case classes. Let's start with binary trees.

    ```
    sealed abstract class BinaryTree
    case class Leaf(value: Int) extends BinaryTree
    case class Node(left: BinaryTree, right: BinaryTree) extends BinaryTree
    ```

    Write a function to compute the sum of all elements in the leaves.

7. Extend the tree in the preceding exercise so that each node can have an arbitrary number of children, and reimplement the `leafSum` function. The tree in Exercise 5 should be expressible as

    ```
    Node(Node(Leaf(3), Leaf(8)), Leaf(2), Node(Leaf(5)))
    ```

8. Extend the tree in the preceding exercise so that each nonleaf node stores an operator in addition to the child nodes. Then write a function `eval` that computes the value. For example, the tree

    ```
        +
       /|\
      * 2 -
     / \  |
    3   8 5
    ```

    has value $(3 \times 8) + 2 + (-5) = 21$.

    Pay attention to the unary minus.

9. Write a function that computes the sum of the non-None values in a `List[Option[Int]]`. Don't use a `match` statement.

10. Write a function that composes two functions of type `Double => Option[Double]`, yielding another function of the same type. The composition should yield `None` if either function does. For example,

    ```
    def f(x: Double) = if (x != 1) Some(1 / (x - 1)) else None
    def g(x: Double) = if (x >= 0) Some(sqrt(x)) else None
    val h = compose(g, f) // h(x) should be g(f(x))
    ```

    Then h(2) is Some(1), and h(1) and h(0) are None.

Annotations

Chapter 15

Annotations let you add information to program items. This information can be processed by the compiler or by external tools. In this chapter, you will learn how to interoperate with Java annotations and how to use the annotations that are specific to Scala.

The key points of this chapter are:

- You can annotate classes, methods, fields, local variables, parameters, expressions, type parameters, and types.

- With expressions and types, the annotation follows the annotated item.

- Annotations have the form @Annotation, @Annotation(value), or @Annotation(name1 = value1, ...).

- @volatile, @transient, @strictfp, and @native generate the equivalent Java modifiers.

- Use @throws to generate Java-compatible throws specifications.

- The @tailrec annotation lets you verify that a recursive function uses tail call optimization.

- The assert function takes advantage of the @elidable annotation. You can optionally remove assertions from your Scala programs.

- Use the @deprecated annotation to mark deprecated features.

15.1 What Are Annotations?

Annotations are tags that you insert into your source code so that some tools can process them. These tools can operate at the source level, or they can process the class files into which the compiler has placed your annotations.

Annotations are widely used in Java, for example by testing tools such as JUnit 4 and enterprise technologies such as Java EE.

The syntax is just like in Java. For example:

```
@Test(timeout = 100) def testSomeFeature() { ... }

@Entity class Credentials {
  @Id @BeanProperty var username : String = _
  @BeanProperty var password : String = _
}
```

You can use Java annotations with Scala classes. The annotations in the preceding examples are from JUnit and JPA, two Java frameworks that have no particular knowledge of Scala.

You can also use Scala annotations. These annotations are specific to Scala and are usually processed by the Scala compiler or a compiler plugin. (Implementing a compiler plugin is a nontrivial undertaking that is not covered in this book.)

Java annotations do not affect how the compiler translates source code into bytecode; they merely add data to the bytecode that can be harvested by external tools. In Scala, annotations can affect the compilation process. For example, the @BeanProperty annotation that you saw in Chapter 5 causes the generation of getter and setter methods.

15.2 What Can Be Annotated?

In Scala, you can annotate classes, methods, fields, local variables, and parameters, just like in Java.

```
@Entity class Credentials
@Test def testSomeFeature() {}
@BeanProperty var username = _
def doSomething(@NotNull message: String) {}
```

You can apply multiple annotations. The order doesn't matter.

```
@BeanProperty @Id var username = _
```

When annotating the primary constructor, place the annotation before the constructor, and add a pair of parentheses if the annotation has no arguments.

```
class Credentials @Inject() (var username: String, var password: String)
```

You can also annotate expressions. Add a colon followed by the annotation, for example:

```
(myMap.get(key): @unchecked) match { ... }
   // The expression myMap.get(key) is annotated
```

You can annotate type parameters:

```
class MyContainer[@specialized T]
```

Annotations on an actual type are placed *after* the type, like this:

```
def country: String @Localized
```

Here, the String type is annotated. The method returns a localized string.

15.3 Annotation Arguments

Java annotations can have named arguments, such as

```
@Test(timeout = 100, expected = classOf[IOException])
```

However, if the argument name is value, it can be omitted. For example:

```
@Named("creds") var credentials: Credentials = _
   // The value argument is "creds"
```

If the annotation has no arguments, the parentheses can be omitted:

```
@Entity class Credentials
```

Most annotation arguments have defaults. For example, the timeout argument of the JUnit @Test annotation has a default value of 0, indicating no timeout. The expected argument has as default a dummy class to signify that no exception is expected. If you use

```
@Test def testSomeFeature() { ... }
```

this annotation is equivalent to

```
@Test(timeout = 0, expected = classOf[org.junit.Test.None])
def testSomeFeature() { ... }
```

Arguments of Java annotations are restricted to the following types:

* Numeric literals
* Strings
* Class literals
* Java enumerations
* Other annotations
* Arrays of the above (but not arrays of arrays)

Arguments of Scala annotations can be of arbitrary types, but only a couple of the Scala annotations take advantage of this added flexibility. For instance, the @deprecatedName annotation has an argument of type Symbol.

15.4 Annotation Implementations

I don't expect that many readers of this book will feel the urge to implement their own Scala annotations. The main point of this section is to be able to decipher the implementation of the existing annotation classes.

An annotation must extend the Annotation trait. For example, the unchecked annotation is defined as follows:

```
class unchecked extends annotation.Annotation
```

A type annotation must extend the TypeAnnotation trait:

```
class Localized extends StaticAnnotation with TypeConstraint
```

 CAUTION: If you want to implement a new Java annotation, you need to write the annotation class in Java. You can, of course, use that annotation for your Scala classes.

Generally, an annotation describes the expression, variable, field, method, class, or type to which it is applied. For example, the annotation

```
def check(@NotNull password: String)
```

applies to the parameter variable password.

However, field definitions in Scala can give rise to multiple features in Java, all of which can potentially be annotated. For example, consider

```
class Credentials(@NotNull @BeanProperty var username: String)
```

Here, there are six items that can be annotation targets:

- The constructor parameter
- The private instance field
- The accessor method username
- The mutator method username_=
- The bean accessor getUsername
- The bean mutator setUsername

By default, constructor parameter annotations are only applied to the parameter itself, and field annotations are only applied to the field. The meta-annotations

@param, @field, @getter, @setter, @beanGetter, and @beanSetter cause an annotation to be attached elsewhere. For example, the @deprecated annotation is defined as:

```
@getter @setter @beanGetter @beanSetter
class deprecated(message: String = "", since: String = "")
  extends annotation.StaticAnnotation
```

You can also apply these annotations in an ad-hoc fashion:

```
@Entity class Credentials {
  @(Id @beanGetter) @BeanProperty var id = 0
  ...
}
```

In this situation, the @Id annotation is applied to the Java getId method, which is a JPA requirement for property access.

15.5 Annotations for Java Features

The Scala library provides annotations for interoperating with Java. They are presented in the following sections.

15.5.1 Java Modifiers

Scala uses annotations instead of modifier keywords for some of the less commonly used Java features.

The @volatile annotation marks a field as volatile:

```
@volatile var done = false // Becomes a volatile field in the JVM
```

A volatile field can be updated in multiple threads.

The @transient annotation marks a field as transient:

```
@transient var recentLookups = new HashMap[String, String]
  // Becomes a transient field in the JVM
```

A transient field is not serialized. This makes sense for cache data that need not be saved, or data that can easily be recomputed.

The @strictfp annotation is the analog of the Java strictfp modifier:

```
@strictfp def calculate(x: Double) = ...
```

This method does its floating-point calculations with IEEE double values, not using the 80 bit extended precision (which Intel processors use by default). The result is slower and less precise but more portable.

The @native annotation marks methods that are implemented in C or C++ code. It is the analog of the native modifier in Java.

```
@native def win32RegKeys(root: Int, path: String): Array[String]
```

15.5.2 Marker Interfaces

Scala uses annotations @cloneable and @remote instead of the Cloneable and java.rmi.Remote marker interfaces for cloneable and remote objects.

```
@cloneable class Employee
```

With serializable classes, you can use the @SerialVersionUID annotation to specify the serial version:

```
@SerialVersionUID(61570324701290704425L)
class Employee extends Person with Serializable
```

 NOTE: For more information about Java concepts such as volatile fields, cloning, or serialization, see C. Horstmann, *Core Java®, Tenth Edition* (Prentice Hall, 2016).

15.5.3 Checked Exceptions

Unlike Scala, the Java compiler tracks checked exceptions. If you call a Scala method from Java code, its signature should include the checked exceptions that can be thrown. Use the @throws annotation to generate the correct signature. For example,

```
class Book {
  @throws(classOf[IOException]) def read(filename: String) { ... }
  ...
}
```

The Java signature is

```
void read(String filename) throws IOException
```

Without the @throws annotation, the Java code would not be able to catch the exception.

```
try { // This is Java
  book.read("war-and-peace.txt");
} catch (IOException ex) {
  ...
}
```

The Java compiler needs to know that the read method can throw an IOException, or it will refuse to catch it.

15.5.4 Variable Arguments

The @varargs annotation lets you call a Scala variable-argument method from Java. By default, if you supply a method such as

```
def process(args: String*)
```

the Scala compiler translates the variable argument into a sequence

```
def process(args: Seq[String])
```

That is cumbersome to use in Java. If you add @varargs,

```
@varargs def process(args: String*)
```

then a Java method

```
void process(String... args) // Java bridge method
```

is generated that wraps the args array into a Seq and calls the Scala method.

15.5.5 JavaBeans

You have seen the @BeanProperty annotation in Chapter 5. When you annotate a field with @scala.reflect.BeanProperty, the compiler generates JavaBeans-style getter and setter methods. For example,

```
class Person {
  @BeanProperty var name : String = _
}
```

generates methods

```
getName() : String
setName(newValue : String) : Unit
```

in addition to the Scala getter and setter.

The @BooleanBeanProperty annotation generates a getter with an is prefix for a Boolean method.

 NOTE: The annotations @BeanDescription, @BeanDisplayName, @BeanInfo, @BeanInfoSkip let you control some of the more obscure features of the JavaBeans specifications. Very few programmers need to worry about these. If you are among them, you'll figure out what to do from the Scaladoc descriptions.

15.6 Annotations for Optimizations

Several annotations in the Scala library let you control compiler optimizations. They are discussed in the following sections.

15.6.1 Tail Recursion

A recursive call can sometimes be turned into a loop, which conserves stack space. This is important in functional programming where it is common to write recursive methods for traversing collections.

Consider this method that computes the sum of a sequence of integers using recursion:

```
object Util {
  def sum(xs: Seq[Int]): BigInt =
    if (xs.isEmpty) 0 else xs.head + sum(xs.tail)
  ...
}
```

This method cannot be optimized because the last step of the computation is addition, not the recursive call. But a slight transformation can be optimized:

```
def sum2(xs: Seq[Int], partial: BigInt): BigInt =
  if (xs.isEmpty) partial else sum2(xs.tail, xs.head + partial)
```

The partial sum is passed as a parameter; call this method as sum2(xs, 0). Since the *last* step of the computation is a recursive call to the same method, it can be transformed into a loop to the top of the method. The Scala compiler automatically applies the "tail recursion" optimization to the second method. If you try

```
sum(1 to 1000000)
```

you will get a stack overflow error (at least with the default stack size of the JVM), but

```
sum2(1 to 1000000, 0)
```

returns the sum 500000500000.

Even though the Scala compiler will try to use tail recursion optimization, it is sometimes blocked from doing so for nonobvious reasons. If you rely on the compiler to remove the recursion, you should annotate your method with @tailrec. Then, if the compiler cannot apply the optimization, it will report an error.

For example, suppose the sum2 method is in a class instead of an object:

```
class Util {
  @tailrec def sum2(xs: Seq[Int], partial: BigInt): BigInt =
    if (xs.isEmpty) partial else sum2(xs.tail, xs.head + partial)
  ...
}
```

Now the program fails with an error message "could not optimize @tailrec annotated method sum2: it is neither private nor final so can be overridden". In this situation, you can move the method into an object, or you can declare it as private or final.

 NOTE: A more general mechanism for recursion elimination is "trampolining." A trampoline implementation runs a loop that keeps calling functions. Each function returns the next function to be called. Tail recursion is a special case where each function returns itself. The more general mechanism allows for mutual calls—see the example that follows.

Scala has a utility object called TailCalls that makes it easy to implement a trampoline. The mutually recursive functions have return type TailRec[A] and return either done(result) or tailcall(fun) where fun is the next function to be called. This needs to be a parameterless function that also returns a TailRec[A]. Here is a simple example:

```
import scala.util.control.TailCalls._
def evenLength(xs: Seq[Int]): TailRec[Boolean] =
  if (xs.isEmpty) done(true) else tailcall(oddLength(xs.tail))
def oddLength(xs: Seq[Int]): TailRec[Boolean] =
  if (xs.isEmpty) done(false) else tailcall(evenLength(xs.tail))
```

To obtain the final result from the TailRec object, use the result method:

```
evenLength(1 to 1000000).result
```

15.6.2 Jump Table Generation and Inlining

In C++ or Java, a switch statement can often be compiled into a jump table, which is more efficient than a sequence of if/else expressions. Scala attempts to generate jump tables for match clauses as well. The @switch annotation lets you check whether a Scala match clause is indeed compiled into one. Apply the annotation to the expression preceding a match clause:

```
(n: @switch) match {
  case 0 => "Zero"
  case 1 => "One"
  case _ => "?"
}
```

A common optimization is method inlining—replacing a method call with the method body. You can tag methods with @inline to suggest inlining, or @noinline to suggest not to inline. Generally, inlining is done in the JVM, whose "just in time" compiler does a good job without any annotations. The @inline and @noinline annotations let you direct the Scala compiler, in case you perceive the need to do so.

15.6.3 Eliding Methods

The @elidable annotation flags methods that can be removed in production code. For example,

```
@elidable(500) def dump(props: Map[String, String]) { ... }
```

If you compile with

```
scalac -Xelide-below 800 myprog.scala
```

then the method code will not be generated. The elidable object defines the following numerical constants:

- MAXIMUM or OFF = Int.MaxValue
- ASSERTION = 2000
- SEVERE = 1000
- WARNING = 900
- INFO = 800
- CONFIG = 700
- FINE = 500
- FINER = 400
- FINEST = 300
- MINIMUM or ALL = Int.MinValue

You can use one of these constants in the annotation:

```
import scala.annotation.elidable._
@elidable(FINE) def dump(props: Map[String, String]) { ... }
```

You can also use these names in the command line:

```
scalac -Xelide-below INFO myprog.scala
```

If you don't specify the -Xelide-below flag, annotated methods with values below 1000 are elided, leaving SEVERE methods and assertions, but removing warnings.

NOTE: The levels ALL and OFF are potentially confusing. The annotation @elide(ALL) means that the method is always elided, and @elide(OFF) means that it is never elided. But -Xelide-below OFF means to elide everything, and -Xelide-below ALL means to elide nothing. That's why MAXIMUM and MINIMUM have been added.

The Predef object defines an elidable assert method. For example,

```
def makeMap(keys: Seq[String], values: Seq[String]) = {
  assert(keys.length == values.length, "lengths don't match")
  ...
}
```

If the method is called with mismatched arguments, the assert method throws an AssertionError with message assertion failed: lengths don't match.

To disable assertions, compile with -Xelide-below 2001 or -Xelide-below MAXIMUM. Note that by default assertions are *not* disabled. This is a welcome improvement over Java assertions.

CAUTION: Calls to elided methods are replaced with Unit objects. If you use the return value of an elided method, a ClassCastException is thrown. It is best to use the @elidable annotation only with methods that don't return a value.

15.6.4 Specialization for Primitive Types

It is inefficient to wrap and unwrap primitive type values—but in generic code, this often happens. Consider, for example,

```
def allDifferent[T](x: T, y: T, z: T) = x != y && x != z && y != z
```

If you call allDifferent(3, 4, 5), each integer is wrapped into a java.lang.Integer before the method is called. Of course, one can manually supply an overloaded version

```
def allDifferent(x: Int, y: Int, z: Int) = ...
```

as well as seven more methods for the other primitive types.

You can generate these methods automatically by annotating the type parameter with @specialized:

```
def allDifferent[@specialized T](x: T, y: T, z: T) = ...
```

You can restrict specialization to a subset of types:

```
def allDifferent[@specialized(Long, Double) T](x: T, y: T, z: T) = ...
```

In the annotation constructor, you can provide any subset of Unit, Boolean, Byte, Short, Char, Int, Long, Float, Double.

15.7 Annotations for Errors and Warnings

If you mark a feature with the @deprecated annotation, the compiler generates a warning whenever the feature is used. The annotation has two optional arguments, message and since.

```
@deprecated(message = "Use factorial(n: BigInt) instead")
def factorial(n: Int): Int = ...
```

The @deprecatedName is applied to a parameter, and it specifies a former name for the parameter.

```
def draw(@deprecatedName('sz) size: Int, style: Int = NORMAL)
```

You can still call draw(sz = 12) but you will get a deprecation warning.

 NOTE: The constructor argument is a *symbol*—a name preceded by a single quote. Symbols with the same name are guaranteed to be unique. Therefore, comparing symbols is a bit more efficient than comparing strings. More importantly, there is a semantic distinction: A symbol denotes a name of some item in a program.

The @deprecatedInheritance and @deprecatedOverriding annotations generate warnings that inheriting from a class or overriding a method is now deprecated.

The @implicitNotFound and @implicitAmbiguous annotations generates meaningful error messages when an implicit value is not available or ambiguous. See Chapter 21 for details about implicits.

The @unchecked annotation suppresses a warning that a match is not exhaustive. For example, suppose we know that a given list is never empty:

```
(lst: @unchecked) match {
  case head :: tail => ...
}
```

The compiler won't complain that there is no Nil option. Of course, if lst is Nil, an exception is thrown at runtime.

The @uncheckedVariance annotation suppresses a variance error message. For example, it would make sense for java.util.Comparator to be contravariant. If Student is a subtype of Person, then a Comparator[Person] can be used when a Comparator[Student] is required. However, Java generics have no variance. We can fix this with the @uncheckedVariance annotation:

```
trait Comparator[-T] extends
    java.lang.Comparator[T @uncheckedVariance]
```

Exercises

1. Write four JUnit test cases that use the @Test annotation with and without each of its arguments. Run the tests with JUnit.

2. Make an example class that shows every possible position of an annotation. Use @deprecated as your sample annotation.

3. Which annotations from the Scala library use one of the meta-annotations @param, @field, @getter, @setter, @beanGetter, or @beanSetter?

4. Write a Scala method sum with variable integer arguments that returns the sum of its arguments. Call it from Java.

5. Write a Scala method that returns a string containing all lines of a file. Call it from Java.

6. Write a Scala object with a volatile Boolean field. Have one thread sleep for some time, then set the field to true, print a message, and exit. Another thread will keep checking whether the field is true. If so, it prints a message and exits. If not, it sleeps for a short time and tries again. What happens if the variable is not volatile?

7. Give an example to show that the tail recursion optimization is not valid when a method can be overridden.

8. Add the allDifferent method to an object, compile and look at the bytecode. What methods did the @specialized annotation generate?

9. The Range.foreach method is annotated as @specialized(Unit). Why? Look at the bytecode by running

    ```
    javap -classpath /path/to/scala/lib/scala-library.jar
        scala.collection.immutable.Range
    ```

    and consider the @specialized annotations on Function1. Click on the Function1.scala link in Scaladoc to see them.

10. Add assert(n >= 0) to a factorial method. Compile with assertions enabled and verify that factorial(-1) throws an exception. Compile without assertions. What happens? Use javap to check what happened to the assertion call.

XML Processing

Chapter 16

Scala has built-in support for XML literals that makes it easy to generate XML fragments in your programs. The Scala library includes support for common XML processing tasks. In this chapter, you will learn how to put these features to use for reading, analyzing, creating, and writing XML.

 NOTE: The XML support in Scala is brilliant because it makes it possible to slice and dice XML data easily and conveniently, in the REPL and in Scala programs. It is also flawed because of some unfortunate design decisions and lack of maintenance. It is difficult to remedy these issues because XML is so tightly integrated into Scala. A future version of Scala will likely abandon this tight integration and instead rely on string interpolation and third-party libraries. But for now, we can enjoy a uniquely powerful way of processing XML.

 NOTE: The API documentation for Scala XML is at www.scala-lang.org/api/current/scala-xml.

The key points of this chapter are:

- XML literals `<like>this</like>` are of type `NodeSeq`.
- You can embed Scala code inside XML literals.
- The `child` property of a `Node` yields the child nodes.

- The `attributes` property of a `Node` yields a `MetaData` object containing the node attributes.
- The \ and \\ operators carry out XPath-like matches.
- You can match node patterns with XML literals in case clauses.
- Use the `RuleTransformer` with `RewriteRule` instances to transform descendants of a node.
- The `XML` object interfaces with Java XML methods for loading and saving.
- The `ConstructingParser` is an alternate parser that preserves comments and `CDATA` sections.

16.1 XML Literals

In Scala, you can define XML *literals*, simply by using the XML code:

```
val doc = <html><head><title>Fred's Memoirs</title></head><body>...</body></html>
```

In this case, doc becomes a value of type `scala.xml.Elem`, representing an XML element.

An XML literal can also be a sequence of nodes. For example,

```
val items = <li>Fred</li><li>Wilma</li>
```

yields a `scala.xml.NodeSeq`. We will discuss the `Elem` and `NodeSeq` classes in the next section.

CAUTION: Sometimes, the compiler suspects XML literals when none are intended. For example,

```
val (x, y) = (1, 2)
x < y // OK
x <y // Error—unclosed XML literal
```

In this case, the remedy is to add a space after the <.

16.2 XML Nodes

The `Node` class is the ancestor of all XML node types. Its two most important subclasses are `Text` and `Elem`. Figure 16–1 shows the complete hierarchy.

The `Elem` class describes an XML element, such as

```
val elem = <a href="http://scala-lang.org">The <em>Scala</em> language</a>
```

The `label` property yields the tag name (here, "a"), and `child` is the child node sequence (two `Text` nodes and an `Elem` node in this example).

CAUTION: Unfortunately, unlike a DOM node, a Scala Node retains no information about its parent.

Node sequences are of type NodeSeq, a subtype of Seq[Node] that adds support for XPath-like operators (see Section 16.7, "XPath-like Expressions," on page 235). You can use any of the Seq operations described in Chapter 13 with XML node sequences. To traverse a sequence, simply use a for loop, for example:

```
for (n <- elem.child) process n
```

 NOTE: The Node class extends NodeSeq. A single node is a sequence of length 1. This is supposed to make it easier to deal with functions that can return a single node or a sequence. (It actually creates as many problems as it solves, so I don't recommend using this trick in your own designs.)

There are also node classes for XML comments (<!-- ... -->), entity references (&...;), and processing instructions (<? ... ?>). Figure 16–1 shows all node types.

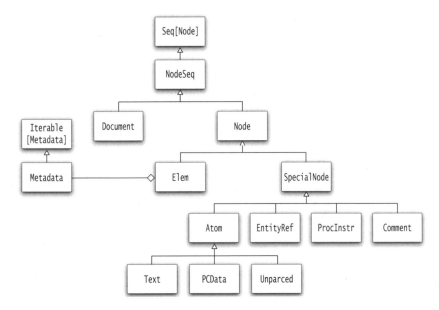

Figure 16–1   XML node types

If you build node sequences programmatically, you can use a NodeBuffer, a subclass of ArrayBuffer[Node].

```
val items = new NodeBuffer
items += <li>Fred</li>
items += <li>Wilma</li>
val nodes: NodeSeq = items
```

 CAUTION: A NodeBuffer is a Seq[Node]. It can be implicitly converted to a NodeSeq. Once this conversion has occurred, you need to be careful not to mutate the node buffer any longer since XML node sequences are supposed to be immutable.

16.3 Element Attributes

To process the attribute keys and values of an element, use the attributes property. It yields an object of type MetaData which is almost, but not quite, a Map from attribute keys to values. You can use the () operator to access the value for a given key:

```
val elem = <a href="http://scala-lang.org">The Scala language</a>
val url = elem.attributes("href")
```

Unfortunately, this yields a node sequence, not a string, because the attribute might contain entity references. For example, consider

```
val image = <img alt="San Jos&eacute; State University Logo"
  src="http://www.sjsu.edu/publicaffairs/pics/sjsu_logo_color_web.jpg"/>
val alt = image.attributes("alt")
```

Here, the value for the key "alt" is a node sequence consisting of a text node for "San Jos", an EntityRef for é, and another text node for " State University Logo".

Why not resolve the entity reference? There is no way to know what é means. In XHTML it means é (the code for é), but in another document type it can be defined as something else.

 TIP: If you find it inconvenient to deal with entity references in XML literals, you can use character references instead: <img alt="San José State University Logo" .../>.

If you are certain you don't have unresolved entities in your attributes, you can simply call the text method to turn the node sequence into a string:

```
val url = elem.attributes("href").text
```

If an attribute is not present, the () operator returns null. If you dislike working with null, use the get method, which returns an Option[Seq[Node]].

Unfortunately, the MetaData class has no getOrElse method, but you can apply getOrElse to the Option that get returns:

```
val url = elem.attributes.get("href").getOrElse(Text(""))
```

To iterate over all attributes, use

```
for (attr <- elem.attributes)
  process attr.key and attr.value.text
```

Alternatively, call the asAttrMap method:

```
val image = <img alt="TODO" src="hamster.jpg"/>
val map = image.attributes.asAttrMap // Map("alt" -> "TODO", "src" -> "hamster.jpg")
```

16.4 Embedded Expressions

You can include blocks of Scala code inside XML literals to dynamically compute items. For example:

```
<ul><li>{items(0)}</li><li>{items(1)}</li></ul>
```

Each block is evaluated, and its result is spliced into the XML tree.

If the block yields a node sequence, the nodes are simply added to the XML. Everything else is turned into an Atom[T], a container for a type T. In this way, you can store arbitrary values in an XML tree. Retrieve the value from an Atom node with the data property.

In many cases, one doesn't care about retrieving the items from the atoms. When the XML document gets saved, each atom is turned into a string, by calling toString on the data property.

 CAUTION: Embedded strings do not get turned into Text nodes but into Atom[String] nodes. That is not quite the same—Text is a subclass of Atom[String]. It doesn't matter when saving a document. But if you later do pattern matching on Text nodes, the match will fail. In that case, you should insert Text nodes instead of strings:

```
<li>{Text("Another item")}</li>
```

Not only can you nest Scala inside XML, but the nested Scala code can again contain XML literals. For example, if you have a list of items, you will want to place each item inside an li element:

```
<ul>{for (i <- items) yield <li>{i}</li>}</ul>
```

We have a Scala block <ul>{...}</ul> inside the ul element. That block yields a sequence of XML expressions.

```
for (i <- items) yield an XML literal
```

That XML literal <li>...</li> contains another Scala block!

```
<li>{i}</li>
```

It's Scala inside XML inside Scala inside XML. The mind reels if you think about it. But if you don't, it's a very natural construction: make a ul that contains an li for every element of items.

 NOTE: To place an opening or closing brace into an XML literal, use two braces:

```
<h1>The Natural Numbers {{1, 2, 3, ...}}</h1>
```

This produces

```
<h1>The Natural Numbers {1, 2, 3, ...}</h1>
```

16.5 Expressions in Attributes

You can compute attribute values with Scala expressions, for example:

```
<img src={makeURL(fileName)}/>
```

Here, the makeURL function returns a string that becomes the attribute value.

 CAUTION: Braces inside quoted strings are *not* evaluated. For example,

```
<img src="{makeURL(fileName)}"/>
```

sets the src attribute to the string "{makeURL(fileName)}", which is probably not what you want.

The embedded block can also yield a node sequence. This is potentially useful if you want to include entity references or atoms in an attribute:

```
<a id={new Atom(1)} ... />
```

If the embedded block returns null or None, the attribute is not set. For example:

```
<img alt={if (description == "TODO") null else description} ... />
```

If description is the string "TODO" or null, the element will have no alt attribute.

You can get the same effect with an Option[Seq[Node]]. For example,

```
<img alt={if (description == "TODO" || description == null) None
  else Some(Text(description))} ... />
```

CAUTION: It is a syntax error if the block yields something other than a `String`, a `Seq[Node]`, or an `Option[Seq[Node]]`. This is inconsistent with blocks inside elements, where the result would be wrapped in an `Atom`. If you want an atom in an attribute value, you must construct it yourself.

16.6 Uncommon Node Types

Sometimes, you need to include non-XML text into an XML document. A typical example is JavaScript code in an XHTML page. You can use `CDATA` markup in XML literals:

```
val js = <script><![CDATA[if (temp < 0) alert("Cold!")]]></script>
```

However, the parser does not retain the fact that the text was marked up with `CDATA`. What you get is a node with a `Text` child. If you want the `CDATA` in the output, include a `PCData` node, like this:

```
val code = """if (temp < 0) alert("Cold!")"""
val js = <script>{PCData(code)}</script>
```

You can include arbitrary text in an `Unparsed` node. It is saved as is. You can generate such nodes as literals or programmatically:

```
val n1 = <xml:unparsed><&></xml:unparsed>
val n2 = Unparsed("<&>")
```

I don't recommend this technique since you can easily end up with malformed XML.

Finally, you can group a node sequence into a single "group" node.

```
val g1 = <xml:group><li>Item 1</li><li>Item 2</li></xml:group>
val g2 = Group(Seq(<li>Item 1</li>, <li>Item 2</li>))
```

Group nodes are "ungrouped" when you iterate over them. Contrast:

```
val items = <li>Item 1</li><li>Item 2</li>
for (n <- <xml:group>{items}</xml:group>) yield n
  // Yields two li elements
for (n <- <ol>{items}</ol>) yield n
  // Yields one ol element
```

16.7 XPath-like Expressions

The `NodeSeq` class provides methods that resemble the / and // operators in XPath (XML Path Language, www.w3.org/TR/xpath). Since // denotes comments and is therefore not a valid operator, Scala uses \ and \\ instead.

The \ operator locates direct descendants of a node or node sequence. For example,

```
val list = <dl><dt>Java</dt><dd>Gosling</dd><dt>Scala</dt><dd>Odersky</dd></dl>
val languages = list \ "dt"
```

sets languages to a node sequence containing <dt>Java</dt> and <dt>Scala</dt>.

A wildcard matches any element. For example,

```
doc \ "body" \ "_" \ "li"
```

finds all li elements, whether they are contained in a ul, an ol, or any other element inside the body.

The \\ operator locates descendants at any depth. For example,

```
doc \\ "img"
```

locates all img elements anywhere inside the doc.

A string starting with @ locates attributes. For example,

```
img \ "@alt"
```

returns the value of the alt attribute of the given node, and

```
doc \\ "@alt"
```

locates all alt attributes of any elements inside doc.

 NOTE: There is no wildcard notation for attributes; img \ "@_" does *not* return all attributes.

 CAUTION: Unlike XPath, you cannot use a single \ to extract attributes from multiple nodes. For example, doc \\ "img" \ "@src" will not work if the document contains more than one img element. Use doc \\ "img" \\ "@src" instead.

The result of \ or \\ is a node sequence. It might be a single node, but unless you know that for sure, you should traverse the sequence. For example,

```
for (n <- doc \\ "img") process n
```

If you simply call text on a result of \ or \\, all texts of the result sequence will be concatenated. For example,

```
(<img src="hamster.jpg"/><img src="frog.jpg"/> \\ "@src).text
```

returns a string "hamster.jpgfrog.jpg".

16.8 Pattern Matching

You can use XML literals in pattern matching expressions. For example,

```
node match {
  case <img/> => ...
    ...
}
```

The first match succeeds if node is an img element with *any* attributes and *no* child elements.

To deal with child elements is a little tricky. You can match a single child with

```
case <li>{_}</li> => ...
```

However, if li has more than one child, for example `<li>An <em>important</em> item</li>`, then the match fails. To match any number of items, use

```
case <li>{_*}</li> => ...
```

Note the braces—they might remind you of the embedded code notation for XML literals. However, inside XML patterns, braces indicate code patterns, not code to be evaluated.

Instead of the wildcard indicators, you can use variable names. The match is bound to the variable.

```
case <li>{child}</li> => child.text
```

To match a text node, use a case class match like this:

```
case <li>{Text(item)}</li> => item
```

To bind a variable to a node sequence, use the following syntax:

```
case <li>{children @ _*}</li> => for (c <- children) yield c
```

 CAUTION: In such a match, children is a Seq[Node] and *not* a NodeSeq.

You can only use one node in the case clause. For example, the following is not legal:

```
case <p>{_*}</p><br/> => ... // Not legal
```

XML patterns can't have attributes.

```
case <img alt="TODO"/> => ... // Not legal
```

To match an attribute, use a guard:

```
case n @ <img/> if (n.attributes("alt").text == "TODO") => ...
```

16.9 Modifying Elements and Attributes

In Scala, XML nodes and node sequences are immutable. If you want to edit a node, you have to create a copy of it, making any needed changes and copying what hasn't changed.

To copy an Elem node, use the copy method. It has five named parameters: the familiar label, attributes, and child, as well as prefix and scope which are used for namespaces (see Section 16.12, "Namespaces," on page 242). Any parameters that you don't specify are copied from the original element. For example,

```
val list = <ul><li>Fred</li><li>Wilma</li></ul>
val list2 = list.copy(label = "ol")
```

makes a copy of list, changing the label from ul to ol. The children are shared, but that's OK since node sequences are immutable.

To add a child, make a call to copy like this:

```
list.copy(child = list.child ++ <li>Another item</li>)
```

To add or change an attribute, use the % operator:

```
val image = <img src="hamster.jpg"/>
val image2 = image % Attribute(null, "alt", "An image of a hamster", Null)
```

The first argument is the namespace. The last one is a list of additional metadata. Just like Node extends NodeSeq, the Attribute trait extends MetaData. To add more than one attribute, you can chain them like this:

```
val image3 = image % Attribute(null, "alt", "An image of a frog",
    Attribute(null, "src", "frog.jpg", Null))
```

 CAUTION: Here, scala.xml.Null is an empty attribute list. It is *not* the scala.Null type.

Adding an attribute with the same key replaces the existing one. The image3 element has a single attribute with key "src"; its value is "frog.jpg".

16.10 Transforming XML

Sometimes, you need to rewrite all descendants that match a particular condition. The XML library provides a `RuleTransformer` class that applies one or more `RewriteRule` instances to a node and its descendants.

For example, suppose you want to change all `ul` nodes in a document to `ol`. Define a `RewriteRule` that overrides the `transform` method:

```
val rule1 = new RewriteRule {
  override def transform(n: Node) = n match {
    case e @ <ul>{_*}</ul> => e.asInstanceOf[Elem].copy(label = "ol")
    case _ => n
  }
}
```

Then you can transform a tree with the command

```
val transformed = new RuleTransformer(rule1).transform(root)
```

You can supply any number of rules in the constructor of the `RuleTransformer`:

```
val transformer = new RuleTransformer(rule1, rule2, rule3);
```

The `transform` method traverses the descendants of a node, applies all rules, and returns the transformed tree.

16.11 Loading and Saving

To load an XML document from a file, call the `loadFile` method of the `XML` object:

```
import scala.xml.XML
val root = XML.loadFile("myfile.xml")
```

You can also load from a `java.io.InputStream`, a `java.io.Reader`, or a URL:

```
val root2 = XML.load(new FileInputStream("myfile.xml"))
val root3 = XML.load(new InputStreamReader(
  new FileInputStream("myfile.xml"), "UTF-8"))
val root4 = XML.load(new URL("http://horstmann.com/index.html"))
```

The document is loaded using the standard SAX parser from the Java library. Unfortunately, the Document Type Definition (DTD) is not made available.

CAUTION: This parser suffers from a problem that is inherited from the Java library. It does not read DTDs from a local catalog. In particular, fetching an XHTML file can take a very long time, or fail altogether, as the parser retrieves the DTDs from the www.w3.org site.

To use a local catalog, you need the CatalogResolver class that is available in the com.sun.org.apache.xml.internal.resolver.tools package of the JDK or, if you are squeamish about using a class outside the official API, in the Apache Commons Resolver project (http://xml.apache.org/commons/components/resolver/resolver-article.html).

Unfortunately, the XML object has no API for installing an entity resolver. Here is how you can do it through the back door:

```scala
val res = new CatalogResolver
val doc = new factory.XMLLoader[Elem] {
  override def adapter = new parsing.NoBindingFactoryAdapter() {
    override def resolveEntity(publicId: String, systemId: String) = {
      res.resolveEntity(publicId, systemId)
    }
  }
}.load(new URL("http://horstmann.com/index.html"))
```

There is another parser that preserves comments, CDATA sections, and, optionally, whitespace:

```scala
import scala.xml.parsing.ConstructingParser
import java.io.File
val parser = ConstructingParser.fromFile(new File("myfile.xml"), preserveWS = true)
val doc = parser.document
val root = doc.docElem
```

Note that the ConstructingParser returns a node of type Document. Call its docElem method to get the document root.

If your document has a DTD and you need it (for example, when saving the document), it is available as doc.dtd.

CAUTION: By default, the `ConstructingParser` does not resolve entities but converts them into useless comments, such as

```
<!-- unknown entity nbsp; -->
```

If you happen to be reading an XHTML file, you can use the `XhtmlParser` subclass:

```
val parser = new XhtmlParser(scala.io.Source.fromFile("myfile.html"))
val doc = parser.initialize.document
```

Otherwise, you need to add entities to the parser's entity map. For example,

```
parser.ent ++= List(
  "nbsp" -> ParsedEntityDecl("nbsp", IntDef("\u00A0")),
  "eacute" -> ParsedEntityDecl("eacute", IntDef("\u00E9")))
```

To save an XML document to a file, use the save method:

```
XML.save("myfile.xml", root)
```

This method takes three optional parameters:

- enc specifies the character encoding (default is "ISO-8859-1").
- xmlDecl specifies whether to emit an XML declaration (<?xml...?>) at the beginning of the output (default is false).
- doctype is an object of the case class scala.xml.dtd.DocType (default is null).

For example, to write an XHTML file, you might use

```
XML.save("myfile.xhtml", root,
  enc = "UTF-8",
  xmlDecl = true,
  doctype = DocType("html",
    PublicID("-//W3C//DTD XHTML 1.0 Strict//EN",
      "http://www.w3.org/TR/xhtml1/DTD/xhtml1-strict.dtd"),
    Nil))
```

The last parameter in the DocType constructor lets you specify internal DTD declarations—an obscure XML feature that I won't discuss here.

You can also save to a java.io.Writer, but then you must specify all parameters.

```
XML.write(writer, root, "UTF-8", false, null)
```

NOTE: When saving an XML file, elements without content are not written with self-closing tags. For example:

```
<img src="hamster.jpg"></img>
```

If you prefer

```
<img src="hamster.jpg"/>
```

use

```
val str = xml.Utility.toXML(node, minimizeTags = true)
```

TIP: If you want your XML code to line up prettily, use the `PrettyPrinter` class:

```
val printer = new PrettyPrinter(width = 100, step = 4)
val str = printer.formatNodes(nodeSeq)
```

16.12 Namespaces

In XML, namespaces are used to avoid name clashes, similar to packages in Java or Scala. However, an XML namespace is a URI (and usually a URL), such as

```
http://www.w3.org/1999/xhtml
```

The `xmlns` attribute declares a namespace, for example:

```
<html xmlns="http://www.w3.org/1999/xhtml">
  <head>...</head>
  <body>...</body>
</html>
```

The `html` element and its descendants (head, body, and so on) are placed in this namespace.

A descendant can introduce its own namespace, for example:

```
<svg xmlns="http://www.w3.org/2000/svg" width="100" height="100">
  <rect x="25" y="25" width="50" height="50" fill="#ff0000"/>
</svg>
```

In Scala, each element has a `scope` property of type `NamespaceBinding`. The `uri` property of that class yields the namespace URI.

If you want to mix elements from multiple namespaces, it is tedious to work with namespace URLs. An alternative is a *namespace prefix*. For example, the tag

```
<html xmlns="http://www.w3.org/1999/xhtml"
  xmlns:svg="http://www.w3.org/2000/svg">
```

introduces the prefix svg for the namespace http://www.w3.org/2000/svg. All elements prefixed with svg: belong to that namespace. For example,

```
<svg:svg width="100" height="100">
  <svg:rect x="25" y="25" width="50" height="50" fill="#ff0000"/>
</svg:svg>
```

As mentioned in Section 16.9, "Modifying Elements and Attributes," on page 238, each Elem object has prefix and scope values. The parser automatically computes these values. To find out the namespace of an element, look at the scope.uri value. If there are multiple namespaces, they are chained together through scope.parent links. This method retrieves them all:

```
def namespaces(node: Node) = {
  def namespaces(scope: NamespaceBinding): List[(String, String)] =
    if (scope == null) List()
    else namespaces(scope.parent) :+ ((scope.prefix, scope.uri))
  namespaces(node.scope)
}
```

To get the namespace of an attribute, use the prefixedKey method.

When you produce XML elements programmatically, you need to set prefixes and scopes. For example,

```
val scope = new NamespaceBinding("svg", "http://www.w3.org/2000/svg", TopScope)
val attrs = Attribute(null, "width", "100",
  Attribute(null, "height", "100", Null))
val elem = Elem(null, "body", Null, TopScope,
  Elem("svg", "svg", attrs, scope))
```

Exercises

1. What is <fred/>(0)? <fred/>(0)(0)? Why?

2. What is the result of

   ```
   <ul>
     <li>Opening bracket: [</li>
     <li>Closing bracket: ]</li>
     <li>Opening brace: {</li>
     <li>Closing brace: }</li>
   </ul>
   ```

   How do you fix it?

3. Contrast

   ```
   <li>Fred</li> match { case <li>{Text(t)}</li> => t }
   ```

and

```
<li>{"Fred"}</li> match { case <li>{Text(t)}</li> => t }
```

Why do they act differently?

4. Read an XHTML file and print all `img` elements that don't have an `alt` attribute.

5. Print the names of all images in an XHTML file. That is, print all `src` attribute values inside `img` elements.

6. Read an XHTML file and print a table of all hyperlinks in the file, together with their URLs. That is, print the child text and the `href` attribute of each a element.

7. Write a function that has a parameter of type `Map[String, String]` and returns a `dl` element with a `dt` for each key and `dd` for each value. For example,

```
Map("A" -> "1", "B" -> "2")
```

should yield `<dl><dt>A</dt><dd>1</dd><dt>B</dt><dd>2</dd></dl>`.

8. Write a function that takes a `dl` element and turns it into a `Map[String, String]`. This function should be the inverse of the function in the preceding exercise, provided all `dt` children are distinct.

9. Transform an XHTML document by adding an `alt="TODO"` attribute to all `img` elements without an `alt` attribute, preserving everything else.

10. Write a function that reads an XHTML document, carries out the transformation of the preceding exercise, and saves the result. Be sure to preserve the DTD and any `CDATA` sections.

Futures

Chapter 17

Writing concurrent applications that work correctly and with high performance is very challenging. The traditional approach, in which concurrent tasks have side effects that mutate shared data, is tedious and error-prone. Scala encourages you to think of a computation in a functional way. A computation yields a value, sometime in the future. As long as the computations don't have side effects, you can let them run concurrently and combine the results when they become available. In this chapter, you will see how to use the Future and Promise traits to organize such computations.

The key points of this chapter are:

- A block of code wrapped in a Future { ... } executes concurrently.

- A future succeeds with a result or fails with an exception.

- You can wait for a future to complete, but you don't usually want to.

- You can use callbacks to get notified when a future completes, but that gets tedious when chaining callbacks.

- Use methods such as map/flatMap, or the equivalent for expressions, to compose futures.

- A promise has a future whose value can be set (once), which gives added flexibility for implementing tasks that produce results.

- Pick an execution context that is suitable for the concurrent workload of your computation.

17.1 Running Tasks in the Future

The scala.concurrent.Future object can execute a block of code "in the future."

```
import java.time._
import scala.concurrent._
import ExecutionContext.Implicits.global

Future {
  Thread.sleep(10000)
  println(s"This is the future at ${LocalTime.now}")
}
println(s"This is the present at ${LocalTime.now}")
```

When running this code, a line similar to the following is printed:

```
This is the present at 13:01:19.400
```

About ten seconds later, a second line appears:

```
This is the future at 13:01:29.140
```

When you create a Future, its code is run on some thread. One could of course create a new thread for each task, but thread creation is not free. It is better to keep some pre-created threads around and use them to execute tasks as needed. A data structure that assigns tasks to threads is usually called a *thread pool*. In Java, the Executor interface describes such a data structure. Scala uses the ExecutionContext trait instead.

Each Future must be constructed with a reference to an ExecutionContext. The simplest way is to import

```
import ExecutionContext.Implicits.global
```

Then the tasks execute on a global thread pool. This is fine for demos, but in a real program, you should make another choice if your tasks block. See Section 17.9, "Execution Contexts," on page 260 for more information.

When you construct multiple futures, they can execute concurrently. For example, try running

```
Future { for (i <- 1 to 100) { print("A"); Thread.sleep(10) } }
Future { for (i <- 1 to 100) { print("B"); Thread.sleep(10) } }
```

You will get an output that looks somewhat like

```
ABABABABABABABABABABABABABABA...AABABBBBABABABABABABABABABBBBBBBBBBBBBBBBBB
```

A future can—and normally will—have a result:

```
val f = Future {
  Thread.sleep(10000)
  42
}
```

When you evaluate f in the REPL immediately after the definition, you will get this output:

```
res12: scala.concurrent.Future[Int] = Future(<not completed>)
```

Wait ten seconds and try again:

```
res13: scala.concurrent.Future[Int] = Future(Success(42))
```

Alternatively, something bad may happen in the future:

```
val f2 = Future {
  if (LocalTime.now.getHour > 12)
    throw new Exception("too late")
  42
}
```

If it is after noon, the task terminates with an exception. In the REPL, you will see

```
res14: scala.concurrent.Future[Int] = Future(Failure(java.lang.Exception: too late))
```

Now you know what a Future is. It is an object that will give you a result (or failure) at some point in the future. In the next section, you will see one way of harvesting the result of a Future.

NOTE: In the Play web framework, you are encouraged to return Future objects in the "action" methods that react to web requests. Then you don't have to worry how the results are harvested—that's the job of the framework.

NOTE: The java.util.concurrent package has a Future interface that is much more limited than the Scala Future trait. A Scala future is equivalent to the CompletionStage interface in Java 8.

NOTE: The Scala language imposes no restrictions on what you can do in concurrent tasks. However, you should stay away from computations with side effects. It is best if you don't increment shared counters—even atomic ones. Don't populate shared maps—even threadsafe ones. Instead, have each future compute a value. Then you can combine the computed values after all contributing futures have completed. That way, each value is only owned by one task at a time, and it is easy to reason about the correctness of the computation.

17.2 Waiting for Results

When you have a Future, you can use the isCompleted method to check whether it is completed. But of course you don't want to wait for completion in a loop.

You can make a blocking call that waits for the result.

```
import scala.concurrent.duration._
val f = Future { Thread.sleep(10000); 42 }
val result = Await.result(f, 10.seconds)
```

The call to Await.result blocks for ten seconds and then yields the result of the future.

The second argument of the Await.result method is a Duration object. Importing scala.concurrent.duration._ enables conversion methods from integers to Duration objects, called seconds, millis, and so on.

If the task is not ready by the allotted time, the Await.ready method throws a TimeoutException.

If the task throws an exception, it is rethrown in the call to Await.result. To avoid that, you can call Await.ready and then get the result.

```
val f = Future { ... }
Await.ready(f, 10.seconds)
val Some(t) = f.value
```

The value method returns an Option[Try[T]], which is None when the future is not completed and Some(t) when it is is. Here, t is an object of the Try class, which holds either the result or the exception that caused the task to fail. In our situation, the value method is only executed if the future is completed, so we can use an extractor to get the Try object. You will see how to look inside it in the next section.

NOTE: In practice, you won't use the Await.result or Await.ready methods much. You run tasks concurrently when they are time-consuming and your program can do something more useful than waiting for the result. Section 17.4, "Callbacks," on page 251 shows you how you can harvest the results without blocking.

CAUTION: In this section, we used the result and ready methods of the Await object. The Future class also has result and ready methods, but you should not call them. If the execution context uses a small number of threads (which is the case for the default fork-join pool), you don't want them all to block. Unlike the Future methods, the Await methods notify the execution context so that it can adjust the pooled threads.

NOTE: Not all exceptions that occur during execution of the future are stored in the result. Virtual machine errors and the InterruptedException are allowed to propagate in the usual way.

17.3 The Try Class

A Try[T] instance is either a Success(v), where v is a value of type T or a Failure(ex), where ex is a Throwable. One way of processing it is with a match statement.

```
t match {
  case Success(v) => println(s"The answer is $v")
  case Failure(ex) => println(ex.getMessage)
}
```

Alternatively, you can use the isSuccess or isFailure methods to find out whether the Try object represents success or failure. In the case of success, you can obtain the value with the get method:

```
if (t.isSuccess) println(s"The answer is ${t.get}")
```

To get the exception in case of failure, first apply the failed method which turns the failed Try[T] object into a Try[Throwable] wrapping the exception. Then call get to get the exception object.

```
if (t.isFailure) println(t.failed.get.getMessage)
```

You can also turn a Try object into an Option with the toOption method if you want to pass it on to a method that expects an option. This turns Success into Some and Failure into None.

To construct a Try object, call Try(block) with some block of code. For example,

```
val result = Try(str.toInt)
```

is either a Success object with the parsed integer, or a Failure wrapping a NumberFormatException.

There are several methods for composing and transforming Try objects. However, analogous methods exist for futures, where they are more commonly used. You will see how to work with multiple futures in Section 17.5, "Composing Future Tasks," on page 252. At the end of that section, you will see how those techniques apply to Try objects.

17.4 Callbacks

As already mentioned, one does not usually use a blocking wait to get the result of a future. For better performance, the future should report its result to a callback function.

This is easy to arrange with the onComplete method.

```
f.onComplete(t => ...)
```

When the future has completed, either successfully or with a failure, it calls the given function with a Try object.

You can then react to the success or failure, for example by passing a match function to the onComplete method.

```
val f = Future { Thread.sleep(10000)
  if (random() < 0.5) throw new Exception
  42
}
f.onComplete {
  case Success(v) => println(s"The answer is $v")
  case Failure(ex) => println(ex.getMessage)
}
```

By using a callback, we avoid blocking. Unfortunately, we now have another problem. In all likelihood, the long computation in one Future task will be followed by another computation, and another. It is possible to nest callbacks within callbacks, but it is profoundly unpleasant. (This technique is sometimes called "callback hell".)

A better approach is to think of futures as entities that can be composed, similar to functions. You compose two functions by calling the first one, then passing its result to the second one. In the next section, you will see how to do the same with futures.

 NOTE: There are callback methods onSuccess and onFailure that are only called on success or failure of a future. However, these are deprecated because they are even bigger contributors to callback hell.

17.5 Composing Future Tasks

Suppose we need to get some information from two web services and then combine the two. Each task is long-running and should be executed in a Future. It is possible to link them together with callbacks:

```
val future1 = Future { getData1() }
val future2 = Future { getData2() }
```

```
future1 onComplete {
  case Success(n1) =>
    future2 onComplete {
      case Success(n2) => {
        val n = n1 + n2
        println(s"Result: $n")
      }
      case Failure(ex) => ...
    }
  case Failure(ex) => ...
}
```

Even though the callbacks are ordered sequentially, the tasks run concurrently. Each task starts after the Future.apply method executes or soon afterwards. We don't know which of f1 and f2 completes first, and it doesn't matter. We can't process the result until both tasks complete. Once f1 completes, its completion handler registers a completion handler on f2. If f2 has already completed, the second handler is called right away. Otherwise, it is called when f2 finally completes.

Even though this chaining of the futures works, it looks very messy, and it will look worse with each additional level of processing.

Instead of nesting callbacks, we will use an approach that you already know from working with Scala collections. Think of a Future as a collection with (hopefully, eventually) one element. You know how to transform the values of a collection—with map:

```
val future1 = Future { getData1() }
val combined = future1.map(n1 => n1 + getData2())
```

Here future1 is a Future[Int]—a collection of (hopefully, eventually) one value. We map a function Int => Int and get another Future[Int]—a collection of (hopefully, eventually) one integer.

But wait—that's not quite the same as in the callback code. The call to getData2 is running *after* getData1, not concurrently. Let's fix that with a second map:

```
val future1 = Future { getData1() }
val future2 = Future { getData2() }
val combined = future1.map(n1 => future2.map(n2 => n1 + n2))
```

When future1 and future2 have delivered their results, the sum is computed.

Unfortunately, now `combined` is a `Future[Future[Int]]`, which isn't so good. That's what `flatMap` is for:

```
val combined = f1.flatMap(n1 => f2.map(n2 => n1 + n2))
```

This looks much nicer when you use a for expression instead of chaining `flatMap` and `map`:

```
val combined = for (n1 <- future1; n2 <- future2) yield n1 + n2
```

This is exactly the same code since for expressions are translated to chains of `map` and `flatMap`.

You can also apply guards in the for expression:

```
val combined =
  for (int n1 <- future1; n2 <- future2 if n1 != n2) yield n1 + n2
```

If the guard fails, the computation fails with a `NoSuchElementException`.

What if something goes wrong? The `map` and `flatMap` implementations take care of all that. As soon as one of the tasks fails, the entire pipeline fails, and the exception is captured. In contrast, when you manually combine callbacks, you have to deal with failure at every step.

 NOTE: If you find the `for/yield` construct unnatural, check out the Scala Async library at `http://github.com/scala/async`. It uses Scala Macros to let you express the flow more naturally as

```
val combined = async { await(future1) + await(future2) }
```

So far, you have seen how to run two tasks concurrently. Sometimes, you need one task to run after another. A `Future` starts execution immediately when it is created. To delay the creation, use functions.

```
def future1 = Future { getData() }
def future2 = Future { getMoreData() } // def, not val
val combined = for (n1 <- future1; n2 <- future2) yield n1 + n2
```

Now future2 is only evaluated when future1 has completed.

It doesn't matter whether you use `val` or `def` for future1. If you use `def`, its creation is slightly delayed to the start of the for expression.

This is particularly useful if the second step depends on the output of the first:

```
def future1 = Future { getData() }
def future2(arg: Int) = Future { getMoreData(arg) }
val combined = for (n1 <- future1; n2 <- future2(n1)) yield n1 + n2
```

NOTE: Like the Future trait, the Try class from Section 17.3, "The Try Class," on page 251 has map and flatMap methods. A Try[T] is a collection of, hopefully, one element. It is just like a Future[T], except you don't have to wait. You can apply map with a function that changes that one element, or flatMap if you have Try-valued function and want to flatten the result. And you can use for expressions. For example, here is how to compute the sum of two function calls that might fail:

```
def readInt(prompt: String) = Try(StdIn.readLine(s"$prompt: ").toInt)
val t = for (n1 <- readInt("n1"); n2 <- readInt("n2")) yield n1 + n2
```

In this way, you can compose Try-valued computations and you don't need to deal with the boring part of error handling.

17.6 Other Future Transformations

The map and flatMap methods that you saw in the preceding section are the most fundamental transformation of Future objects.

Table 17–1 shows several ways of applying functions to the contents of a future that differ in subtle details.

The foreach method works exactly like it does for collections, applying a method for its side effect. The method is applied to the single value in the future. It is convenient for harvesting the answer when it materializes.

```
val combined = for (n1 <- future1; n2 <- future2) yield n1 + n2
combined.foreach(n => println(s"Result: $n"))
```

The recover method accepts a partial function that can turn an exception into a successful result. Consider this call:

```
val f = Future { persist(data) } recover { case e: SQLException => 0 }
```

If a SQLException occurs, the future succeeds with result 0.

The fallbackTo method provides a different recovery mechanism. When you call f.fallbackTo(f2), then f2 is executed if f fails, and its value becomes the value of the future. However, f2 cannot inspect the reason for the failure.

The failed method turns a failed Future[T] into a successful Future[Throwable], just like the Try.failed method. You can retrieve the failure in a for expression like this:

```
val f = Future { ... }
for (ex <- f.failed) println(ex)
```

Finally, you can zip two futures together. The call f1.zip(f2) yields a future whose result is a pair (v, w) if v was the result of f1 and w the result of f2, or an exception if either f1 or f2 failed. (If both fail, the exception of f1 is reported.)

Table 17–1 Transformations on a `Future[T]` with success value v or exception ex

Method	Result	Description
collect(pf: PartialFunction[T, S])	Future[S]	Like map, but with a partial function. The result fails with a NoSuchElementException if pf(v) is not defined.
foreach(f: T => U)	Unit	Calls f(v) like map, but only for its side effect.
andThen(pf: PartialFunction[Try[T], U])	Future[T]	Calls pf(v) for its side effect and returns a future with v.
filter(p: T => Boolean)	Future[T]	Calls p(v) and returns a future with v or a NoSuchElementException.
recover(pf: PartialFunction[Throwable, U]) recoverWith(pf: PartialFunction[Throwable, Future[U]])	Future[U] (where U is a supertype of T)	A future with value v or pf(ex), flattened in the asynchronous case.
fallbackTo(f2: Future[U])	Future[U] (where U is a supertype of T)	A future with value v, or if this future failed, with the value of f2, or if that also failed, with exception ex.
failed	Future[Throwable]	A future with value ex.
transform(s: T => S, f: Throwable => Throwable) transform(f: Try[T] => Try[S]) transformWith(f: Try[T] => Future[Try[S]])	Future[S]	Transforms both the success and failure.

The zipWith method is similar, but it takes a method to combine the two results instead of returning a pair. For example, here is another way of obtaining the sum of two computations:

```
val future1 = Future { getData1() }
val future2 = Future { getData2() }
val combined = future1.zipWith(future2)(_ + _)
```

17.7 Methods in the Future Object

The Future companion object contains useful methods for working on collections of futures.

Suppose that, as you are computing a result, you organize the work so that you can concurrently work on different parts. For example, each part might be a range of the inputs. Make a future for each part:

```
val futures = parts.map(p => Future { compute result in p })
```

Now you have a collection of futures. Often, you want to combine the results. By using the Future.sequence method, you can get a collection of all results for further processing:

```
val result = Future.sequence(futures);
```

Note that the call doesn't block—it gives you a future to a collection. For example, assume futures is a Set[Future[T]]. Then the result is a Future[Set[T]]. When the results for all elements of futures are available, the result future will complete with a set of the results.

If any of the futures fail, then the resulting future fails as well with the exception of the leftmost failed future. If multiple futures fail, you don't get to see the remaining failures.

The traverse method combines the map and sequence steps. Instead of

```
val futures = parts.map(p => Future { compute result in p })
val result = Future.sequence(futures);
```

you can call

```
val result = Future.traverse(parts)(p => Future { compute result in p })
```

The function in the second curried argument is applied to each element of parts. You get a future to a collection of all results.

There are also reduceLeft and foldLeft operations that are analogous to the reductions and folds described in Section 13.9, "Reducing, Folding, and Scanning," on page 184. You supply an operation that combines the results of all futures as they become available. For example, here is how you can compute the sum of the results:

```
val result = Future.reduceLeft(futures)(_ + _)
    // Yields a future to the sum of the results of all futures
```

So far, we have collected the results from all futures. Suppose you are willing to accept a result from any of the parts. Then call

```
Future[T] result = Future.firstCompletedOf(futures)
```

You get a future that, when it completes, has the result or failure of the first completed element of futures.

The find method is similar, but you also supply a predicate.

```
val result = Future.find(futures)(predicate)
    // Yields a Future[Option[T]]
```

You get a future that, when it completes successfully, yields Some(r), where r is the result of one of the given futures that fulfills the predicate. Failed futures are ignored. If all futures complete but none yields a result that matches the predicate, then find returns None.

 CAUTION: A potential problem with firstCompletedOf and find is that the other computations keep on going even when the result has been determined. Scala futures do not have a mechanism for cancellation. If you want to stop unnecessary work, you have to provide your own mechanism.

Finally, the Future object provides convenience methods for generating simple futures:

- Future.successful(r) is an already completed future with result r.

- Future.failed(e) is an already completed future with exception e.

- Future.fromTry(t) is an already completed future with the result or exception given in the Try object t.

- Future.unit is an already completed future with Unit result.

- Future.never is a future that never completes.

17.8 Promises

A Future object is read-only. The value of the future is set implicitly when the task has finished or failed. A Promise is similar, but the value can be set explicitly.

Consider this method that yields a Future:

```
def computeAnswer(arg: String) = Future {
 val n = workHard(arg)
 n
}
```

With a Promise, it looks like this:

```
def computeAnswer(arg: String) = {
  val p = Promise[Int]()
  Future {
    val n = workHard(arg)
    p.success(n)
    workOnSomethingElse()
  }
  p.future
}
```

Calling future on a promise yields the associated Future object. Note that the method returns the Future right away, immediately after starting the task that will eventually yield the result. That task is run in another Future, defined by the expression Future { ... }, that is unrelated to the promise's future.

Calling success on a promise sets the result. Alternatively, you can call failure with an exception to make the promise fail. As soon as one of these methods is called, the associated future is completed, and neither method can be called again. (An IllegalStateException is thrown otherwise.)

From the point of view of the consumer (that is, caller of the computeAnswer method), there is no difference between the two approaches. Either way, the consumer has a Future and eventually gets the result.

The producer, however, has more flexibility when using a Promise. As suggested in the code sample, the producer can do other work besides fulfilling this promise. For example, the producer might work on fulfilling multiple promises.

```
val p1 = Promise[Int]()
val p2 = Promise[Int]()
Future {
  val n1 = getData1()
  p1.success(n1)
  val n2 = getData2()
  p2.success(n2)
}
```

It is also possible to have multiple tasks that work concurrently to fulfill a single promise. When one of the tasks has a result, it calls trySuccess on the promise. Unlike the success method, that method accepts the result and returns true if the promise has not yet completed; otherwise it returns false and ignores the result.

```
val p = Promise[Int]()
Future {
  var n = workHard(arg)
  p.trySuccess(n)
}
Future {
  var n = workSmart(arg)
  p.trySuccess(n)
}
```

The promise is completed by the first task that manages to produce the result. With this approach, the tasks might want to periodically call p.isCompleted to check whether they should continue.

NOTE: Scala promises are equivalent to the `CompletableFuture` class in Java 8.

17.9 Execution Contexts

By default, Scala futures are executed on the global fork-join pool. That works well for computationally intensive tasks. However, the fork-join pool only manages a small number of threads (by default, equal to the number of cores of all processors). This is a problem when tasks have to wait, for example when communicating with a remote resource. A program could exhaust all available threads, waiting for results.

You can notify the execution context that you are about to block, by placing the blocking code inside `blocking { ... }`:

```
val f = Future {
  val url = ...
  blocking {
    val contents = Source.fromURL(url).mkString
    ...
  }
}
```

The execution context may then increase the number of threads. The fork-join pool does exactly that, but it isn't designed for perform well for many blocking threads. If you do input/output or connect to databases, you are better off using a different thread pool. The `Executors` class from the Java concurrency library gives you several choices. A cached thread pool works well for I/O intensive workloads. You can pass it explicitly to the `Future.apply` method, or you can set it as the implicit execution context:

```
val pool = Executors.newCachedThreadPool()
implicit val ec = ExecutionContext.fromExecutor(pool)
```

Now this pool is used by all futures when ec is in scope.

Exercises

1. Consider the expression

```
for (n1 <- Future { Thread.sleep(1000) ; 2 }
     n2 <- Future { Thread.sleep(1000); 40 })
  println(n1 + n2)
```

How is the expression translated to map and flatMap calls? Are the two futures executed concurrently or one after the other? In which thread does the call to println occur?

2. Write a function doInOrder that, given two functions f: T => Future[U] and g: U => Future[V], produces a function T => Future[U] that, for a given t, eventually yields g(f(t)).

3. Repeat the preceding exercise for any sequence of functions of type T => Future[T].

4. Write a function doTogether that, given two functions f: T => Future[U] and g: U => Future[V], produces a function T => Future[(U, V)], running the two computations in parallel and, for a given t, eventually yielding (f(t), g(t)).

5. Write a function that receives a sequence of futures and returns a future that eventually yields a sequence of all results.

6. Write a method

    ```
    Future[T] repeat(action: => T, until: T => Boolean)
    ```

    that asynchronously repeats the action until it produces a value that is accepted by the until predicate, which should also run asynchronously. Test with a function that reads a password from the console, and a function that simulates a validity check by sleeping for a second and then checking that the password is "secret". Hint: Use recursion.

7. Write a program that counts the prime numbers between 1 and n, as reported by BigInt.isProbablePrime. Divide the interval into p parts, where p is the number of available processors. Count the primes in each part in concurrent futures and combine the results.

8. Write a program that asks the user for a URL, reads the web page at that URL, and displays all the hyperlinks. Use a separate Future for each of these three steps.

9. Write a program that asks the user for a URL, reads the web page at that URL, finds all the hyperlinks, visits each of them concurrently, and locates the Server HTTP header for each of them. Finally, print a table of which servers were found how often. The futures that visit each page should return the header.

10. Change the preceding exercise where the futures that visit each header update a shared Java ConcurrentHashMap or Scala TrieMap. This isn't as easy as it sounds. A threadsafe data structure is safe in the sense that you cannot corrupt its implementation, but you have to make sure that sequences of reads and updates are atomic.

11. Using futures, run four tasks that each sleep for ten seconds and then print the current time. If you have a reasonably modern computer, it is very likely that it reports four available processors to the JVM, and the futures should all complete at around the same time. Now repeat with forty tasks. What happens? Why? Replace the execution context with a cached thread pool. What happens now? (Be careful to define the futures *after* replacing the implicit execution context.)

12. Write a method that, given a URL, locates all hyperlinks, makes a promise for each of them, starts a task in which it will eventually fulfill all promises, and returns a sequence of futures for the promises. Why would it not be a good idea to return a sequence of promises?

13. Use a promise for implementing cancellation. Given a range of big integers, split the range into subranges that you concurrently search for palindromic primes. When such a prime is found, set it as the value of the future. All tasks should periodically check whether the promise is completed, in which case they should terminate.

Type Parameters

Topics in This Chapter L2

Chapter 18

In Scala, you can use type parameters to implement classes and functions that work with multiple types. For example, an Array[T] stores elements of an arbitrary type T. The basic idea is very simple, but the details can get tricky. Sometimes, you need to place restrictions on the type. For example, to sort elements, T must provide an ordering. Furthermore, if the parameter type varies, what should happen with the parameterized type? For example, can you pass an Array[String] to a function that expects an Array[Any]? In Scala, you specify how your types should vary depending on their parameters.

The key points of this chapter are:

- Classes, traits, methods, and functions can have type parameters.

- Place the type parameters after the name, enclosed in square brackets.

- Type bounds have the form T <: UpperBound, T >: LowerBound, T : ContextBound.

- You can restrict a method with a type constraint such as (implicit ev: T <:< UpperBound).

- Use +T (covariance) to indicate that a generic type's subtype relationship is in the same direction as the parameter T, or -T (contravariance) to indicate the reverse direction.

- Covariance is appropriate for parameters that denote outputs, such as elements in an immutable collection.

• Contravariance is appropriate for parameters that denote inputs, such as function arguments.

18.1 Generic Classes

As in Java or C++, classes and traits can have type parameters. In Scala, you use square brackets for type parameters, for example:

```
class Pair[T, S](val first: T, val second: S)
```

This defines a class with two type parameters T and S. You use the type parameters in the class definition to define the types of variables, method parameters, and return values.

A class with one or more type parameters is *generic*. If you substitute actual types for the type parameters, you get an ordinary class, such as Pair[Int, String].

Pleasantly, Scala attempts to infer the actual types from the construction parameters:

```
val p = new Pair(42, "String") // It's a Pair[Int, String]
```

You can also specify the types yourself:

```
val p2 = new Pair[Any, Any](42, "String")
```

18.2 Generic Functions

Functions and methods can also have type parameters. Here is a simple example:

```
def getMiddle[T](a: Array[T]) = a(a.length / 2)
```

As with generic classes, you place the type parameter after the name.

Scala infers the actual types from the arguments in the call.

```
getMiddle(Array("Mary", "had", "a", "little", "lamb")) // Calls getMiddle[String]
```

If you need to, you can specify the type:

```
val f = getMiddle[String] _ // The function, saved in f
```

18.3 Bounds for Type Variables

Sometimes, you need to place restrictions on type variables. Consider a Pair type where both components have the same type, like this:

```
class Pair[T](val first: T, val second: T)
```

Now we want to add a method that produces the smaller value:

```
class Pair[T](val first: T, val second: T) {
  def smaller = if (first.compareTo(second) < 0) first else second // Error
}
```

That's wrong—we don't know if first has a compareTo method. To solve this, we can add an *upper bound* T <: Comparable[T].

```
class Pair[T <: Comparable[T]](val first: T, val second: T) {
  def smaller = if (first.compareTo(second) < 0) first else second
}
```

This means that T must be a subtype of Comparable[T].

Now we can instantiate Pair[java.lang.String] but not Pair[java.net.URL], since String is a subtype of Comparable[String] but URL does not implement Comparable[URL]. For example:

```
val p = new Pair("Fred", "Brooks")
println(p.smaller) // Prints Brooks
```

 CAUTION: This example is a bit simplistic. If you try a new Pair(4, 2), you will be told that for T = Int, the bound T <: Comparable[T] is not fulfilled. See Section 18.4, "View Bounds," on page 268 for a remedy.

You can also specify a lower bound for a type. For example, suppose we want to define a method that replaces the first component of a pair with another value. Our pairs are immutable, so we need to return a new pair. Here is a first attempt:

```
class Pair[T](val first: T, val second: T) {
  def replaceFirst(newFirst: T) = new Pair[T](newFirst, second)
}
```

But we can do better than that. Suppose we have a Pair[Student]. It should be possible to replace the first component with a Person. Of course, then the result must be a Pair[Person]. In general, the replacement type must be a supertype of the pair's component type.

```
def replaceFirst[R >: T](newFirst: R) = new Pair[R](newFirst, second)
```

Here, I included the type parameter in the returned pair for greater clarity. You can also write

```
def replaceFirst[R >: T](newFirst: R) = new Pair(newFirst, second)
```

Then the return type is correctly inferred as new Pair[R].

CAUTION: If you omit the lower bound,

```
def replaceFirst[R](newFirst: R) = new Pair(newFirst, second)
```

the method will compile, but it will return a Pair[Any].

18.4 View Bounds

In the preceding section, we had an example of an upper bound:

```
class Pair[T <: Comparable[T]]
```

Unfortunately, if you try constructing a new Pair(4, 2), the compiler complains that Int is not a subtype of Comparable[Int]. Unlike the java.lang.Integer wrapper type, the Scala Int type does not implement Comparable. However, RichInt does implement Comparable[Int], and there is an implicit conversion from Int to RichInt. (See Chapter 21 for more information on implicit conversions.)

A solution is to use a "view bound" like this:

```
class Pair[T <% Comparable[T]]
```

The <% relation means that T can be converted to a Comparable[T] through an implicit conversion.

However, view bounds are on their way out in Scala. If you compile with the -future flag, you'll get a warning when you use them. You can replace a view bound with a "type constraint" (see Section 18.8, "Type Constraints," on page 269), like this:

```
class Pair[T](val first: T, val second: T)(implicit ev: T => Comparable[T]) {
  def smaller = if (first.compareTo(second) < 0) first else second
  ...
}
```

18.5 Context Bounds

A view bound T <% V requires the existence of an implicit conversion from T to V. A *context bound* has the form T : M, where M is another generic type. It requires that there is an "implicit value" of type M[T]. We discuss implicit values in detail in Chapter 21.

For example,

```
class Pair[T : Ordering]
```

requires that there is an implicit value of type Ordering[T]. That implicit value can then be used in the methods of the class. When you declare a method that uses the implicit value, you have to add an "implicit parameter." Here is an example:

```
class Pair[T : Ordering](val first: T, val second: T) {
  def smaller(implicit ord: Ordering[T]) =
    if (ord.compare(first, second) < 0) first else second
}
```

As you will see in Chapter 21, implicit values are more flexible than implicit conversions.

18.6 The ClassTag Context Bound

To instantiate a generic Array[T], one needs a ClassTag[T] object. This is required for primitive type arrays to work correctly. For example, if T is Int, you want an int[] array in the virtual machine. If you write a generic function that constructs a generic array, you need to help it out and pass that class tag object. Use a context bound, like this:

```
import scala.reflect._
def makePair[T : ClassTag](first: T, second: T) = {
  val r = new Array[T](2); r(0) = first; r(1) = second; r
}
```

If you call makePair(4, 9), the compiler locates the implicit ClassTag[Int] and actually calls makePair(4, 9)(classTag). Then the new operator is translated to a call classTag.newArray, which in the case of a ClassTag[Int] constructs a primitive array int[2].

Why all this complexity? In the virtual machine, generic types are erased. There is only a single makePair method that needs to work for *all* types T.

18.7 Multiple Bounds

A type variable can have both an upper and a lower bound. The syntax is this:

```
T >: Lower <: Upper
```

You can't have multiple upper or lower bounds. However, you can still require that a type implements multiple traits, like this:

```
T <: Comparable[T] with Serializable with Cloneable
```

You can have more than one context bound:

```
T : Ordering : ClassTag
```

18.8 Type Constraints **L3**

Type constraints give you another way of restricting types. There are three relationships that you can use:

```
T =:= U
T <:< U
T => U
```

These constraints test whether T equals U, is a subtype of U, or is convertible to U. To use such a constraint, you add an "implicit evidence parameter" like this:

```
class Pair[T](val first: T, val second: T)(implicit ev: T <:< Comparable[T])
```

 NOTE: See Chapter 21 for an explanation of the curious syntax, and for an analysis of the inner workings of the type constraints.

In the example above, there is no advantage to using a type constraint over a type bound class Pair[T <: Comparable[T]]. However, type constraints are useful in some specialized circumstances. In this section, you will see two uses of type constraints.

Type constraints let you supply a method in a generic class that can be used only under certain conditions. Here is an example:

```
class Pair[T](val first: T, val second: T) {
  def smaller(implicit ev: T <:< Ordered[T]) =
    if (first < second) first else second
}
```

You can form a Pair[URL], even though URL is not ordered. You will get an error only if you invoke the smaller method.

Another example is the orNull method in the Option class:

```
val friends = Map("Fred" -> "Barney", ...)
val friendOpt = friends.get("Wilma") // An Option[String]
val friendOrNull = friendOpt.orNull // A String or null
```

The orNull method can be useful when working with Java code where it is common to encode missing values as null. But it can't be applied to value types such as Int that don't have null as a valid value. Because orNull is implemented using a constraint Null <:< A, you can still instantiate Option[Int], as long as you stay away from orNull for those instances.

Another use of type constraints is for improving type inference. Consider

```
def firstLast[A, C <: Iterable[A]](it: C) = (it.head, it.last)
```

When you call

```
firstLast(List(1, 2, 3))
```

you get a message that the inferred type arguments [Nothing, List[Int]] don't conform to [A, C <: Iterable[A]]. Why Nothing? The type inferencer cannot figure out what A is from looking at List(1, 2, 3), because it matches A and C in a single step. To help it along, first match C and then A:

```
def firstLast[A, C](it: C)(implicit ev: C <:< Iterable[A]) =
  (it.head, it.last)
```

> **NOTE:** You saw a similar trick in Chapter 12. The corresponds method checks whether two sequences have corresponding entries:
>
> ```
> def corresponds[B](that: Seq[B])(match: (A, B) => Boolean): Boolean
> ```
>
> The match predicate is a curried parameter so that the type inferencer can first determine the type of B and then use that information to analyze match. In the call
>
> ```
> Array("Hello", "Fred").corresponds(Array(5, 4))(_.length == _)
> ```
>
> the compiler can infer that B is Int. Then it can make sense of _.length == _.

18.9 Variance

Suppose we have a function that does something with a Pair[Person]:

```
def makeFriends(p: Pair[Person])
```

If Student is a subclass of Person, can I call makeFriend with a Pair[Student]? By default, this is an error. Even though Student is a subtype of Person, there is *no* relationship between Pair[Student] and Pair[Person].

If you want such a relationship, you have to indicate it when you define the Pair class:

```
class Pair[+T](val first: T, val second: T)
```

The + means that the type is *covariant* in T—that is, it varies in the same direction. Since Student is a subtype of Person, a Pair[Student] is now a subtype of Pair[Person].

It is also possible to have variance in the other direction. Consider a generic type Friend[T], which denotes someone who is willing to befriend anyone of type T.

```
trait Friend[-T] {
  def befriend(someone: T)
}
```

Now suppose you have a function

```
def makeFriendWith(s: Student, f: Friend[Student]) { f.befriend(s) }
```

Can you call it with a Friend[Person]? That is, if you have

```
class Person extends Friend[Person] { ... }
class Student extends Person
val susan = new Student
val fred = new Person
```

will the call `makeFriendWith(susan, fred)` succeed? It seems like it should. If Fred is willing to befriend any person, he'll surely like to be friends with Susan.

Note that the type varies in the opposite direction of the subtype relationship. `Student` is a subtype of `Person`, but `Friend[Student]` is a supertype of `Friend[Person]`. In that case, you declare the type parameter to be *contravariant*:

```
trait Friend[-T] {
  def befriend(someone: T)
}
```

You can have both variance types in a single generic type. For example, single-argument functions have the type `Function1[-A, +R]`. To see why these are the appropriate variances, consider a function

```
def friends(students: Array[Student], find: Function1[Student, Person]) =
  // You can write the second parameter as find: Student => Person
  for (s <- students) yield find(s)
```

Suppose you have a function

```
def findStudent(p: Person) : Student
```

Can you call `friends` with that function? Of course you can. It's willing to take any person, so surely it will take a `Student`. It yields `Student` results, which can be put into an `Array[Person]`.

18.10 Co- and Contravariant Positions

In the preceding section, you saw that functions are contravariant in their arguments and covariant in their results. Generally, it makes sense to use contravariance for the values an object consumes, and covariance for the values it produces. (Aide-mémoire: **con**travariance **con**sumes.)

If an object does both, then the type should be left *invariant*. This is generally the case for mutable data structures. For example, in Scala, arrays are invariant. You can't convert an `Array[Student]` to an `Array[Person]` or the other way around. This would not be safe. Consider the following:

```
val students = new Array[Student](length)
val people: Array[Person] = students // Not legal, but suppose it was . . .
people(0) = new Person("Fred") // Oh no! Now students(0) isn't a Student
```

Conversely,

```
val people = new Array[Person](length)
val students: Array[Student] = people // Not legal, but suppose it was ...
people(0) = new Person("Fred") // Oh no! Now students(0) isn't a Student
```

 NOTE: In Java, it is possible to convert a Student[] array to a Person[] array, but if you try to add a nonstudent into such an array, an ArrayStoreException is thrown. In Scala, the compiler rejects programs that could cause type errors.

Suppose we tried to declare a covariant *mutable* pair. This wouldn't work. It would be like an array with two elements, and one could produce the same kind of error that you just saw.

Indeed, if you try

```
class Pair[+T](var first: T, var second: T) // Error
```

you get an error complaining that the covariant type T occurs in a *contravariant position* in the setter

```
first_=(value: T)
```

Parameters are contravariant positions, and return types are covariant.

However, inside a function parameter, the variance flips—its parameters are covariant. For example, look at the foldLeft method of Iterable[+A]:

```
foldLeft[B](z: B)(op: (B, A) => B): B
          -      +  +    -  +
```

Note that A is now in a covariant position.

These position rules are simple and safe, but they sometimes get in the way of doing something that would be risk-free. Consider the replaceFirst method from Section 18.3, "Bounds for Type Variables," on page 266 in an immutable pair:

```
class Pair[+T](val first: T, val second: T) {
  def replaceFirst(newFirst: T) = new Pair[T](newFirst, second) // Error
}
```

The compiler rejects this, because the parameter type T is in a contravariant position. Yet this method cannot damage the pair—it returns a new pair.

The remedy is to come up with a second type parameter for the method, like this:

```
def replaceFirst[R >: T](newFirst: R) = new Pair[R](newFirst, second)
```

Now the method is a generic method with another type parameter R. But R is *invariant*, so it doesn't matter that it appears in a contravariant position.

18.11 Objects Can't Be Generic

It is not possible to add type parameters to objects. Consider, for example, immutable lists. A list with element type T is either empty, or it is a node with a head of type T and a tail of type List[T]:

```
abstract class List[+T] {
  def isEmpty: Boolean
  def head: T
  def tail: List[T]
}

class Node[T](val head: T, val tail: List[T]) extends List[T] {
  def isEmpty = false
}

class Empty[T] extends List[T] {
  def isEmpty = true
  def head = throw new UnsupportedOperationException
  def tail = throw new UnsupportedOperationException
}
```

 NOTE: Here I use Node and Empty to make the discussion easier to follow for Java programmers. If you are experienced with Scala lists, just substitute :: and Nil in your mind.

It seems silly to define Empty as a class. It has no state. But you can't simply turn it into an object:

```
object Empty[T] extends List[T] // Error
```

You can't add a parameterized type to an object. In this case, a remedy is to inherit List[Nothing]:

```
object Empty extends List[Nothing]
```

Recall from Chapter 8 that the Nothing type is a subtype of all types. Thus, when we make a one-element list

```
val lst = new Node(42, Empty)
```

type checking is successful. Due to covariance, a List[Nothing] is convertible into a List[Int], and the Node[Int] constructor can be invoked.

18.12 Wildcards

In Java, all generic types are invariant. However, you can vary the types where you use them, using wildcards. For example, a method

```
void makeFriends(List<? extends Person> people) // This is Java
```

can be called with a `List<Student>`.

You can use wildcards in Scala too. They look like this:

```
def process(people: java.util.List[_ <: Person]) // This is Scala
```

In Scala, you don't need the wildcard for a covariant `Pair` class. But suppose `Pair` is invariant:

```
class Pair[T](var first: T, var second: T)
```

Then you can define

```
def makeFriends(p: Pair[_ <: Person]) // OK to call with a Pair[Student]
```

You can also use wildcards for contravariance:

```
import java.util.Comparator
def min[T](p: Pair[T])(comp: Comparator[_ >: T])
```

Wildcards are "syntactic sugar" for existential types, which we will discuss in detail in Chapter 19.

 CAUTION: In certain complex situations, Scala wildcards are still a work in progress. For example, the following declaration does not work in Scala 2.12:

```
def min[T <: Comparable[_ >: T]](p: Pair[T]) = ...
```

A workaround is the following:

```
type SuperComparable[T] = Comparable[_ >: T]
def min[T <: SuperComparable[T]](p: Pair[T]) = ...
```

Exercises

1. Define an immutable class `Pair[T, S]` with a method `swap` that returns a new pair with the components swapped.

2. Define a mutable class `Pair[T]` with a method `swap` that swaps the components of the pair.

3. Given a class Pair[T, S], write a generic method swap that takes a pair as its argument and returns a new pair with the components swapped.

4. Why don't we need a lower bound for the replaceFirst method in Section 18.3, "Bounds for Type Variables," on page 266 if we want to replace the first component of a Pair[Person] with a Student?

5. Why does RichInt implement Comparable[Int] and not Comparable[RichInt]?

6. Write a generic method middle that returns the middle element from any Iterable[T]. For example, middle("World") is 'r'.

7. Look through the methods of the Iterable[+A] trait. Which methods use the type parameter A? Why is it in a covariant position in these methods?

8. In Section 18.10, "Co- and Contravariant Positions," on page 272, the replaceFirst method has a type bound. Why can't you define an equivalent method on a mutable Pair[T]?

   ```
   def replaceFirst[R >: T](newFirst: R) { first = newFirst } // Error
   ```

9. It may seem strange to restrict method parameters in an immutable class Pair[+T]. However, suppose you could define

   ```
   def replaceFirst(newFirst: T)
   ```

   in a Pair[+T]. The problem is that this method can be overridden in an unsound way. Construct an example of the problem. Define a subclass NastyDoublePair of Pair[Double] that overrides replaceFirst so that it makes a pair with the square root of newFirst. Then construct the call replaceFirst("Hello") on a Pair[Any] that is actually a NastyDoublePair.

10. Given a mutable Pair[S, T] class, use a type constraint to define a swap method that can be called if the type parameters are the same.

Advanced Types

Topics in This Chapter L2

Chapter 19

In this chapter, you will see all the types that Scala has to offer, including some of the more technical ones. We will end with a discussion of self types and dependency injection.

The key points of this chapter are:

- Singleton types are useful for method chaining and methods with object parameters.

- A type projection includes inner class instances for all objects of an outer class.

- A type alias gives a short name for a type.

- Structural types are equivalent to "duck typing."

- Existential types provide the formalism for wildcard parameters of generic types.

- Use a self type declaration to indicate that a trait requires another type.

- The "cake pattern" uses self types to implement a dependency injection mechanism.

- An abstract type must be made concrete in a subclass.

- A higher-kinded type has a type parameter that is itself a parameterized type.

19.1 Singleton Types

Given any reference v, you can form the type v.type, which has two values: v and null. This sounds like a curious type, but it has a couple of useful applications.

First, consider a method that returns this so you can chain method calls:

```
class Document {
  def setTitle(title: String) = { ...; this }
  def setAuthor(author: String) = { ...; this }
  ...
}
```

You can then call

```
article.setTitle("Whatever Floats Your Boat").setAuthor("Cay Horstmann")
```

However, if you have a subclass, there is a problem:

```
class Book extends Document {
  def addChapter(chapter: String) = { ...; this }
  ...
}

val book = new Book()
book.setTitle("Scala for the Impatient").addChapter(chapter1) // Error
```

Since the setTitle method returns this, Scala infers the return type as Document. But Document doesn't have an addChapter method.

The remedy is to declare the return type of setTitle as this.type:

```
def setTitle(title: String): this.type = { ...; this }
```

Now the return type of book.setTitle("...") is book.type, and since book has an addChapter method, the chaining works.

You can also use a singleton type if you want to define a method that takes an object instance as parameter. You may wonder why you would ever want to do that—after all, if there is just one instance, the method could simply use it instead of making the caller pass it.

However, some people like to construct "fluent interfaces" that read like English, for example:

```
book set Title to "Scala for the Impatient"
```

This is parsed as

```
book.set(Title).to("Scala for the Impatient")
```

For this to work, set is a method whose argument is the singleton Title:

```
object Title

class Document {
  private var useNextArgAs: Any = null
  def set(obj: Title.type): this.type = { useNextArgAs = obj; this }
  def to(arg: String) = if (useNextArgAs == Title) title = arg; else ...
  ...
}
```

Note the Title.type parameter. You can't use

```
def set(obj: Title) ... // Error
```

since Title denotes the singleton *object*, not a type.

19.2 Type Projections

In Chapter 5, you saw that a nested class belongs to the *object* in which it is nested. Here is the example:

```
import scala.collection.mutable.ArrayBuffer
class Network {
  class Member(val name: String) {
    val contacts = new ArrayBuffer[Member]
  }

  private val members = new ArrayBuffer[Member]

  def join(name: String) = {
    val m = new Member(name)
    members += m
    m
  }
}
```

Each Network instance has its own Member class. For example, here are two networks:

```
val chatter = new Network
val myFace = new Network
```

Now chatter.Member and myFace.Member are *different classes*.

You can't add a member from one network to another:

```
val fred = chatter.join("Fred") // Has type chatter.Member
val barney = myFace.join("Barney") // Has type myFace.Member
fred.contacts += barney // Error
```

If you don't want this restriction, you should simply move the Member type outside the Network class. A good place would be the Network companion object.

If what you want is fine-grained classes, with an occasional loose interpretation, use a *type projection* `Network#Member`, which means "a `Member` of *any* `Network`."

```
class Network {
  class Member(val name: String) {
    val contacts = new ArrayBuffer[Network#Member]
  }
  ...
}
```

You would do that if you want the fine-grained "inner class per object" feature in some places of your program, but not everywhere.

 CAUTION: A type projection such as `Network#Member` is not considered a "path," and you cannot import it. We discuss paths in the next section.

19.3 Paths

Consider a type such as

```
com.horstmann.impatient.chatter.Member
```

or, if we nest `Member` inside the companion object,

```
com.horstmann.impatient.Network.Member
```

Such an expression is called a *path*.

Each component of the path before the final type must be "stable," that is, it must specify a single, definite scope. Each such component is one of the following:

- A package
- An object
- A val
- `this`, `super`, `super[S]`, `C.this`, `C.super`, or `C.super[S]`

A path component can't be a class because, as you have seen, a nested class isn't a single type, but it gives rise to a separate type for each instance.

Moreover, a path element can't be a var. For example,

```
var chatter = new Network
...
val fred = new chatter.Member // Error—chatter is not stable
```

Since you might assign a different value to `chatter`, the compiler can't assign a definite meaning to the type `chatter.Member`.

NOTE: Internally, the compiler translates all nested type expressions a.b.c.T to type projections a.b.c.type#T. For example, chatter.Member becomes chatter.type#Member—any Member inside the singleton chatter.type. That is not something you generally need to worry about. However, sometimes you will see an error message with a type of the form a.b.c.type#T. Just translate it back to a.b.c.T.

19.4 Type Aliases

You can create a simple *alias* for a complicated type with the type keyword, like this:

```
class Book {
  import scala.collection.mutable._
  type Index = HashMap[String, (Int, Int)]
  ...
}
```

Then you can refer to Book.Index instead of the cumbersome type scala.collection. mutable.HashMap[String, (Int, Int)].

A type alias must be nested inside a class or object. It cannot appear at the top level of a Scala file. However, in the REPL, you can declare a type at the top level, since everything in the REPL is implicitly contained in a top-level object.

 NOTE: The type keyword is also used for *abstract types* that are made concrete in a subclass, for example:

```
abstract class Reader {
  type Contents
  def read(fileName: String): Contents
}
```

We will discuss abstract types in Section 19.12, "Abstract Types," on page 291.

19.5 Structural Types

A "structural type" is a specification of abstract methods, fields, and types that a conforming type should possess. For example, this method has a structural type parameter:

```
def appendLines(target: { def append(str: String): Any },
    lines: Iterable[String]) {
  for (l <- lines) { target.append(l); target.append("\n") }
}
```

You can call the appendLines method with an instance of *any* class that has an append method. This is more flexible than defining a Appendable trait, because you might not always be able to add that trait to the classes you are using.

Under the hood, Scala uses reflection to make the calls to target.append(...). Structural typing gives you a safe and convenient way of making such calls.

However, a reflective call is *much* more expensive than a regular method call. For that reason, you should only use structural typing when you model common behavior from classes that cannot share a trait.

 NOTE: Structural types are similar to "duck typing" in dynamically typed programming languages such as JavaScript or Ruby. In those languages, variables have no type. When you write obj.quack(), the runtime figures out whether the particular object to which obj refers at this point has a quack method. In other words, you don't have to declare obj as a Duck as long as it walks and quacks like one.

19.6 Compound Types

A compound type has the form

T_1 with T_2 with T_3 ...

where T_1, T_2, T_3, and so on are types. In order to belong to the compound type, a value must belong to all of the individual types. Therefore, such a type is also called an intersection type.

You can use a compound type to manipulate values that must provide multiple traits. For example,

```
val image = new ArrayBuffer[java.awt.Shape with java.io.Serializable]
```

You can draw the image object as for (s <- image) graphics.draw(s). You can serialize the image object because you know that all elements are serializable.

Of course, you can only add elements that are both shapes and serializable objects:

```
val rect = new Rectangle(5, 10, 20, 30)
image += rect // OK—Rectangle is Serializable
image += new Area(rect) // Error—Area is a Shape but not Serializable
```

NOTE: When you have a declaration

```
trait ImageShape extends Shape with Serializable
```

this means that ImageShape extends the intersection type Shape with Serializable.

You can add a structural type declaration to a simple or compound type. For example,

```
Shape with Serializable { def contains(p: Point): Boolean }
```

An instance of this type must be a subtype of Shape and Serializable, and it must have a contains method with a Point parameter.

Technically, the structural type

```
{ def append(str: String): Any }
```

is an abbreviation for

```
AnyRef { def append(str: String): Any }
```

and the compound type

```
Shape with Serializable
```

is a shortcut for

```
Shape with Serializable {}
```

19.7 Infix Types

An infix type is a type with two type parameters, written in "infix" syntax, with the type name between the type parameters. For example, you can write

```
String Map Int
```

instead of

```
Map[String, Int]
```

The infix notation is common in mathematics. For example, $A \times B = \{ (a, b) \mid a \in A, b \in B \}$ is the set of pairs with components of types A and B. In Scala, this type is written as (A, B). If you prefer the mathematical notation, you can define

```
type x[A, B] = (A, B)
```

Then you can write String x Int instead of (String, Int).

All infix type operators have the same precedence. As with regular operators, they are left-associative unless their names end in :. For example,

```
String x Int x Int
```

means ((String, Int), Int). This type is similar to, but not the same, as (String, Int, Int), which could not be written in infix form in Scala.

 NOTE: An infix type name can be any sequence of operator characters, except for a single ∗. This rule avoids confusion with variable argument declarations T∗.

19.8 Existential Types

Existential types were added to Scala for compatibility with Java wildcards. An existential type is a type expression followed by forSome { ... }, where the braces contain type and val declarations. For example,

```
Array[T] forSome { type T <: JComponent }
```

This is the same as the wildcard type

```
Array[_ <: JComponent]
```

that you saw in Chapter 18.

Scala wildcards are syntactic sugar for existential types. For example,

```
Array[_]
```

is the same as

```
Array[T] forSome { type T }
```

and

```
Map[_, _]
```

is the same as

```
Map[T, U] forSome { type T; type U }
```

The forSome notation allows for more complex relationships than wildcards can express, for example:

```
Map[T, U] forSome { type T; type U <: T }
```

You can use val declarations in the forSome block because a val can have its own nested types (see Section 19.2, "Type Projections," on page 281). Here is an example:

```
n.Member forSome { val n: Network }
```

By itself, that's not so interesting—you could just use a type projection Network#Member. But consider

```
def process[M <: n.Member forSome { val n: Network }](m1: M, m2: M) = (m1, m2)
```

This method will accept members from the same network, but reject members from different ones:

```
val chatter = new Network
val myFace = new Network
val fred = chatter.join("Fred")
val wilma = chatter.join("Wilma")
val barney = myFace.join("Barney")
process(fred, wilma) // OK
process(fred, barney) // Error
```

 NOTE: To use existential types without warnings, you must import `scala.language.existentials` or use the compiler option `-language:existentials`.

19.9 The Scala Type System

The Scala language reference gives an exhaustive list of all Scala types, which is reproduced in Table 19–1, with brief explanations for each type.

Table 19–1 Scala Types

Type	Syntax	Notes
Class or trait	`class C ...`, `trait C ...`	See Chapter 5, Chapter 10
Tuple type	$(T_1, \ldots, T_n)$	Section 4.7
Function type	$(T_1, \ldots, T_n)$ => T	
Annotated type	T `@A`	See Chapter 15
Parameterized type	`A[`$T_1, \ldots, T_n$`]`	See Chapter 18
Singleton type	*value*`.type`	See Section 19.1
Type projection	$O\#I$	See Section 19.2
Compound type	T_1 `with` T_2 `with` ... `with` T_n { *declarations* }	See Section 19.6
Infix type	T_1 `A` T_2	See Section 19.7
Existential type	T `forSome` { *type and val declarations* }	See Section 19.8

NOTE: This table shows the types that you, the programmer, can declare. There are a few types that the Scala compiler uses internally. For example, a *method type* is denoted by $(T_1, \ldots, T_n)T$ without a =>. You will occasionally see such types. For example, when you enter

```
def square(x: Int) = x * x
```

in the Scala REPL, it responds with

```
square (x: Int)Int
```

This is different from

```
val triple = (x: Int) => 3 * x
```

which yields

```
triple: Int => Int
```

You can turn a method into a function by appending a _. The type of

```
square _
```

is Int => Int.

19.10 Self Types

In Chapter 10, you saw how a trait can require that it is mixed into a class that extends another type. You define the trait with a *self type* declaration:

```
this: Type =>
```

Such a trait can only be mixed into a subclass of the given type. In the following example, the LoggedException trait can only be mixed into a class that extends Exception:

```
trait Logged {
  def log(msg: String)
}

trait LoggedException extends Logged {
  this: Exception =>
    def log() { log(getMessage()) }
      // OK to call getMessage because this is an Exception
}
```

If you try to mix the trait into a class that doesn't conform to the self type, an error occurs:

```
val f = new JFrame with LoggedException
  // Error: JFrame isn't a subtype of Exception, the self type of LoggedException
```

If you want to require multiple types, use a compound type:

```
this: T with U with ... =>
```

NOTE: You can combine the self type syntax with the "alias for enclosing this" syntax that I briefly introduced in Chapter 5. If you give a name other than this to the variable, then it can be used in subtypes by that name. For example,

```
trait Group {
  outer: Network =>
  class Member {
    ...
  }
}
```

The Group trait requires that it is added to a subtype of Network, and inside Member, you can refer to Group.this as outer.

This syntax seems to have grown organically over time; unfortunately, it introduces a great deal of confusion for a small amount of added functionality.

CAUTION: Self types do not automatically inherit. If you define

```
trait ManagedException extends LoggedException { ... }
```

you get an error that ManagedException doesn't supply Exception. In this situation, you need to repeat the self type:

```
trait ManagedException extends LoggedException {
  this: Exception =>
  ...
}
```

19.11 Dependency Injection

When building a large system out of components, with different implementations for each component, one needs to assemble the component choices. For example, there may be a mock database and a real database, or console logging and file logging. A particular implementation may want the real database and console logging for running an experiment, or the mock database and file logging for running an automated test script.

Usually, there is some dependency among the components. For example, the data access component may require logging.

Java has several tools that allow programmers to express dependencies through frameworks such as Spring or module systems such as OSGi. Each component describes on which other component interfaces it depends. References to actual component implementations are "injected" when the application is assembled.

In Scala, you can achieve a simple form of dependency injection with traits and self types.

For logging, suppose we have a trait

```
trait Logger { def log(msg: String) }
```

with implementations ConsoleLogger and FileLogger.

The user authentication trait has a logging dependency to log authentication failures:

```
trait Auth {
  this: Logger =>
    def login(id: String, password: String): Boolean
}
```

The application depends on both:

```
trait App {
  this: Logger with Auth =>
    ...
}
```

Now we can assemble an application as

```
object MyApp extends App with FileLogger("test.log") with MockAuth("users.txt")
```

It's a bit awkward to use trait composition in this way. After all, an application isn't an authenticator and a file logger. It has these components, and it is more natural to use instance variables for the components than to glue them all into one huge type. A better design is given by the *cake pattern*. In this pattern, you supply a component trait for each service that contains

- Any dependent components, expressed as self types
- A trait describing the service interface
- An abstract val that will be instantiated with an instance of the service
- Optionally, implementations of the service interface

```
trait LoggerComponent {
  trait Logger { ... }
  val logger: Logger
  class FileLogger(file: String) extends Logger { ... }
  ...
}

trait AuthComponent {
  this: LoggerComponent => // Gives access to logger

  trait Auth { ... }
  val auth: Auth
  class MockAuth(file: String) extends Auth { ... }
  ...
}
```

Note the use of the self type to indicate that the authentication component requires the logger component.

Now the component configuration can happen in one central place:

```
object AppComponents extends LoggerComponent with AuthComponent {
  val logger = new FileLogger("test.log")
  val auth = new MockAuth("users.txt")
}
```

Either approach is better than component wiring in an XML file because the compiler can verify that the module dependencies are satisfied.

19.12 Abstract Types L3

A class or trait can define an *abstract type* that is made concrete in a subclass. For example:

```
trait Reader {
  type Contents
  def read(fileName: String): Contents
}
```

Here, the type Contents is abstract. A concrete subclass needs to specify the type:

```
class StringReader extends Reader {
  type Contents = String
  def read(fileName: String) = Source.fromFile(fileName, "UTF-8").mkString
}

class ImageReader extends Reader {
  type Contents = BufferedImage
  def read(fileName: String) = ImageIO.read(new File(fileName))
}
```

The same effect could be achieved with a type parameter:

```
trait Reader[C] {
  def read(fileName: String): C
}

class StringReader extends Reader[String] {
  def read(fileName: String) = Source.fromFile(fileName, "UTF-8").mkString
}

class ImageReader extends Reader[BufferedImage] {
  def read(fileName: String) = ImageIO.read(new File(fileName))
}
```

Which is better? In Scala, the rule of thumb is:

- Use type parameters when the types are supplied as the class is instantiated. For example, when you construct a HashMap[String, Int], you want control over the types.

- Use abstract types when the types are expected to be supplied in a subclass. That is the case in our Reader example.

Nothing bad will happen if you specify type parameters as you form a subclass. But abstract types can work better when there are many type dependencies—you avoid long lists of type parameters. For example,

```
trait Reader {
  type In
  type Contents
  def read(in: In): Contents
}

class ImageReader extends Reader {
  type In = File
  type Contents = BufferedImage
  def read(file: In) = ImageIO.read(file)
}
```

With type parameters, ImageReader would extend Reader[File, BufferedImage]. That's still OK, but you can see that this technique doesn't scale so well in more complex situations.

Also, abstract types can express subtle interdependencies between types. The next section has an example.

Abstract types can have type bounds, just like type parameters. For example:

```
trait Listener {
  class EventObject { ... }
  type Event <: EventObject
  ...
}
```

A subclass must provide a compatible type, for example:

```
trait ActionListener extends Listener {
  class ActionEvent extends EventObject { ... }
  type Event = ActionEvent // OK, it's a subtype
  ...
}
```

Note that this example could not have been done with type parameters since the bound is an inner class.

19.13 Family Polymorphism L3

It is a challenge to model families of types that vary together, share common code, and preserve type safety. For example, consider event handling in client-side Java. There are different types of events (such as ActionEvent, ChangeEvent, and so on). Each type has a separate listener interface (ActionListener, ChangeListener, and so on). This is an example of "family polymorphism."

Let's design a generic mechanism for listener management. We'll start using generic types, and then switch to abstract types.

In Java, each listener interface has a different name for the method called when an event occurs: actionPerformed, stateChanged, itemStateChanged, and so on. We'll unify those:

```
trait Listener[E] {
  def occurred(e: E): Unit
}
```

An event source needs a collection of listeners, and a method to fire them all:

```
trait Source[E, L <: Listener[E]] {
  private val listeners = new ArrayBuffer[L]
  def add(l: L) { listeners += l }
  def remove(l: L) { listeners -= l }
  def fire(e: E) {
    for (l <- listeners) l.occurred(e)
  }
}
```

Now consider a button firing action events. We define a listener type

```
trait ActionListener extends Listener[ActionEvent]
```

The Button class can mix in the Source trait:

```
class Button extends Source[ActionEvent, ActionListener] {
  def click() {
    fire(new ActionEvent(this, ActionEvent.ACTION_PERFORMED, "click"))
  }
}
```

Mission accomplished: The Button class didn't need to replicate the code for listener management, and the listeners are typesafe. You can't add a ChangeListener to a button.

The ActionEvent class sets the event source to this, but the type of the event source is Object. We can make this typesafe with a self type:

```
trait Event[S] {
  var source: S = _
}

trait Listener[S, E <: Event[S]] {
  def occurred(e: E): Unit
}

trait Source[S, E <: Event[S], L <: Listener[S, E]] {
  this: S =>
  private val listeners = new ArrayBuffer[L]
  def add(l: L) { listeners += l }
  def remove(l: L) { listeners -= l }
  def fire(e: E) {
    e.source = this // Self type needed here
    for (l <- listeners) l.occurred(e)
  }
}
```

Note the self type this: S => that is required for setting the source to this. Otherwise, this would only be some Source, not necessarily the one required by Event[S].

Here is how you define a button:

```
class ButtonEvent extends Event[Button]

trait ButtonListener extends Listener[Button, ButtonEvent]

class Button extends Source[Button, ButtonEvent, ButtonListener] {
  def click() { fire(new ButtonEvent) }
}
```

You can see the proliferation of the type parameters. With abstract types, this looks a little nicer.

```
trait ListenerSupport {
  type S <: Source
  type E <: Event
  type L <: Listener

  trait Event {
    var source: S = _
  }

  trait Listener {
    def occurred(e: E): Unit
  }

  trait Source {
    this: S =>
      private val listeners = new ArrayBuffer[L]
    def add(l: L) { listeners += l }
    def remove(l: L) { listeners -= l }
    def fire(e: E) {
      e.source = this
      for (l <- listeners) l.occurred(e)
    }
  }
}
```

But there is a price to pay. You can't have top-level type declarations. That's why everything is wrapped in the ListenerSupport trait.

Now when you want to define a button with a button event and a button listener, enclose the definitions in a module that extends this trait:

```
object ButtonModule extends ListenerSupport {
  type S = Button
  type E = ButtonEvent
  type L = ButtonListener

  class ButtonEvent extends Event
  trait ButtonListener extends Listener
  class Button extends Source {
    def click() { fire(new ButtonEvent) }
  }
}
```

To use the button, import the module:

```
object Main {
  import ButtonModule._

  def main(args: Array[String]) {
    val b = new Button
    b.add(new ButtonListener {
      override def occurred(e: ButtonEvent) { println(e) }
    })
    b.click()
  }
}
```

 NOTE: In this example, I used single-letter names for the abstract types, to show the analogy with the version that uses type parameters. It is common in Scala to use more descriptive type names, which leads to more self-documenting code:

```
object ButtonModule extends ListenerSupport {
  type SourceType = Button
  type EventType = ButtonEvent
  type ListenerType = ButtonListener
  ...
}
```

19.14 Higher-Kinded Types L3

The generic type List depends on a type T and produces a type. For example, given the type Int, you get the type List[Int]. For that reason, a generic type such as List is sometimes called a *type constructor*. In Scala, you can go up another level and define types that depend on types that depend on types.

To see why this can be useful, consider the following simplified Iterable trait:

```
trait Iterable[E] {
  def iterator(): Iterator[E]
  def map[F](f: (E) => F): Iterable[F]
}
```

Now consider a class implementing this trait:

```
class Buffer[E] extends Iterable[E] {
  def iterator(): Iterator[E] = ...
  def map[F](f: (E) => F): Buffer[F] = ...
}
```

For a buffer, we expect that map returns a Buffer, not a mere Iterable. That means we cannot implement map in the Iterable trait itself, which we would like to do. A remedy is to parameterize the Iterable with a type constructor, like this:

```
trait Iterable[E, C[_]] {
  def iterator(): Iterator[E]
  def build[F](): C[F]
  def map[F](f : (E) => F) : C[F]
}
```

Now an Iterable depends on a type constructor for the result, denoted as C[_]. This makes Iterable a higher-kinded type.

The type returned by map may or may not be the same as the type of the Iterable on which map was invoked. For example, if you invoke map on a Range, the result is not generally a range, so map must construct a different type such as a Buffer[F]. Such a Range type is declared as

```
class Range extends Iterable[Int, Buffer]
```

Note that the second parameter is the type constructor Buffer.

To implement map in Iterable, we need a bit more support. An Iterable needs to be able to produce a container that holds values of any type F. Let's define a Container trait—it is something to which you can add values:

```
trait Container[E] {
  def +=(e: E): Unit
}
```

The build method is required to yield such an object:

```
trait Iterable[E, C[X] <: Container[X]] {
  def build[F](): C[F]
  ...
}
```

The type constructor C has now been constrained to be a Container, so we know that we can add items to the object that build returns. We can no longer use a wildcard for the parameter of C since we need to indicate that C[X] is a container for the same X.

 NOTE: The Container trait is a simpler version of the builder mechanism that is used in the Scala collections library.

The map method can be implemented in the Iterable trait:

```
def map[F](f : (E) => F) : C[F] = {
  val res = build[F]()
  val iter = iterator()
  while (iter.hasNext) res += f(iter.next())
  res
}
```

Iterable classes no longer need to supply their own map. Here is the Range class:

```
class Range(val low: Int, val high: Int) extends Iterable[Int, Buffer] {
  def iterator() = new Iterator[Int] {
    private var i = low
    def hasNext = i <= high
    def next() = { i += 1; i - 1 }
  }

  def build[F]() = new Buffer[F]
}
```

Note that a Range is an Iterable: You can iterate over its contents. But it is not a Container: You can't add values to it.

A Buffer, on the other hand, is both:

```
class Buffer[E : ClassTag] extends Iterable[E, Buffer] with Container[E] {
  private var capacity = 10
  private var length = 0
  private var elems = new Array[E](capacity) // See note

  def iterator() = new Iterator[E] {
    private var i = 0
    def hasNext = i < length
    def next() = { i += 1; elems(i - 1) }
  }

  def build[F : ClassTag]() = new Buffer[F]
```

```
def +=(e: E) {
  if (length == capacity) {
    capacity = 2 * capacity
    val nelems = new Array[E](capacity) // See note
    for (i <- 0 until length) nelems(i) = elems(i)
    elems = nelems
  }
  elems(length) = e
  length += 1
}
}
```

 NOTE: There is one additional complexity in this example, and it has nothing to do with higher-kinded types. In order to construct a generic Array[E], the type E must fulfill the ClassTag context bound that was discussed in Chapter 18.

 NOTE: To use higher-kinded types without a warning, add the statement import scala.language.higherKinds or use the compiler option -language:higherKinds.

This example showed a typical use of higher-kinded types. An Iterator depends on Container, but Container isn't a type—it is a mechanism for making types.

The Iterable trait of the Scala collections library doesn't have an explicit parameter for making collections. Instead, Scala uses an *implicit parameter* to conjure up an object for building the target collection. See Chapter 21 for more information.

Exercises

1. Implement a Bug class modeling a bug that moves along a horizontal line. The move method moves in the current direction, the turn method makes the bug turn around, and the show method prints the current position. Make these methods chainable. For example,

   ```
   bugsy.move(4).show().move(6).show().turn().move(5).show()
   ```

   should display 4 10 5.

2. Provide a fluent interface for the Bug class of the preceding exercise, so that one can write

   ```
   bugsy move 4 and show and then move 6 and show turn around move 5 and show
   ```

3. Complete the fluent interface in Section 19.1, "Singleton Types," on page 280 so that one can call

   ```
   book set Title to "Scala for the Impatient" set Author to "Cay Horstmann"
   ```

4. Implement the `equals` method for the `Member` class that is nested inside the `Network` class in Section 19.2, "Type Projections," on page 281. For two members to be equal, they need to be in the same network.

5. Consider the type alias

   ```
   type NetworkMember = n.Member forSome { val n: Network }
   ```

   and the function

   ```
   def process(m1: NetworkMember, m2: NetworkMember) = (m1, m2)
   ```

   How does this differ from the `process` function in Section 19.8, "Existential Types," on page 286?

6. The `Either` type in the Scala library can be used for algorithms that return either a result or some failure information. Write a function that takes two parameters: a sorted array of integers and an integer value. Return either the index of the value in the array or the index of the element that is closest to the value. Use an infix type as the return type.

7. Implement a method that receives an object of any class that has a method

   ```
   def close(): Unit
   ```

   together with a function that processes that object. Call the function and invoke the `close` method upon completion, or when any exception occurs.

8. Write a function `printValues` with three parameters f, from, to that prints all values of f with inputs from the given range. Here, f should be any object with an `apply` method that consumes and yields an `Int`. For example,

   ```
   printValues((x: Int) => x * x, 3, 6) // Prints 9 16 25 36
   printValues(Array(1, 1, 2, 3, 5, 8, 13, 21, 34, 55), 3, 6) // Prints 3 5 8 13
   ```

9. Consider this class that models a physical dimension:

   ```
   abstract class Dim[T](val value: Double, val name: String) {
     protected def create(v: Double): T
     def +(other: Dim[T]) = create(value + other.value)
     override def toString() = s"$value $name"
   }
   ```

   Here is a concrete subclass:

   ```
   class Seconds(v: Double) extends Dim[Seconds](v, "s") {
     override def create(v: Double) = new Seconds(v)
   }
   ```

But now a knucklehead could define

```
class Meters(v: Double) extends Dim[Seconds](v, "m") {
  override def create(v: Double) = new Seconds(v)
}
```

allowing meters and seconds to be added. Use a self type to prevent that.

10. Self types can usually be replaced with traits that extend classes, but there can be situations where using self types changes the initialization and override orders. Construct such an example.

Parsing

Chapter 20

In this chapter, you will see how to use the "parser combinators" library to analyze data with fixed structure. Examples of such data are programs in a programming language or data in formats such as HTTP or JSON. Not everyone needs to write parsers for these languages, so you may not find this chapter useful for your work. If you are familiar with the basic concepts of grammars and parsers, glance through the chapter anyway because the Scala parser library is a good example of a sophisticated *domain-specific language* embedded in the Scala language.

 NOTE: The API documentation for Scala parser combinators is at `www.scala-lang.org/api/current/scala-parser-combinators`.

The key points of this chapter are:

* Alternatives, concatenation, options, and repetitions in a grammar turn into `|`, `~`, `opt`, and `rep` in Scala combinator parsers.
* With `RegexParsers`, literal strings and regular expressions match tokens.
* Use `^^` to process parse results.
* Use pattern matching in a function supplied to `^^` to take apart `~` results.
* Use `~>` and `<~` to discard tokens that are no longer needed after matching.
* The `repsep` combinator handles the common case of repeated items with a separator.

- A token-based parser is useful for parsing languages with reserved words and operators. Be prepared to define your own lexer.

- Parsers are functions that consume a reader and yield a parse result: success, failure, or error.

- For a practical parser, you need to implement robust error reporting.

- Thanks to operator symbols, implicit conversions, and pattern matching, the parser combinator library makes parser writing easy for anyone who understands context-free grammars. Even if you don't feel the urge to write your own parsers, you may find this an interesting case study for an effective domain-specific language.

20.1 Grammars

To understand the Scala parsing library, you need to know a few concepts from the theory of formal languages. A *grammar* is a set of rules for producing all strings that follow a particular format. For example, we can say that an arithmetic expression is given by the following rules:

- Each whole number is an arithmetic expression.

- + - * are operators.

- If *left* and *right* are arithmetic expressions and *op* is an operator, then *left op right* is an arithmetic expression.

- If *expr* is an arithmetic expression, then (*expr*) is an arithmetic expression.

According to these rules, 3+4 and (3+4)*5 are arithmetic expressions, but 3+) or 3^4 or 3+x are not.

A grammar is usually written in a notation called Backus-Naur Form (BNF). Here is the BNF for our expression language:

```
op ::= "+" | "-" | "*"
expr ::= number | expr op expr | "(" expr ")"
```

Here, number is undefined. We could define it as

```
digit ::= "0" | "1" | "2" | "3" | "4" | "5" | "6" | "7" | "8" | "9"
number ::= digit | digit number
```

But in practice, it is more efficient to collect numbers before parsing starts, in a separate step called *lexical analysis*. A *lexer* discards whitespace and comments, and forms *tokens*—identifiers, numbers, or symbols. In our expression language, tokens are number and the symbols + - * ( ).

Note that op and expr are not tokens. They are structural elements that were invented by the author of the grammar, in order to produce correct token sequences.

Such symbols are called *nonterminal symbols*. One of the nonterminal symbols is at the root of the hierarchy; in our case, that is expr. It is called the *start symbol*. To produce correctly formatted strings, you start with the start symbol and apply the grammar rules until all nonterminals have been replaced and only tokens remain. For example, the derivation

```
expr -> expr op expr -> number op expr ->
  -> number "+" expr -> number "+" number
```

shows that 3+4 is a valid expression.

The most often used "extended Backus-Naur form," or EBNF, allows specifying optional elements and repetition. I will use the familiar regex operators ? * + for 0 or 1, 0 or more, 1 or more, correspondingly. For example, a comma-separated list of numbers can be described with the grammar

```
numberList ::= number ( "," numberList )?
```

or with

```
numberList ::= number ( "," number )*
```

As another example of EBNF, let's make an improvement to the grammar for arithmetic expressions to support operator precedence. Here is the revised grammar:

```
expr ::= term ( ( "+" | "-" ) expr )?
term ::= factor ( "*" factor )*
factor ::= number | "(" expr ")"
```

20.2 Combining Parser Operations

To use the Scala parsing library, provide a class that extends the Parsers trait and defines parsing operations that are combined from primitive operations, such as

- Matching a token
- Choosing between two operations (|)
- Performing two operations in sequence (~)
- Repeating an operation (rep)
- Optionally performing an operation (opt)

The following parser recognizes arithmetic expressions. It extends RegexParsers, a subtrait of Parsers that can match tokens against regular expressions. Here, we specify number with the regular expression "[0-9]+".r:

```
class ExprParser extends RegexParsers {
  val number = "[0-9]+".r

  def expr: Parser[Any] = term ~ opt(("+" | "-") ~ expr)
  def term: Parser[Any] = factor ~ rep("*" ~ factor)
  def factor: Parser[Any] = number | "(" ~ expr ~ ")"
}
```

Note that the parser is a straightforward translation from the EBNF of the preceding section.

Simply use the ~ operator to join the parts, and use opt and rep instead of ? and *.

In our example, each function has return type Parser[Any]. This type isn't very useful, and we will improve it in the next section.

To run the parser, invoke the inherited parse method, for example:

```
val parser = new ExprParser
val result = parser.parseAll(parser.expr, "3-4*5")
if (result.successful) println(result.get)
```

The parseAll method receives the method to be invoked—that is, the method associated with the grammar's start symbol—and the string to be parsed.

 NOTE: There is also a parse method that parses a prefix of a string, stopping when it can't find another match. That method isn't very useful; for example, parser.parse(parser.expr, "3-4/5") parses 3-4, then quietly stops at the / which it cannot handle.

The output of the program snippet is

```
((3~List())~Some((-~((4~List((*~5)))~None))))
```

To interpret this output, you need to know the following:

- Literal strings and regular expressions return String values.
- p ~ q returns an instance of the ~ case class, which is very similar to a pair.
- opt(p) returns an Option, either Some(...) or None.
- rep(p) returns a List.

The call to expr returns the result from term (shown in bold) joined with something optional—the Some(...) part which I won't analyze.

Since term is defined as

```
def term = factor ~ rep(("*" | "/" ) ~ factor)
```

it returns the result from factor joined with a List. That's an empty list because there is no * in the subexpression to the left of the -.

Of course, this result is quite tedious. In the next section, you will see how to transform it to something more useful.

20.3 Transforming Parser Results

Instead of having a parser build up a complex structure of ~, options, and lists, you should transform intermediate outputs to a useful form. Consider, for example, the arithmetic expression parser. If it is our goal to evaluate the expression, then each of the functions expr, term, and factor should return the value of the parsed subexpression. Let's start with

```
def factor: Parser[Any] = number | "(" ~ expr ~ ")"
```

We want it to return an Int:

```
def factor: Parser[Int] = ...
```

When a whole number is received, we want its integer value:

```
def factor: Parser[Int] = number ^^ { _.toInt } | ...
```

Here, the ^^ operator applies the function { _.toInt } to the result of number.

NOTE: There is no particular significance to the ^^ symbol. It conveniently has lower precedence than ~ but higher precedence than |.

Assuming that expr has been changed to return a Parser[Int], we can evaluate "(" ~ expr ~ ")" simply by returning expr, which yields an Int. Here is one way of doing that (you'll see a simpler one in the next section):

```
def factor: Parser[Int] = ... | "(" ~ expr ~ ")" ^^ {
  case _ ~ e ~ _ => e
}
```

In this case, the argument of the ^^ operator is the partial function { case _ ~ e ~ _ => e }.

NOTE: The ~ combinator returns an instance of the ~ case class instead of a pair to make matching easier. If ~ returned a pair, then you would have to write case ((_, e), _) instead of case _ ~ e ~ _.

A similar pattern match yields the sum or difference. Note that opt yields an Option: either None or Some(...).

```
def expr: Parser[Int] = term ~ opt(("+" | "-") ~ expr) ^^ {
  case t ~ None => t
  case t ~ Some("+" ~ e) => t + e
  case t ~ Some("-" ~ e) => t - e
}
```

Finally, to multiply the factors, note that rep("*" ~ factor) yields a List of items of the form "*" ~ f, where f is an Int. We extract the second component of each ~ pair and compute their product:

```
def term: Parser[Int] = factor ~ rep("*" ~ factor) ^^ {
  case f ~ r => f * r.map(_._2).product
}
```

In this example, we simply computed the value of the expression. When building a compiler or interpreter, the usual goal is to build a *parse tree*—a tree structure that describes the parsed result; see Section 20.5, "Generating Parse Trees," on page 309.

 CAUTION: If you turn off the warning against postfix operators, you can write p? instead of opt(p) and p* instead of rep(p):

```
def expr: Parser[Any] = term ~ (("+" | "-") ~ expr)?
def term: Parser[Any] = factor ~ ("*" ~ factor)*
```

It seems a good idea to use these familiar operators, but they conflict with the ^^ operator. You'll have to add another set of parentheses, such as

```
def term: Parser[Any] = factor ~ (("*" ~ factor)*) ^^ { ... }
```

For that reason, I prefer opt and rep.

20.4 Discarding Tokens

As you saw in the preceding section, it can be tedious to deal with tokens when analyzing a match. The tokens are required for parsing, but they can often be discarded after they have been matched. The ~> and <~ operators are used to match and discard a token. For example, the result of "*" ~> factor is just the result of factor, not a value of the form "*" ~ f. With that notation, we can simplify the term function to

```
def term = factor ~ rep("*" ~> factor) ^^ {
  case f ~ r => f * r.product
}
```

Similarly, we can discard the parentheses around an expression, like this:

```
def factor = number ^^ { _.toInt } | "(" ~> expr <~ ")"
```

A transformation is no longer required in the expression "(" ~> expr <~ ")", since the value is now simply e, which already yields an Int.

Note that the "arrow tip" of the ~> or <~ operator points to the part that is retained.

 CAUTION: You need to be careful when using multiple ~, ~>, and <~ in the same expression. <~ has a lower precedence than ~ and ~>. Consider, for example:

```
"if" ~> "(" ~> expr <~ ")" ~ expr
```

Unfortunately, this doesn't just discard ")", but the subexpression ")" ~ expr. The remedy is to use parentheses: "if" ~> "(" ~> (expr <~ ")") ~ expr.

20.5 Generating Parse Trees

The parsers of the preceding examples simply computed numeric results. When you build an interpreter or compiler, you will want to build up a parse tree instead. This is usually done with case classes. For example, the following classes can represent an arithmetic expression:

```
class Expr
case class Number(value: Int) extends Expr
case class Operator(op: String, left: Expr, right: Expr) extends Expr
```

The parser's job is to turn an input such as 3+4*5 into a value

```
Operator("+", Number(3), Operator("*", Number(4), Number(5)))
```

In an interpreter, such an expression can be evaluated. In a compiler, it can be used for generating code.

To generate a parse tree, use ^^ with functions that yield tree nodes. For example,

```
class ExprParser extends RegexParsers {
  ...
  def term: Parser[Expr] = (factor ~ opt("*" ~> term)) ^^ {
    case a ~ None => a
    case a ~ Some(b) => Operator("*", a, b)
  }
  def factor: Parser[Expr] = wholeNumber ^^ (n => Number(n.toInt)) |
    "(" ~> expr <~ ")"
}
```

20.6 Avoiding Left Recursion

If a parser function calls itself without first consuming some input, the recursion will never stop. Consider this function that is supposed to consume any sequence of ones:

```
def ones: Parser[Any] = ones ~ "1" | "1"
```

Such a function is called *left-recursive*. To avoid the recursion, you can reformulate the grammar. Here are two alternatives:

```
def ones: Parser[Any] = "1" ~ ones | "1"
```

or

```
def ones: Parser[Any] = rep1("1")
```

This problem occurs commonly in practice. For example, consider our arithmetic expression parser:

```
def expr: Parser[Any] = term ~ opt(("+" | "-") ~ expr)
```

The rule for expr has an unfortunate effect with subtraction. The expressions are grouped in the wrong order. When the input is 3-4-5, the expression is parsed as

```
      -
     / \
    3   -
       / \
      4   5
```

That is, 3 is accepted as term, and -4-5 as "-" ~ expr. This yields a wrong answer of 4 instead of -6.

Could we turn the grammar around?

```
def expr: Parser[Any] = expr ~ opt(("+" | "-") ~ term)
```

Then we would get the correct parse tree. But that doesn't work—this expr function is left-recursive.

The original version eliminates the left recursion, but at a cost—it is harder to compute the parse result. You need to collect the intermediate results and then combine them in the correct order.

Collecting intermediate results is easier if you can use a repetition, which yields a List of the collected values. For example, an expr is a sequence of term values, joined by + or -:

```
def expr: Parser[Any] = term ~ rep(("+" | "-") ~ term)
```

To evaluate the expression, replace each s ~ t in the repetition with t or -t, depending on whether s is "+" or "-". Then compute the sum of the list.

```
def expr: Parser[Int] = term ~ rep(
  ("+" | "-") ~ term ^^ {
    case "+" ~ t => t
    case "-" ~ t => -t
  }) ^^ { case t ~ r => t + r.sum }
```

If rewriting the grammar is too cumbersome, see Section 20.9, "Packrat Parsers," on page 314 for another remedy.

20.7 More Combinators

The rep method matches zero or more repetitions. Table 20–1 shows several variations of this combinator. The most commonly used among them is repsep. For example, a list of comma-separated numbers can be defined as

```
def numberList = number ~ rep("," ~> number)
```

or more concisely as

```
def numberList = repsep(number, ",")
```

Table 20–2 shows additional combinators that are occasionally useful. The into combinator can come in handy to store information from an earlier combinator in a variable so that it can be used later. For example, in the grammar rule

```
def term: Parser[Any] = factor ~ rep("*" ~> factor)
```

you can store the first factor in a variable, like this:

```
def term: Parser[Int] = factor into { first =>
  rep("*" ~> factor) ^^ { first * _.product }
}
```

The log combinator can help debug a grammar. Replace a parser p with log(p)(str), and you get a printout whenever p is called. For example,

```
def factor: Parser[Int] = log(number)("number") ^^ { _.toInt } | ...
```

yields outputs such as

```
trying number at scala.util.parsing.input.CharSequenceReader@76f7c5
number --> [1.2] parsed: 3
```

Table 20–1 Combinators for Repetitions

Combinator	Description	Notes
rep(p)	0 or more matches of p.	
rep1(p)	1 or more matches of p.	rep1("[" ~> expr <~ "]") yields a list of expressions that were included inside brackets—for example, to specify bounds of a multidimensional array.
rep1(p, q), p and q are Parser[P]	1 match of p followed by 0 or more matches of q.	
repN(n, p)	n matches of p.	repN(4, number) matches a sequence of four numbers—for example, to specify a rectangle.
repsep(p, s) rep1sep(p, s) p is a Parser[P]	0 or more/1 or more matches of p, separated by matches of s. The result is a List[P]; the s are discarded.	repsep(expr, ",") yields a list of expressions that were separated by commas. Useful for parsing the arguments to a function call.
chainl1(p, s)	Like rep1sep, but s must, upon matching each separator, produce a binary function that is used to combine neighboring values. If p produces values v_0, v_1, v_2, . . . and s produces functions $f_1, f_2, . . .$, then the result is $(v_0\, f_1\, v_1)\, f_2\, v_2\, . . .$	chainl1(number ^^ { _.toInt }, "*" ^^ { _ * _ }) computes the product of a sequence of integers separated by *.

Table 20–2 Additional Combinators

Combinator	Description	Notes
p ^^^ v	Like ^^, but returns a constant result.	Useful for parsing literals: "true" ^^^ true.
p into f or p >> f	f is a function whose argument is the result of p. Useful to bind the result of p to a variable.	(number ^^ { _.toInt }) >> { n => repN(n, number) } parses a sequence of numbers, where the first number indicates how many numbers follow.

(Continues)

Table 20–2 Additional Combinators *(Continued)*

Combinator	Description	Notes
p ∧? f p ∧? (f, error)	Like ∧∧, but takes a partial function f. Fails if f can't be applied to the result of p. In the second version, error is a function from the result type of p, yielding an error message string.	ident ∧? (symbols, "undefined symbol " + _) looks up ident in the map symbols and reports an error if it is not contained in the map. Note that a map can be converted to a partial function.
log(p)(str)	Executes p and prints a logging message.	log(number)("number") ∧∧ { _.toInt } prints a message whenever a number is parsed.
guard(p)	Calls p, succeeds or fails, then restores the input as if p had not been called.	Useful for looking ahead. For example, to distinguish between a variable and a function call, you can use a guard(ident ~ "(").
not(p)	Calls p and succeeds if p fails, or fails if p succeeds.	
p ~! q	Like ~, but if the second match fails, the failure turns into an error, inhibiting backtracking in an enclosing |.	See Section 20.8.
accept(descr, f)	Accepts an item that is accepted by the partial function f, returning the function result. The string descr is used to describe the expected item in the failure message.	accept("string literal", { case t: lexical.StringLit => t.chars })
success(v)	Always succeeds with value v.	Can be used to add a value v to a result.
failure(msg) err(msg)	Fails with the given error message.	See Section 20.13 on how to improve error messages.
phrase(p)	Succeeds if p succeeds and no input is left over.	Useful for defining a parseAll method; see, for example, Section 20.12.
positioned(p)	Adds position to the result of p (must extend Positional).	Useful for reporting errors after parsing has finished.

20.8 Avoiding Backtracking

Whenever an alternative p | q is parsed and p fails, the parser tries q on the same input. This is called *backtracking*. Backtracking also happens when there is a failure in an opt or rep. Clearly, backtracking can be inefficient. For example, consider an arithmetic expression parser with the rules

```
def expr: Parser[Any] = term ~ ("+" | "-") ~ expr | term
def term: Parser[Any] = factor ~ "*" ~ term | factor
def factor: Parser[Any] = "(" ~ expr ~ ")" | number
```

If the expression (3+4)*5 is parsed, then term matches the entire input. Then the match for + or - fails, and the compiler backtracks to the second alternative, parsing term again.

It is often possible to rearrange the grammar rules to avoid backtracking. For example:

```
def expr: Parser[Any] = term ~ opt(("+" | "-") ~ expr)
def term: Parser[Any] = factor ~ rep("*" ~ factor)
```

You can then use the ~! operator instead of ~ to express that there is no need to backtrack.

```
def expr: Parser[Any] = term ~ opt(("+" | "-") ~! expr)
def term: Parser[Any] = factor ~ rep("*" ~! factor)
def factor: Parser[Any] = "(" ~! expr ~! ")" | number
```

When p ~! q is evaluated and q fails, no other alternatives are tried in an enclosing |, opt, or rep. For example, if factor finds a "(" and then expr doesn't match, the parser won't even try matching number.

20.9 Packrat Parsers

A packrat parser uses an efficient parsing algorithm that caches previous parse results. This has two advantages:

- Parse time is guaranteed to be proportional to the length of the input.

- The parser can accept left-recursive grammars.

In order to use packrat parsing in Scala, follow these steps:

1. Mix the PackratParsers trait into your parser.

2. Use val or lazy val, not def, for each parser function. This is important because the parser caches these values, and it relies on them being identical. (A def would return a different value each time it is called.)

3. Have each parser function return PackratParser[T] instead of Parser[T].

4. Use a PackratReader and supply a parseAll method (which is annoyingly missing from the PackratParsers trait).

For example,

```
class OnesPackratParser extends RegexParsers with PackratParsers {
  lazy val ones: PackratParser[Any] = ones ~ "1" | "1"

  def parseAll[T](p: Parser[T], input: String) =
    phrase(p)(new PackratReader(new CharSequenceReader(input)))
}
```

20.10 What Exactly Are Parsers?

Technically, a Parser[T] is a function with one argument, of type Reader[Elem], and a return value of type ParseResult[T]. In this section, we will have a closer look at these types.

The type Elem is an abstract type of the Parsers trait. (See Section 19.12, "Abstract Types," on page 291 for more information about abstract types.) The RegexParsers trait defines Elem as Char, and the StdTokenParsers trait defines Elem as Token. (We will have a look at token-based parsing in Section 20.12, "Token-Based Parsers," on page 317.)

A Reader[Elem] reads a sequence of Elem values (that is, characters or tokens) from some source and tracks their positions for error reporting.

When a Parser[T] is invoked on a reader, it returns an object of one of three subclasses of ParseResult[T]: Success[T], Failure, or Error.

An Error terminates the parser and anything that called it. It can arise in one of these circumstances:

• A parser p ~! q fails to match q.

• A commit(p) fails.

• The err(msg) combinator is encountered.

A Failure simply arises from a failure to match; it normally triggers alternatives in an enclosing |.

A Success[T] has, most importantly, a result of type T. It also has a Reader[Elem] called next, containing the input beyond the match that is yet to be consumed.

Consider this part of our arithmetic expression parser:

```
val number = "[0-9]+".r
def expr = number | "(" ~ expr ~ ")"
```

Our parser extends RegexParsers, which has an implicit conversion from a Regex to a Parser[String]. The regular expression number is converted into such a parser—a function that consumes a Reader[Char].

If the initial characters in the reader match the regular expression, the function returns a Success[String]. The result property of the returned object is the matched input, and the next property is the reader with the match removed.

If the initial characters in the reader don't match the regular expression, the parser function returns a Failure object.

The | method combines two parsers. That is, if p and q are functions, then p | q is again a function. The combined function consumes a reader, say r. It calls p(r). If that call returns Success or Error, then that's the return value of p | q. Otherwise, the return value is the result of q(r).

20.11 Regex Parsers

The RegexParsers trait, which we have used in all examples up to this point, provides two implicit conversions for defining parsers:

- literal makes a Parser[String] from a literal string (such as "+").

- regex makes a Parser[String] from a regular expression (such as "[0-9]".r).

By default, regex parsers skip whitespace. If your notion of whitespace is different from the default of """\s+""".r (for example, if you want to skip comments), override whiteSpace with your definition. If you don't want whitespace skipped, use

```
override val whiteSpace = "".r
```

The JavaTokenParsers trait extends RegexParsers and specifies five tokens, shown in Table 20–3. None of them correspond exactly to their Java forms, which makes that trait of limited utility.

Table 20–3 Predefined Tokens in JavaTokenParsers

Token	Regular Expression
ident	[a-zA-Z_]\w*
wholeNumber	-?\d+
decimalNumber	\d+(\.\d*)?|\d*\.\d+
stringLiteral	"([^"\p{Cntrl}\\]|\\[\\/bfnrt]|\\u[a-fA-F0-9]{4})*"
floatingPointNumber	-?(\d+(\.\d*)?|\d*\.\d+)([eE][+-]?\d+)?[fFdD]?

20.12 Token–Based Parsers

Token-based parsers use a `Reader[Token]` instead of a `Reader[Char]`. The `Token` type is defined in the trait `scala.util.parsing.combinator.token.Tokens`. The `StdTokens` subtrait defines four types of tokens that one commonly finds when parsing a programming language:

- `Identifier`
- `Keyword`
- `NumericLit`
- `StringLit`

The `StandardTokenParsers` class provides a parser that produces these tokens. Identifiers consist of letters, digits, or _ but don't start with a digit.

 CAUTION: The rules for letters and digits are subtly different from those in Java or Scala. Digits in any script are supported, but letters in the "supplementary" range (above U+FFFF) are excluded.

Numeric literals are sequences of digits. String literals are enclosed in "..." or '...', with no escapes. Comments, enclosed in /* ... */ or from // to the end of the line, are considered whitespace.

When you extend this parser, add any reserved words and special tokens to the `lexical.reserved` and `lexical.delimiters` sets:

```
class MyLanguageParser extends StandardTokenParser {
  lexical.reserved += ("auto", "break", "case", "char", "const", ...)
  lexical.delimiters += ("=", "<", "<=", ">", ">=", "==", "!=", ...)
  ...
}
```

When a reserved word is encountered, it becomes a `Keyword`, not an `Identifier`.

The parser sorts the delimiters according to the "maximum munch" rule. For example, when the input contains <=, you will get that as a single token, not as a sequence of tokens < and =.

The `ident` function parses an identifier; `numericLit` and `stringLit` parse literals.

For example, here is our arithmetic expression grammar, using `StandardTokenParsers`:

```
class ExprParser extends StandardTokenParsers {
  lexical.delimiters += ("+", "-", "*", "(", ")")

  def expr: Parser[Any] = term ~ rep(("+" | "-") ~ term)
  def term: Parser[Any] = factor ~ rep("*" ~> factor)
```

```
    def factor: Parser[Any] = numericLit  | "(" ~> expr <~ ")"

    def parseAll[T](p: Parser[T], in: String): ParseResult[T] =
      phrase(p)(new lexical.Scanner(in))
  }
```

Note that you need to supply a parseAll method, which is annoyingly missing from the StandardTokenParsers class. In that method, you use a lexical.Scanner, which is the Reader[Token] supplied by the StdLexical trait.

TIP: If you need to process a language with different tokens, it is easy to adapt the token parser. Extend StdLexical and override the token method to recognize the token types you need. Consult the source code of StdLexical for guidance—it is quite short. Then extend StdTokenParsers and override lexical:

```
    class MyParser extends StdTokenParsers {
      val lexical = new MyLexical

      ...

    }
```

TIP: The token method in StdLexical is a bit tedious. It's nicer to define tokens with regular expressions. Add this definition when you extend StdLexical:

```
    def regex(r: Regex): Parser[String] = new Parser[String] {
      def apply(in: Input) = r.findPrefixMatchOf(
        in.source.subSequence(in.offset, in.source.length)) match {
          case Some(matched) =>
            Success(in.source.subSequence(in.offset,
              in.offset + matched.end).toString, in.drop(matched.end))
          case None =>
            Failure("string matching regex `$r' expected but
              ${in.first} found", in)
        }
    }
```

Then you can use regular expressions in your token method, like this:

```
    override def token: Parser[Token] = {
      regex("[a-z][a-zA-Z0-9]*".r) ^^ { processIdent(_) } |
      regex("0|[1-9][0-9]*".r) ^^ { NumericLit(_) } |

      ...

    }
```

20.13 Error Handling

When a parser can't accept an input, you want to get an accurate message indicating where the failure occurred.

The parser generates an error message that describes the position at which the parser was unable to continue. If there were several failure points, the one that was visited last is reported.

You may want to keep error reporting in mind when you order alternatives. For example, if you have a rule

```
def value: Parser[Any] = numericLit | "true" | "false"
```

and the parser doesn't match any of them, then it's not so useful to know that the input failed to match "false". You can add a failure clause with an explicit error message:

```
def value: Parser[Any] = numericLit | "true" | "false" |
    failure("Not a valid value")
```

The failure combinator only reports an error when it is visited. It does not change the error messages that another combinator reports. For example, a RegexParser has an error message such as

```
string matching regex `\d+' expected but `x' found
```

Then use the withFailureMessage method, like this:

```
def value = opt(sign) ~ digits withFailureMessage "Not a valid number"
```

When the parser fails, the parseAll method returns a Failure result. Its msg property is an error message that you can display to the user. The next property is the Reader that points to the unconsumed input at the point of failure. You will want to display the line number and column, which are available as next.pos.line and next.pos.column.

Finally, next.first is the lexical element at which the failure occurred. If you use the RegexParsers trait, that element is a Char, which is not very useful for error reporting. But with a token parser, next.first is a token, which is worth reporting.

 TIP: If you want to report errors that you detect after a successful parse (such as type errors in a programming language), use the positioned combinator to add a position to a parse result. The result type must extend the Positional trait. For example,

```
def vardecl = "var" ~ positioned(ident ^^ { Ident(_) }) ~ "=" ~ value
```

Exercises

1. Add / and % operations to the arithmetic expression evaluator.

2. Add a ∧ operator to the arithmetic expression evaluator. As in mathematics, ∧ should have a higher precedence than multiplication, and it should be right-associative. That is, 4∧2∧3 should be 4∧(2∧3), or 65536.

3. Write a parser that parses a list of integers (such as (1, 23, -79)) into a List[Int].

4. Write a parser that can parse date and time expressions in ISO 8601. Your parser should return a java.time.LocalDateTime object.

5. Write a parser that parses a subset of XML. Handle tags of the form <ident> ... </ident> or <ident/>. Tags can be nested. Handle attributes inside tags. Attribute values can be delimited by single or double quotes. You don't need to deal with character data (that is, text inside tags or CDATA sections). Your parser should return a Scala XML Elem value. The challenge is to reject mismatched tags. Hint: into, accept.

6. Assume that the parser in Section 20.5, "Generating Parse Trees," on page 309 is completed with

   ```
   class ExprParser extends RegexParsers {
     def expr: Parser[Expr] = (term ~ opt(("+" | "-") ~ expr)) ^^ {
       case a ~ None => a
       case a ~ Some(op ~ b) => Operator(op, a, b)
     }
     ...
   }
   ```

   Unfortunately, this parser computes an incorrect expression tree—operators with the same precedence are evaluated right-to-left. Modify the parser so that the expression tree is correct. For example, 3-4-5 should yield an Operator("-", Operator("-", 3, 4), 5).

7. Suppose in Section 20.6, "Avoiding Left Recursion," on page 310, we first parse an expr into a list of ~ with operations and values:

   ```
   def expr: Parser[Int] = term ~ rep(("+" | "-") ~ term) ^^ {...}
   ```

   To evaluate the result, we need to compute $((t_0 \pm t_1) \pm t_2) \pm \ldots$ Implement this computation as a fold (see Chapter 13).

8. Add variables and assignment to the calculator program. Variables are created when they are first used. Uninitialized variables are zero. To print a value, assign it to the special variable out.

9. Extend the preceding exercise into a parser for a programming language that has variable assignments, Boolean expressions, and if/else and while statements.

10. Add function definitions to the programming language of the preceding exercise.

Implicits

Chapter 21

Implicit conversions and implicit parameters are Scala's power tools that do useful work behind the scenes. In this chapter, you will learn how implicit conversions can be used to enrich existing classes, and how implicit objects are summoned automatically to carry out conversions or other tasks. With implicits, you can provide elegant libraries that hide tedious details from library users.

The key points of this chapter are:

- Implicit conversions are used to convert between types.

- You must import implicit conversions so that they are in scope.

- An implicit parameter list requests objects of a given type. They can be obtained from implicit objects that are in scope, or from the companion object of the desired type.

- If an implicit parameter is a single-argument function, it is also used as an implicit conversion.

- A context bound of a type parameter requires the existence of an implicit object of the given type.

- If it is possible to locate an implicit object, this can serve as evidence that a type conversion is valid.

21.1 Implicit Conversions

An *implicit conversion function* is a function with a single parameter that is declared with the `implicit` keyword. As the name suggests, such a function is automatically applied to convert values from one type to another.

Consider the `Fraction` class from Section 11.2, "Infix Operators," on page 143 with a method `*` for multiplying a fraction with another. We want to convert integers *n* to fractions *n* / 1.

```
implicit def int2Fraction(n: Int) = Fraction(n, 1)
```

Now we can evaluate

```
val result = 3 * Fraction(4, 5) // Calls int2Fraction(3)
```

The implicit conversion function turns the integer 3 into a `Fraction` object. That object is then multiplied by `Fraction(4, 5)`.

You can give any name to the conversion function. Since you don't call it explicitly, you may be tempted to use something short such as `i2f`. But, as you will see in Section 21.3, "Importing Implicits," on page 325, sometimes it is useful to import a conversion function. I suggest that you stick with the *source2target* convention.

Scala is not the first language that allows the programmer to provide automatic conversions. However, Scala gives programmers a great deal of control over when to apply these conversions. In the following sections, we will discuss exactly when the conversions happen, and how you can fine-tune the process.

NOTE: Even though Scala gives you tools to fine-tune implicit conversions, the language designers realize that implicit conversions are potentially problematic. To avoid a warning when using implicit functions, add the statement `import scala.language.implicitConversions` or the compiler option `-language:implicitConversions`.

NOTE: In C++, you specify implicit conversions as one-argument constructors or member functions with the name `operator` *Type*(). However, in C++, you cannot selectively allow or disallow these functions, and it is common to run into unwanted conversions.

21.2 Using Implicits for Enriching Existing Classes

Did you ever wish that a class had a method its creator failed to provide? For example, wouldn't it be nice if the `java.io.File` class had a `read` method for reading a file:

```
val contents = new File("README").read
```

As a Java programmer, your only recourse is to petition Oracle Corporation to add that method. Good luck!

In Scala, you can define an enriched class that provides what you want:

```
class RichFile(val from: File) {
  def read = Source.fromFile(from.getPath).mkString
}
```

Then, provide an implicit conversion to that type:

```
implicit def file2RichFile(from: File) = new RichFile(from)
```

Now it is possible to call read on a File object. It is implicitly converted to a RichFile.

Instead of providing a conversion function, you can declare RichFile as an implicit class:

```
implicit class RichFile(val from: File) { ... }
```

An implicit class must have a primary constructor with exactly one argument. That constructor becomes the implicit conversion function.

It is a good idea to declare the enriched class as a value class:

```
implicit class RichFile(val from: File) extends AnyVal { ... }
```

In that case, no RichFile objects are created. A call file.read is directly compiled into a static method call RichFile$.read$extension(file).

 CAUTION: An implicit class cannot be a top-level class. You can place it inside the class that uses the type conversion, or inside another object or class that you import, as explained in the next section.

21.3 Importing Implicits

Scala will consider the following implicit conversion functions:

1. Implicit functions or classes in the companion object of the source or target type

2. Implicit functions or classes that are in scope

For example, consider the int2Fraction function. We can place it into the Fraction companion object, and it will be available for converting fractions.

Alternatively, let's suppose we put it inside a FractionConversions object, which we define in the com.horstmann.impatient package. If you want to use the conversion, import the FractionConversions object, like this:

```
import com.horstmann.impatient.FractionConversions._
```

For an implicit conversion to be in scope, it must be imported *without a prefix*. For example, if you import com.horstmann.impatient.FractionConversions or com.horstmann, then the int2Fraction method is in scope as FractionConversions.int2Fraction or impatient.FractionConversions.int2Fraction, to anyone who wants to call it explicitly. But if the function is not available as int2Fraction, without a prefix, the compiler won't use it implicitly.

 TIP: In the REPL, type :implicits to see all implicits that have been imported from a source other than Predef, or :implicits -v to see all implicits.

You can localize the import to minimize unintended conversions. For example,

```
object Main extends App {
  import com.horstmann.impatient.FractionConversions._
  val result = 3 * Fraction(4, 5) // Uses imported conversion
  println(result)
}
```

You can even select the specific conversions that you want. Suppose you have a second conversion

```
object FractionConversions {
  ...
  implicit def fraction2Double(f: Fraction) = f.num * 1.0 / f.den
}
```

If you prefer this conversion over int2Fraction, you can import it:

```
import com.horstmann.impatient.FractionConversions.fraction2Double
val result = 3 * Fraction(4, 5) // result is 2.4
```

You can also exclude a specific conversion if it causes you trouble:

```
import com.horstmann.impatient.FractionConversions.{fraction2Double => _, _}
  // Imports everything but fraction2Double
```

 TIP: If you want to find out why the compiler *doesn't* use an implicit conversion that you think it should use, try adding it explicitly, for example by calling fraction2Double(3) * Fraction(4, 5). You may get an error message that shows the problem.

21.4 Rules for Implicit Conversions

In this section, you will see when implicit conversions are attempted. To illustrate the rules, we again use the Fraction class and assume that the implicit conversions int2Fraction and fraction2Double are both available.

Implicit conversions are considered in three distinct situations:

- If the type of an expression differs from the expected type:

  ```
  3 * Fraction(4, 5) // Calls fraction2Double
  ```

  The Int class doesn't have a method *(Fraction), but it has a method *(Double).

- If an object accesses a nonexistent member:

  ```
  3.den // Calls int2Fraction
  ```

  The Int class doesn't have a den member but the Fraction class does.

- If an object invokes a method whose parameters don't match the given arguments:

  ```
  Fraction(4, 5) * 3
    // Calls int2Fraction
  ```

  The * method of Fraction doesn't accept an Int but it accepts a Fraction.

On the other hand, there are three situations when an implicit conversion is *not* attempted:

- No implicit conversion is used if the code compiles without it. For example, if a * b compiles, the compiler won't try a * convert(b) or convert(a) * b.

- The compiler will never attempt multiple conversions, such as convert1(convert2(a)) * b.

- Ambiguous conversions are an error. For example, if both convert1(a) * b and convert2(a) * b are valid, the compiler will report an error.

 CAUTION: It is *not* an ambiguity that

```
3 * Fraction(4, 5)
```

could be either

```
3 * fraction2Double(Fraction(4, 5))
```

or

```
int2Fraction(3) * Fraction(4, 5)
```

The first conversion wins over the second, since it does not require modification of the object to which the * method is applied.

 TIP: If you want to find out which implicit conversion the compiler uses, compile your program as

```
scalac -Xprint:typer MyProg.scala
```

You will see the source after implicit conversions have been added.

21.5 Implicit Parameters

A function or method can have a parameter list that is marked `implicit`. In that case, the compiler will look for default values to supply with the function call. Here is a simple example:

```
case class Delimiters(left: String, right: String)

def quote(what: String)(implicit delims: Delimiters) =
  delims.left + what + delims.right
```

You can call the `quote` method with an explicit `Delimiters` object, like this:

```
quote("Bonjour le monde")(Delimiters("«", "»")) // Returns «Bonjour le monde»
```

Note that there are two argument lists. This function is "curried"—see Chapter 12.

You can also omit the implicit parameter list:

```
quote("Bonjour le monde")
```

In that case, the compiler will look for an implicit value of type `Delimiters`. This must be a value that is declared as `implicit`. The compiler looks for such an object in two places:

* Among all `val` and `def` of the desired type that are in scope without a prefix.
* In the companion object of a type that is *associated* with the desired type. Associated types include the desired type itself and, if it is a parameterized type, its type parameters.

In our example, it is useful to make an object, such as

```
object FrenchPunctuation {
  implicit val quoteDelimiters = Delimiters("«", "»")
  ...
}
```

Then one imports all values from the object:

```
import FrenchPunctuation._
```

or just the specific value:

```
import FrenchPunctuation.quoteDelimiters
```

Now the French delimiters are supplied implicitly to the `quote` function.

 NOTE: There can only be one implicit value for a given data type. Thus, it is not a good idea to use implicit parameters of common types. For example,

```
def quote(what: String)(implicit left: String, right: String) // No!
```

would not work—one could not supply two different strings.

21.6 Implicit Conversions with Implicit Parameters

An implicit function parameter is also usable as an implicit conversion. To understand the significance, consider first this simple generic function:

```
def smaller[T](a: T, b: T) = if (a < b) a else b // Not quite
```

That doesn't actually work. The compiler won't accept the function because it doesn't know that a and b belong to a type with a < operator.

We can supply a conversion function for that purpose:

```
def smaller[T](a: T, b: T)(implicit order: T => Ordered[T])
  = if (order(a) < b) a else b
```

Since the Ordered[T] trait has a < operator that consumes a T, this version is correct.

As it happens, this is such a common situation that the Predef object defines implicit values of type T => Ordered[T] for a large number of types, including all types that already implement Ordered[T] or Comparable[T]. Therefore, you can call

```
smaller(40, 2)
```

and

```
smaller("Hello", "World")
```

If you want to call

```
smaller(Fraction(1, 7), Fraction(2, 9))
```

then you need to define a function Fraction => Ordered[Fraction] and either supply it in the call or make it available as an implicit val. I leave this as an exercise because it moves us too far from the point that I want to make in this section.

Here, finally, is the point. Look again at

```
def smaller[T](a: T, b: T)(implicit order: T => Ordered[T])
```

Note that order is a function that is tagged implicit and is in scope. Therefore, *it is an implicit conversion*, in addition to being an implicit parameter. So, we can omit the call to order in the body of the function:

```
def smaller[T](a: T, b: T)(implicit order: T => Ordered[T])
  = if (a < b) a else b // Calls order(a) < b if a doesn't have a < operator
```

21.7 Context Bounds

A type parameter can have a *context bound* of the form T : M, where M is another generic type. It requires that there is an implicit value of type M[T] in scope.

For example,

```
class Pair[T : Ordering]
```

requires that there is an implicit value of type Ordering[T]. That implicit value can then be used in the methods of the class. Consider this example:

```
class Pair[T : Ordering](val first: T, val second: T) {
  def smaller(implicit ord: Ordering[T]) =
    if (ord.compare(first, second) < 0) first else second
}
```

If we form a new Pair(40, 2), then the compiler infers that we want a Pair[Int]. Since there is an implicit value of type Ordering[Int] in the Ordering companion object, Int fulfills the context bound. That ordering becomes a field of the class, and it is passed to the methods that need it.

If you prefer, you can retrieve the ordering with the implicitly method in the Predef class:

```
class Pair[T : Ordering](val first: T, val second: T) {
  def smaller =
    if (implicitly[Ordering[T]].compare(first, second) < 0) first else second
}
```

The implicitly function is defined as follows in Predef.scala:

```
def implicitly[T](implicit e: T) = e
  // For summoning implicit values from the nether world
```

 NOTE: The comment is apt—the implicit objects live in the "nether world" and are invisibly added to methods.

Alternatively, you can take advantage of the fact that the Ordered trait defines an implicit conversion from Ordering to Ordered. If you import that conversion, you can use relational operators:

```
class Pair[T : Ordering](val first: T, val second: T) {
  def smaller = {
    import Ordered._;
    if (first < second) first else second
  }
}
```

These are just minor variations; the important point is that you can instantiate Pair[T] whenever there is an implicit value of type Ordering[T]. For example, if you want a Pair[Point], arrange for an implicit Ordering[Point] value:

```
implicit object PointOrdering extends Ordering[Point] {
  def compare(a: Point, b: Point) = ...
}
```

21.8 Type Classes

Have another look at the Ordering trait in the preceding section. We had an algorithm that required the parameters to have an ordering. Normally, in object-oriented programming, we would require the parameter types to extend a trait. But that's not what happened here. In order to make a class usable with the algorithm, it is not necessary to modify the class at all. Instead, one provides an implicit conversion. This is much more flexible than the object-oriented approach.

A trait such as Ordering is called a *type class*. A type class defines some behavior, and a type can join the class by providing that behavior. (The term comes from Haskell, and "class" is not used in the same way as in object-oriented programming. Think of "class" as in a "class action"—types banding together for a common purpose.)

To see how a type joins a type class, let us look at a simple example. We want to compute averages, $(x_1 + \ldots + x_n) / n$. To do that, we need to be able to add two values and divide a value by an integer. There is a type class Numeric in the Scala library, which requires that values can be added, multiplied, and compared. But it doesn't have any requirement that values can be divided by an integer. Therefore, let's define our own:

```
trait NumberLike[T] {
  def plus(x: T, y: T): T
  def divideBy(x: T, n: Int): T
}
```

Next, to make sure that the type class is useful out of the gate, let's add some common types as members. That's easy to do by providing implicit objects in the companion object:

```
object NumberLike {
  implicit object NumberLikeDouble extends NumberLike[Double] {
    def plus(x: Double, y: Double) = x + y
    def divideBy(x: Double, n: Int) = x / n
  }

  implicit object NumberLikeBigDecimal extends NumberLike[BigDecimal] {
    def plus(x: BigDecimal, y: BigDecimal) = x + y
    def divideBy(x: BigDecimal, n: Int) = x / n
  }
}
```

Now we are ready to put the type class to use. In the average method, we need an instance of the type class so that we can call plus and divideBy. (Note that these are methods of the type class, not the member types.)

Here, we'll just compute the average of two values. The general case is left as an exercise. There are two ways in which we can supply the type class instance: as an implicit parameter, or with a context bound. Here is the first approach:

```
def average[T](x: T, y: T)(implicit ev: NumberLike[T]) =
  ev.divideBy(ev.plus(x, y), 2)
```

The parameter name ev is shorthand for "evidence"—see the next section.

When using a context bound, we retrieve the implicit object from the "nether world."

```
def average[T : NumberLike](x: T, y: T) = {
  val ev = implicitly[NumberLike[T]]
  ev.divideBy(ev.plus(x, y), 2)
}
```

That's all there is to it. Finally, let's see what a type needs to do to join the NumberLike type class. It must provide an implicit object, just like the NumberLikeDouble and NumberLikeBigDecimal objects that we provided out of the gate. Here is how Point can join:

```
class Point(val x: Double, val y: Double) {
  ...
}

object Point {
  def apply(x: Double, y: Double) = new Point(x, y)
  implicit object NumberLikePoint extends NumberLike[Point] {
    def plus(p: Point, q: Point) = Point(p.x + q.x, p.y + q.y)
    def divideBy(p: Point, n: Int) = Point(p.x * 1.0 / n, p.y * 1.0 / n)
  }
}
```

Here we added the implicit object to the companion object of Point. If you can't modify the Point class, you can put the implicit object elsewhere and import it as needed.

The standard Scala library provides useful type classes, such as Equiv, Ordering, Numeric, Fractional, Hashing, IsTraversableOnce, IsTraversableLike. As you have seen, it is easy to provide your own.

The important point about type classes is that they provide an "ad-hoc" way of providing polymorphism that is less rigid than inheritance.

21.9 Evidence

In Chapter 18, you saw the type constraints

```
T =:= U
T <:< U
T => U
```

The constraints test whether T equals U, is a subtype of U, or is convertible to U. To use such a type constraint, you supply an implicit parameter, such as

```
def firstLast[A, C](it: C)(implicit ev: C <:< Iterable[A]) =
  (it.head, it.last)
```

The =:= and <:< are classes with implicit values, defined in the Predef object. For example, <:< is essentially

```
abstract class <:<[-From, +To] extends Function1[From, To]

object <:< {
  implicit def conforms[A] = new (A <:< A) { def apply(x: A) = x }
}
```

Suppose the compiler processes a constraint implicit ev: String <:< AnyRef. It looks in the companion object for an implicit object of type String <:< AnyRef. Note that <:< is contravariant in From and covariant in To. Therefore the object

```
<:<.conforms[String]
```

is usable as a String <:< AnyRef instance. (The <:<.conforms[AnyRef] object is also usable, but it is less specific and therefore not considered.)

We call ev an "evidence object"—its existence is evidence of the fact that, in this case, String is a subtype of AnyRef.

Here, the evidence object is the identity function. To see why the identity function is required, have a closer look at

```
def firstLast[A, C](it: C)(implicit ev: C <:< Iterable[A]) =
  (it.head, it.last)
```

The compiler doesn't actually know that C is an Iterable[A]—recall that <:< is not a feature of the language, but just a class. So, the calls it.head and it.last are not valid. But ev is a function with one parameter, and therefore an implicit conversion from C to Iterable[A]. The compiler applies it, computing ev(it).head and ev(it).last.

 TIP: To test whether a generic implicit object exists, you can call the implicitly function in the REPL. For example, type implicitly[String <:< AnyRef] in the REPL, and you get a result (which happens to be a function). But implicitly[AnyRef <:< String] fails with an error message.

21.10 The @implicitNotFound Annotation

The @implicitNotFound annotation raises an error message when the compiler cannot construct an implicit parameter of the annotated type. The intent is to give a useful error message to the programmer. For example, the <:< class is annotated as

```
@implicitNotFound(msg = "Cannot prove that ${From} <:< ${To}.")
abstract class <:<[-From, +To] extends Function1[From, To]
```

For example, if you call

```
firstLast[String, List[Int]](List(1, 2, 3))
```

then the error message is

```
Cannot prove that List[Int] <:< Iterable[String]
```

That is more likely to give the programmer a hint than the default

```
Could not find implicit value for parameter ev: <:<[List[Int],Iterable[String]]
```

Note that ${From} and ${To} in the error message are replaced with the type parameters From and To of the annotated class.

21.11 CanBuildFrom Demystified

In Chapter 1, I wrote that you should ignore the implicit CanBuildFrom parameter. Now you are finally ready to understand how it works.

Consider the map method. Simplifying slightly, map is a method of Iterable[A, Repr] with the following implementation:

```
def map[B, That](f : (A) => B)(implicit bf: CanBuildFrom[Repr, B, That]): That = {
  val builder = bf()
  val iter = iterator()
  while (iter.hasNext) builder += f(iter.next())
  builder.result
}
```

Here, Repr is the "representation type." That parameter will enable us to select appropriate builder factories for unusual collections such as Range or String.

 NOTE: In the Scala library, map is actually defined in the TraversableLike[A, Repr] trait. That way, the more commonly used Iterable trait doesn't need to carry with it the Repr type parameter.

The CanBuildFrom[From, E, To] trait provides evidence that it is possible to create a collection of type To, holding values of type E, that is compatible with type From. Before discussing how these evidence objects are generated, let's see what they do.

The CanBuildFrom trait has an apply method that yields an object of type Builder[E, To]. A Builder has methods += for adding elements into an internal buffer, and result for producing the desired collection.

```
trait Builder[-E, +To] {
  def +=(e: E): Unit
  def result(): To
}

trait CanBuildFrom[-From, -E, +To] {
  def apply(): Builder[E, To]
}
```

Therefore, the map method simply constructs a builder for the target type, fills the builder with the values of the function f, and yields the resulting collection.

Each collection provides an implicit CanBuildFrom object in its companion object. Consider a simplified version of the standard ArrayBuffer class:

```
class Buffer[E : ClassTag] extends Iterable[E, Buffer[E]]
    with Builder[E, Buffer[E]] {
  private var elems = new Array[E](10)
  ...
  def iterator() = ...
    private var i = 0
    def hasNext = i < length
    def next() = { i += 1; elems(i - 1) }
  }
  def +=(e: E) { ... }
  def result() = this
}

object Buffer {
  implicit def canBuildFrom[E : ClassTag] =
      new CanBuildFrom[Buffer[_], E, Buffer[E]] {
    def apply() = new Buffer[E]
  }
}
```

Consider a call buffer.map(f), where f is a function of type A => B. The implicit bf parameter is obtained by calling the canBuildFrom[B] method in the Buffer companion object. Its apply method returns the builder, in this case a Buffer[B].

As it happens, the Buffer class already has a += method, and its result method is defined to return itself. Therefore, a Buffer is its own builder.

However, a builder for the Range class doesn't return a Range, and clearly it can't. For example, (1 to 10).map(x => x * x) has a value that isn't a Range. In the actual

Scala library, Range extends IndexedSeq[Int], and the IndexedSeq companion object defines a builder that constructs a Vector.

Here is a simplified Range class that provides a Buffer as builder:

```
class Range(val low: Int, val high: Int) extends Iterable[Int, Range] {
  def iterator() = ...
}

object Range {
  implicit def canBuildFrom[E : ClassTag] = new CanBuildFrom[Range, E, Buffer[E]] {
    def apply() = new Buffer[E]
  }
}
```

Now consider a call Range(1, 10).map(f). That method needs an implicit bf: CanBuildFrom[Repr, B, That]. Since Repr is Range, the associated types are CanBuildFrom, Range, B, and the unknown That. The Range object yields a match by calling its canBuildFrom[B] method, which returns a CanBuildFrom[Range, B, Buffer[B]]. That object is bf, and its apply method yields a Buffer[B] for building the result.

As you just saw, the implicit CanBuildFrom[Repr, B, That] parameter locates a factory object that can produce a builder for the target collection. The builder factory is defined as implicit in the companion object of Repr.

Exercises

1. How does -> work? That is, how can "Hello" -> 42 and 42 -> "Hello" be pairs ("Hello", 42) and (42, "Hello")? Hint: Predef.ArrowAssoc.

2. Define an operator +% that adds a given percentage to a value. For example, 120 +% 10 should be 132. Use an implicit class.

3. Define a ! operator that computes the factorial of an integer. For example, 5.! is 120. Use an implicit class.

4. Some people are fond of "fluent APIs" that read vaguely like English sentences. Create such an API for reading integers, floating-point numbers, and strings from the console. For example: Read in aString askingFor "Your name" and anInt askingFor "Your age" and aDouble askingFor "Your weight".

5. Provide the machinery that is needed to compute

   ```
   smaller(Fraction(1, 7), Fraction(2, 9))
   ```

   with the Fraction class of Chapter 11. Supply an implicit class RichFraction that extends Ordered[Fraction].

6. Compare objects of the class java.awt.Point by lexicographic comparison.

7. Continue the previous exercise, comparing two points according to their distance to the origin. How can you switch between the two orderings?

8. Use the `implicitly` command in the REPL to summon the implicit objects described in Section 21.5, "Implicit Parameters," on page 328 and Section 21.6, "Implicit Conversions with Implicit Parameters," on page 329. What objects do you get?

9. Explain why `Ordering` is a type class and why `Ordered` is not.

10. Generalize the `average` method in Section 21.8, "Type Classes," on page 331 to a `Seq[T]`.

11. Make `String` a member of the `NumberLike` type class in Section 21.8, "Type Classes," on page 331. The `divBy` method should retain every nth letter, so that `average("Hello", "World")` becomes `"Hlool"`.

12. Look up the `=:=` object in `Predef.scala`. Explain how it works.

13. The result of `"abc".map(_.toUpper)` is a `String`, but the result of `"abc".map(_.toInt)` is a `Vector`. Find out why.

Index

Symbols and Numbers

- (minus sign)
  in identifiers, 142
  operator:
    arithmetic, 6
    for collections, 178–179
    for maps, 49
    for type parameters, 271
    left-associative, 145
    precedence of, 145
    unary (negation), 14, 143
-- operator, 177–179
  not used for arithmetic decrements, 7
-= operator
  arithmetic, 7
  for collections, 178–179
  for maps, 49
--= operator, 178–179
_ (underscore)
  as wildcard:
    for XML elements, 236
    in case clauses, 30, 198–199, 237
    in imports, 8, 76, 85–86
    in tuples, 52
  for function calls, 158, 288
  for function parameters, 161
  in identifiers, 142, 317
_* syntax
  for arrays, 201
  for nested structures, 207
  in function parameters, 27
  in pattern matching, 237
_=, in setter methods, 57
_1, _2, _3 methods (tuples), 51
; (semicolon)
  after statements, 5, 18–20
  inside loops, 24–25

: (colon)
  followed by annotations, 217
  in case clauses, 200–201
  in identifiers, 142
  in implicits, 329–330
  in operator names, 285
    and precedence, 145
    right-associative, 146, 185
  in type parameters, 268–269
:: operator
  for lists, 175–176, 178–179
  in case clauses, 201, 206
  right-associative, 146, 176
:::, :+ operators, 178–179
:\, /: operators, 185
:+= operator, 179
! (exclamation mark)
  in identifiers, 142
  operator:
    in shell scripts, 114–115
    precedence of, 145
    unary, 143
!! operator, in shell scripts, 114
!= operator, 144
? (question mark)
  in identifiers, 142
  in parsers, 308
?: operator, 18
??? method, 101
/ (slash)
  in identifiers, 142
  in XPath, 235
  operator, 6
    precedence of, 145
//
  for comments, 317
  in XPath, 235
/* ... */ comments, parsing, 317

REGISTER YOUR PRODUCT at informit.com/register
Access Additional Benefits and SAVE 35% on Your Next Purchase

- Download available product updates.

- Access bonus material when applicable.

- Receive exclusive offers on new editions and related products.
  (Just check the box to hear from us when setting up your account.)

- Get a coupon for 35% for your next purchase, valid for 30 days. Your code will
  be available in your InformIT cart. (You will also find it in the Manage Codes
  section of your account page.)

Registration benefits vary by product. Benefits will be listed on your account page
under Registered Products.

InformIT.com—The Trusted Technology Learning Source
InformIT is the online home of information technology brands at Pearson, the world's foremost
education company. At InformIT.com you can

- Shop our books, eBooks, software, and video training.
- Take advantage of our special offers and promotions (informit.com/promotions).
- Sign up for special offers and content newsletters (informit.com/newsletters).
- Read free articles and blogs by information technology experts.
- Access thousands of free chapters and video lessons.

Connect with InformIT—Visit informit.com/community
Learn about InformIT community events and programs.

the trusted technology learning source

Addison-Wesley • Cisco Press • IBM Press • Microsoft Press • Pearson IT Certification • Prentice Hall • Que • Sams • VMware Press